MADE IN JAPAN

AKIO MORITA and SONY

Akio Morita
with Edwin M. Reingold and Mitsuko Shimomura

E. P. DUTTON   NEW YORK

Published in the United States by
E. P. Dutton, a division of New American Library,
2 Park Avenue, New York, N.Y. 10016.

Library of Congress Cataloging-in-Publication Data
Morita, Akio, 1921–
Made in Japan.
1. Morita, Akio, 1921–   . 2. Industrialists—Japan—Biography.
3. Sonī Kabushiki Kaisha—History.
4. Electronic industries—Japan—History.
I. Reingold, Edwin M.   II. Shimomura, Mitsuko, 1938–   III. Title.
HD9696.A3J3658   1986   338.7'6213'0924   [B]   86-11479

ISBN: 0-525-24465-4

Published simultaneously in Canada
by Fitzhenry & Whiteside Limited, Toronto

COBE

Designed by Nancy Etheredge

10 9 8 7 6 5 4 3 2 1

First Edition

Contents

Acknowledgements
vii

WAR
Survival and Hope
1

PEACE
Our New Life Begins
35

SELLING TO THE WORLD
My Learning Curve
74

ON MANAGEMENT
It's All in the Family
130

AMERICAN AND JAPANESE STYLES
The Difference
171

COMPETITION
The Fuel of Japanese Enterprise
203

TECHNOLOGY
Survival Exercise
226

JAPAN AND THE WORLD
Alienation and Alliance
254

WORLD TRADE
Averting Crisis
280

Eight pages of photographs follow page 150.

Acknowledgments

Forty years ago, on the afternoon of May 7, 1946, some twenty people gathered on the third floor of a burned-out department store building in war-devastated downtown Tokyo to establish a new company: Tokyo Telecommunications Engineering Corporation, which was later to become the Sony Corporation. The founder of this company, Masaru Ibuka, was thirty-eight years old. I was twenty-five. Knowing him has been one of the greatest blessings in my life, and working with him has been a source of immense joy. This book owes its existence to my long association with Masaru Ibuka.

Almost a week after the fortieth anniversary of Sony, my wife Yoshiko and I celebrated our thirty-fifth wedding anniversary. Yoshiko has played a great role as my diplomat and partner, and together with my sons Hideo and Masao, and my daughter Naoko, she has provided me with the support and understanding that allowed me to devote myself to my work.

I cannot express enough thanks to my parents, to my mentors, and to my innumerable friends and colleagues within and outside Sony who have helped to nurture an environment of creativity and support.

My deepest gratitude goes to Edwin Reingold and Mitsuko Shimomura, who listened with endless patience and enthusiasm to my thoughts and long stories. Without them this book could not have been completed.

Also I wish to express my sincere appreciation to many others, particularly my assistants, Megumi Yoshii and Lidia Maruyama, for their important staff work in the preparation of materials for this book.

MADE IN JAPAN

WAR

Survival and Hope

I

I was having lunch with my navy colleagues when the incredible news of the atomic bombing of Hiroshima arrived. The information was sketchy—we were not even told what kind of bomb had been dropped—but as a technical officer just out of college with a degree in physics, I understood what the bomb was and what it meant to Japan, and to me. The future had never been more uncertain—Japan had never lost a war—and only a young man could be optimistic. Yet I had confidence in myself and in my future even then.

For many months, I had known that Japan was losing the war and that continuing it was futile, but I also knew that the military would want to fight to the last man. I was twenty-four, with a degree from Osaka Imperial University, and was working with an interdisciplinary team of scientists and engineers trying to perfect thermal-guidance weapons and night-vision gunsights. The military authorities hoped that Japanese technology would turn the tide of the war, but although we worked diligently, we knew that it was late and that our projects were not destined to succeed. We were lacking in resources and in time. And now, after Hiroshima, it was obvious to me that time had run out.

Unlike the civilian population at the time, which was under the strict surveillance and control of the police and the military, I had access to naval information and I could listen to short-wave radio broadcasts, although it was illegal even for a naval officer off duty. I knew before August 6, 1945, that American strength was overwhelming and that the war was as much as lost. Yet I was not prepared for the news of the atomic bomb. The bomb took everyone by surprise.

On that hot, humid summer day, we knew nothing of the horror of the bomb that was dropped. The news bulletin we got at our navy lunch table said only that the bomb that fell was "a new kind of weapon that flashed and shone," but that description told us this surely had to be an atomic device. Actually, Japanese military authorities withheld the details of what happened at Hiroshima for quite a long time, and some officers refused to believe that the Americans had the bomb. We had not come far enough in our theoretical research to know the dimensions of the destructive power of such a weapon, to realize the tremendous loss of life it could cause. We didn't know how horrible an atomic weapon could be, but I had seen the terrible results of conventional firebombing, and, in fact, I was in Tokyo just after the night of March 9–10, when the incendiary bombs from wave after wave of B-29's had whipped up a fire storm that killed one hundred thousand people in just a few hours. I had also seen the horror of the bombing of Nagoya, my hometown. Parts of all of Japan's major industrial cities, with the exception of Kyoto, were charred wastelands in 1945, depressing heaps of blackened remains: the homes of millions of Japanese. That an atomic bomb could be worse was almost unimaginable.

Although the bomb was dropped at 8:15 A.M. on August 6, we didn't hear about it until noon on August 7. My reaction to the Hiroshima bomb was the reaction of a scientist. Sitting there at lunch, I lost all interest in the rice in front of me, as much of a luxury as it was in wartime Japan. I looked around at my colleagues and said to everyone at the table, "We might as well give up our research right now. If the Americans can build an atomic bomb, we must be too far behind in every field to catch up." My superior officer got very angry with me.

I knew something about the potential of atomic power, but I thought it would take at least twenty years for an atomic bomb to be developed, and it was shocking to realize that the Americans had done it. It was obvious that if the Americans had come this far, our technology had to be primitive in comparison. No weapon we could devise could possibly match it, I said, and it seemed to me there was nothing, no new weapon or defensive device, that we could build in time to counter it. The news of Hiroshima was something truly incredible to me. The technology gap it represented was tremendous.

Although we knew there was a difference between American and Japanese technology, we thought ours was very good, and it was, but we still tried to get as many new ideas as we could from elsewhere. Once, for example, we got some salvaged equipment from a shot-down B-29 bomber, and we noticed that the Americans were using some advanced technology and different electrical circuitry, but it wasn't a great deal better than our own.

That is why when I first heard of the atomic attack on Hiroshima, it struck me that American industrial might was greater than we realized, simply overwhelming. I, for one, should have been prepared for it. In fact, as a boy in high school I had seen a film of the construction of the Ford Motor Company River Rouge complex in Dearborn, Michigan, and was thrilled by the concept of this gigantic project. The film showed big ships bringing iron ore from faraway mines to the Ford River Rouge steel mill, which turned it into different kinds and shapes of steel. When the steel was finished, it was moved to another part of the complex, where it was molded or stamped into parts for automobiles, and the parts were then assembled into cars in another part of the same plant. Japan had no integrated manufacturing like that at the time. It is ironic, though, that many years later, when Japan was recovering from the war and developing its own new industrial system, building new and efficient plants on tidewater locations and developing integration like we had seen in the Ford prewar operation, I had an opportunity to visit the River Rouge complex. I was surprised and puzzled and disappointed to see the very same scenes that I remembered from that film made almost twenty years before—the same equipment seemed to be in service, and it made me wonder then about the future of America's industrial plant and its supreme position, the envy of the world.

But in August 1945, I was still reeling from the realization that there would be dramatic changes in store for Japan and me. I had been thinking for a long time about my future. I had been persuaded by an officer to enlist in the navy while in college under a program that would allow me to continue my studies and to avoid throwing my life away in some futile sea battle thousands of miles from home. And then after Hiroshima and the second atomic bombing at Nagasaki, it was brought home to me more than ever that Japan would need all the talent it could save for the future. I don't mind saying that even then, as a young man, I felt that somehow I had a role to play in that future. I didn't know how big a role it would turn out to be.

Neither did I realize then how in later years I would devote many hours, weeks, and months, and travel literally millions of miles to help bring Japan and the United States and other Western nations closer together.

I was born the first son and fifteenth-generation heir to one of Japan's finest and oldest sake-brewing families. The sake of Japan is not only the national drink but also a cultural symbol to the Japanese people. It is even a part of many religious rituals—at traditional marriage ceremonies the couple shares a cup of sake. The Morita family of Kosugaya village, near the industrial city of Nagoya, has been making sake for three hundred years under the brand name "Nenohimatsu." The name was taken from the title of a poem in the *Man'yoshu*, Japan's famous anthology of poetry, which was compiled in the eighth century. The name comes from the traditional court custom of going into the countryside on the first day of the Year of the Rat, in the zodiacal counting of the years, and selecting a pine seedling to bring home and plant in the garden. The pine symbolizes longevity and happiness, and by planting a pine tree at the beginning of the new year, the people were wishing for health and prosperity throughout the year.

The Morita company also produced soy sauce and miso paste, a staple ingredient of the Japanese diet for making soup and for flavoring other foods. Being in a business so central to the life of the community, the Morita family has always taken a position of civic leadership as well.

My father was a very good businessman, but he took over a fine old business that was in serious financial trouble. Grandfather and his father were aesthetic persons who were devoted to the fine arts and crafts of Japan and China, and they both spent much of their time and money in their civic work and in patronizing artists, craftsmen, and art dealers. Fine ceramics and utensils for the tea ceremony, beautiful furniture, paintings, and the other objects that accompany the social rituals of upper-class Japanese life have always been highly prized—and also very highly priced. For many years, Japan has bestowed the title Living National Treasure on the best craftsmen and artists of traditional Japanese culture—painters, potters, textile makers, swordsmiths, weavers, designers, calligraphers, and others. The works of these superb craftsmen are always in great demand among lovers of fine things. Unfortunately, the taste of a couple of generations of Morita family heads was so refined and their collecting skills so acute that the business suffered while they pursued their artistic interests, letting the business take care of itself, or, rather, putting it in other hands.

They relied on hired managers to run the Morita company, but to these managers the business was no more than a livelihood, and if the business did not do well, that was to be regretted, but it was not crucial to their personal survival. In the end, all the managers stood to lose was a job. They did not carry the responsibility of the generations, of maintaining the continuity and prosperity of the enterprise and the financial well-being of the Morita family. And so that is why when the business fell into my father's hands, as the first son of the family, he was faced with the immediate task of bringing the company back to profitability and restoring the Morita family fortunes. No outside manager could be counted on to do that for him.

It was not a simple matter. When he was called away from his studies to take over the business, my father, Kyuzaemon Morita, was a student of business administration at Keio University in Tokyo. The company was facing bankruptcy, and father understood that, although he was being forced to abandon his academic studies, he was being tested with a real-life crisis—not a textbook problem or case study, but the future of the Morita family. He returned home and began to set the company on its feet with hands-on management.

Ironically, and fortunately for all of us in the family, he got some of the money to pay off the company debts and put the neglected factory back into good condition by selling many of the fine art objects his father and grandfather had purchased. These things had appreciated in value over the years, and so the family's investment in art, while it was not too wise from the point of view of running a business, turned out to be beneficial and in fact was crucial in helping to rescue the business. Among the treasures he had to sell were three especially valuable items: a Chinese scroll, a bronze mirror from China, and an ancient ornament of jade dating back to Japan's Yayoi period somewhere between 350 B.C. and A.D. 250. My father was a serious and conservative man, and he knew how much these special items meant to his father, and so he vowed that as soon as the family fortunes could afford it, the items would be bought back. Indeed, in several years they were "redeemed" and once again added to the family collection.

By the time I was born, the first son of Kyuzaemon and Shuko Morita, the business was on its feet again, and I never had to know privation at home as a child. On the contrary, I was always privileged. We were a rich family, and we lived in a huge (by Japanese standards), rambling house on Shirakabe-cho, one of the finest residential streets of Nagoya. People called it a rich man's street. We had a tennis court on our property, and the Toyodas across the street had one, and so did our other neighbors on either side. We needed a big house in those days because there were so many of us living under the same big tile roof: myself and my brothers, Kazuaki, who is two years younger than I am, and Masaaki, who is six years younger, and my sister, Kikuko, who is three years younger than I am. Then, of course, there were my father and mother, and an aunt whose husband had died young before they could have any children, and my father's younger brother, who had spent four years in France studying painting, and my father's parents, and six servants, and three or four young people from our ancestral village that our family was helping to send through school in exchange for work around the house.

It seemed as though something was always going on in

the house, and I guess it is no wonder, considering the crowd that inhabited it. We maintained our privacy, though, and my parents and their children usually dined separately from the rest of the household. But on special occasions, like a birthday, we would open all the sliding doors between the rooms and have a big party with twenty or thirty of us and our friends. On a birthday, we would gather for the party and have a lottery. Everybody won a prize and there was a lot of laughing and joking and eating. Of course, managing such a full household, and mediating the disputes and disagreements that came up among the children and the young servants and the students who lived with us, was a full-time job for my mother, a clever woman of great patience.

My mother was only seventeen when she married my father, and she and father worried for some time that they might not be able to have a child. Having a son and heir was very important then, as it still is in Japan, and it was seven years before I made my appearance, to their great relief. Mother was a quiet, artistic, and gentle woman who took her responsibility of managing the house very seriously, and she was constantly busy seeing that the work was done and that relations were smooth, or at least civil, among all those people. She was very assertive for a Japanese housewife, which in those days was very unusual. She had firm opinions, especially about my education, although she was never like today's pushy "education mothers" who force their children through cram courses to make sure they get into the "right" schools and universities. I felt she understood everything, and she was easy to talk to, certainly easier than my father, whose life was dominated by the business he had to save, rebuild, and nurture, and so I went to her more often than to my father for advice and help.

My mother changed many traditions in our family. Although she came from a samurai family on one side and was aware of the traditions—she always wore kimono—she was also willing to accept new ways. Of course we children did a fair amount of arguing and fighting, but as I grew older, actually even before my teens, I withdrew to the study of my own interests and I relied on her more and more for advice. She was in charge of our home, completely, and she gave me a room of my own with a desk. I got a second desk when I started my experiments, because I needed a workbench. She also bought me a bed, so I didn't have to use quilted bedding on the tatami mats as most others in the house did. I was being modernized even as a child. My mother and father wanted it that way because they were grooming me to carry on as the heir to the family business and as the next head of the Morita family, literally the fifteenth Morita to take the name Kyuzaemon.

It has been customary in our family that when the son takes over as family head he abandons his given name and assumes the traditional given name, Kyuzaemon. Most of the first sons for fifteen generations have alternatively been given at birth the first names Tsunesuke or Hikotaro. My father was Hikotaro Morita until he assumed the role of head of the family and became the fourteenth Kyuzaemon. His father, who was born Tsunesuke Morita, became Kyuzaemon Morita when he took over, and when he retired and passed the duties and responsibilities to my father, Kyuzaemon took another first name, Nobuhide Morita.

But when I was born, my father thought the name waiting for me, Tsunesuke, was too old-fashioned for the twentieth century, so he called on a venerable Japanese scholar of Chinese lore and literature for advice on naming me. This man was a renowned scholar, and a friend of my grandfather, and he recommended the name Akio, which uses the character for "enlightened," pronounced "aki." The character also appeared in my grandfather's name. Chinese characters usually have more than one pronunciation, and some have dozens, and so my first name could be read to mean enlightened or uncommon, and coupled with Morita, which means "prosperous rice field," it seemed an optimistic and hopeful identity to carry through life. My parents liked my name very much and used the syllable in the given names of both of my brothers, Masaaki and Kazuaki. Imperial reigns in Japan are given era names, and years in the official calendar are counted from one at the beginning of each era. When Hirohito became emperor after the death of his father in 1926, the imperial family consulted the same famous scholar of Chinese in seeking an auspicious name for his reign. He named the era "Showa," meaning "enlightened peace," using the same character as the "aki" in my name, but pronounced "sho." (The year 1986 is officially known as Showa 61, the sixty-first year of this imperial era called Showa.)

My family has suggested to me that I should really take

the name Kyuzaemon now. It is possible to go into family court and have your name changed if you can prove the historical precedent, but I think it would not be wise for me, because so many people know me as Akio all over the world. But I sometimes sign my name with the initials AKM, which could mean Akio Kyuzaemon Morita, and I have a personalized license plate on the Lincoln Continental I keep in the United States, AKM-15. One day my first son, Hideo, will take over as head of the family, but whether he will become Kyuzaemon or not is up to him, although my wife and I would like him to do it. But that is really getting ahead of my story.

I was made aware of my family tradition and my ancestors from early childhood. My family was blessed with men of culture and lovers of art, like my grandfather and his father. They were also civic leaders and officials of our village going back to the era of the Tokugawa Shogunate, in the seventeenth century. They were an elite, and they were accorded the privilege in those days of using a surname and carrying a sword. Whenever my parents would take me back to Kosugaya for a visit or just a day's trip, the people there would fuss over me and build up my ego.

My father's great-grandfather, the eleventh Kyuzaemon, liked new things and new ideas and during the Meiji era, before the beginning of this century, he invited a Frenchman to Japan to help him with an idea he had of growing grapes and making wine. He had a name picked out and was excited about producing Western-style wine as well as sake. Japan was opening to the world then after over two hundred and fifty years of self-imposed seclusion. New things were in vogue and Emperor Meiji was encouraging the Japanese to learn from the West, especially Western life-styles and technologies. In Tokyo they were holding formal ballroom dances, and people were emulating European clothing and hairstyles and trying Western food, even at the palace.

There were other reasons for trying to produce wine. The government of Emperor Meiji foresaw a coming rice shortage, and rice was the basis of sake. The planting of vineyards, and substitution of wine for sake, where possible, would make it easier to withstand the rice harvest shortfalls that some were predicting. Historians also say the government was looking for employment for many samurai warriors who were out of work

under the new government. We had a large amount of farm-
land, and so in 1880, with the encouragement of the Meiji government, the grape root stock was brought from France and
planted there. My ancestor installed a machine for processing
the grapes and built proper winery facilities, importing people
from nearby areas to work the vineyards. Four years later a
small amount of wine was produced, and hopes were raised
that this new industry could flourish. But it was not to be.

This was the time when the French vineyards were being
devastated, first by the oidium mildew and then by the disastrous phylloxera, small licelike insects that attacked the vines.
Apparently the root stock that was brought from France was
infected, and despite all the elaborate preparations the project
was a failure. Phylloxera were found in Kyuzaemon's vineyards
in 1885, and the vines had to be destroyed. Kyuzaemon had to
sell the land to pay off his debts. The vineyards were converted
to mulberry fields, for silkworm cultivation. But other traditional Morita products, such as soy sauce and sake, found their
way to a Paris international exposition in 1899, and one of them
won a gold medal, a very impressive thing for a Japanese company in those days. Anyway, this ancestor of mine had the
eagerness to try something new and had the courage and strength
not to give up if a single project failed. His predecessor as family
head had started a beer business by hiring a Chinese brew-
master who had learned his trade in England. He also founded
a baking company, now called Pasco, which prospered and
today has overseas branches. Tenacity, perseverance, and optimism are traits that have been handed down to me through
the family genes. I think my father recognized this in me.

My father's great-grandfather died in 1894, and in 1918 a
bronze statue of him was put up in Kosugaya in recognition of
the service he gave to the community. He had used his own
money to build roads and make other community improvements and did so many other good works that Emperor Meiji,
who once visited the vicinity of our little village, decorated
him. Unfortunately, during the war the statue was melted down
for use in the war effort, but a mold was taken and a porcelain
bust was made, which still stands in a wooded area in front of
a shrine in Kosugaya.

Although our family history seems to revolve around Kosugaya, my parents moved from the quiet little village to the

city of Nagoya, the capital of our prefecture, and I was born there on January 26, 1921. The move to Nagoya, a bustling industrial city, which was the capital of Aichi Prefecture, was part of father's campaign to modernize the Morita company and instill a new spirit in the old firm. Besides, the city was a more convenient place from which to run a modern business than a charming little countryside village. So I grew up in the city rather than in the tiny village of my ancestors, although we still consider our roots to be in Kosugaya.

Recently we discovered many of the ancient records of the village in our family's storehouses, and we have found them so interesting that I have formed a foundation for the preservation and study of this library of historical documents. The material is all very detailed and tells a great deal about rural life in Japan three hundred years ago from a very practical point of view. We have catalogued these records and delivered bound copies of the catalogue to major libraries and universities in Japan. We have built a glassed-in enclosure to cover the old storehouses and a three-story building as part of the same structure, where scholars now come to study the documents, which we still keep in their original place in the storehouses. I have often thought that if I ever retire I can spend many more busy years studying history and working with those historical records in Kosugaya.

My father was quite generous in his treatment of me, but I was, after all, carrying the first son's burden, and he was determined to give me a business education starting very early in life. Father was conditioned by the times, and because, as the family's eldest son, he had had to give up his schooling to rescue the family fortunes, he remained a very practical, and I think conservative—almost too conservative, I thought at the time—businessman when it came to making decisions on new ventures or doing things out of the ordinary. He seemed to take too long to make a decision, and he was always worrying about something. Sometimes I thought he worried that he didn't have anything to worry about. I often quarreled with him about some of the obligations that fell to me, and I think he liked these little disputes as a way of bringing me out, getting me to reason and to try to present arguments logically. He even turned my anger into training. As I got older, I continued to disagree with him often about his conservatism, but it served the family well. And in contrast to his serious and cautious business personality, he was a warm and generous father. He spent all his leisure time with his children, and I have many fond memories of my father teaching us how to swim and fish and hike.

But business was business to him, and there was not much fun involved. When I was as young as ten or eleven, I was first taken to the company office and the sake brewery. I was shown how the business was run, and I had to sit at my father's side through long and boring board meetings. But I was taught how to talk to people who work for you, and I learned while I was still in elementary school something about what goes on in business discussions. Since my father was the boss, he could call his managers to our home for reports and for conferences, and he would always insist that I listen in. After a while I got to enjoy it.

I was always told, "You are the boss from the start. You are the eldest son in the family. Remember that." I was not allowed to forget that I was to be my father's successor in the top management of our company and the head of our household one day. I think it was very important that I was also cautioned time and again as a young man, "Don't think that because you are at the top you can boss others around. Be very clear on what you have decided to do and what you ask others to do and take full responsibility for it." I was taught that scolding subordinates and looking for people to blame for problems— seeking scapegoats—is useless. The proper thing, to the Japanese way of thinking that I was taught at home, is to make use of the motivations you share with people to accomplish something that will be to the advantage of both. Everybody wants to succeed. In learning to work with employees, I discovered, a manager needs to cultivate the traits of patience and understanding. You can't make selfish moves or get mean with people. These concepts have stayed with me and helped me develop the philosophy of management that served me very well in the past and continues to serve me and my company today.

My family was also guided by family precepts stemming from our Buddhist religion. The family was devout, and we held the usual religious services at home. We children would be handed a book of sutras and would be required to try to read the complicated characters along with the adults. I wouldn't say I am a religious man, but these customs and traditions have been important in my family and we still adhere to them. In later years, when we would go home to visit my father and mother, we would always first go to the family altar and bow to it before doing anything.

As a young boy in middle school, my holidays were consumed by business, business, business. My father would take me to the office when he had a meeting and I would sit through it, or listen when reports were made to him. Then there was inventory. We used to call it stock-checking, and we used the ancient, traditional, and very accurate way of doing it: we would go into the plant, with the president of the company looking over our shoulders, and count everything. Then there was the sake-tasting from the barrels in midwinter to check its development in the complicated maturing and refining process. I often had to go along. I was taught to inspect the brewing process, then take a small sip of sake to get the flavor, and then spit it out. I never developed a taste for anything alcoholic despite this, or maybe because of it.

Although my father was by nature a very conservative person, he wanted his family to have the things they needed and desired. He was always interested in new, imported technologies and foreign products. When the family still lived in Kosugaya, he started a taxi and bus service there by importing a Ford touring car. For the first company driver, he chose the man who pulled the *jinriksha*, the two-wheeled, man-powered taxi that was then quite common in Japan. In my childhood recollections, I remember Sunday outings, riding in an open Model T or Model A Ford, bumping along the rutted, narrow, and dusty roads at a very slow speed, my mother sitting in the back seat in a very dignified and stately way holding her parasol upright to shade her from the sun. Later, father used to go to work in his chauffeur-driven Buick. At home we had a General Electric washing machine and a Westinghouse refrigerator.

But even though the family was to some degree Westernized, I think the first really strong foreign influence in my life was my Uncle Keizo, who came home from Paris after about four years abroad and brought the first truly Western wind into our house. He was very sophisticated, much more than any of us. Even before he came, I was never required to wear kimono, and my father wore Western clothing at work and changed into traditional dress at home; even his father often wore Western clothing. My grandfather was intrigued by the West—he liked American movies, and I remember he took me to see *King Kong* when I was a very small boy. But Uncle Keizo brought a personal account of the outside world to us, and we were all intrigued. He brought back his paintings of Paris, photographs of France, and pictures taken on his trips to London and New York, and he also showed us films he had taken with a Pathé movie camera, which used 9.5-millimeter film. He owned a Renault car in Paris, which he drove himself, and had pictures to prove it. Although I was only eight years old, it made such an impression on me that I learned all the foreign words I could—Place de la Concorde, Montmartre, Coney Island. When he told us about Coney Island, I was fascinated, and years later, on my very first trip to New York in 1953, I went to Coney Island on my first Sunday because of his stories. I had a wonderful time; I rode the roller coaster and even tried the parachute drop.

My father followed the example of his father. He used to say that all the money in the world cannot give a person education unless that person is willing to sit down by himself and study hard. But money can provide one kind of education, the education you can get by travel. That is what happened with my uncle, who came home and set up his atelier in our house and stayed with us for a long time until he got married. My grandfather supported him those four years he was studying abroad. Years later my father would give me money to travel on my high school vacations, and with a schoolmate I visited many places in Japan. We had a relative in Korea, which had been under Japanese occupation since 1904 and was annexed to Japan in 1910, and I visited there, and after Korea I went as far as Manchuria—I even rode on the first all air-conditioned, streamlined train, which was called "the Asia," in 1939 or 1940, and my next trip would have been to the United States, but the war postponed that trip for more than a decade.

At home we were an unusually modern family. My mother was very fond of Western classical music, and she bought many phonograph records for our old Victrola. My grandfather often took her to concerts, and I believe my interest in electronics and sound reproduction began because of her. We would listen to the scratchy-sounding recordings of the great music masters of Europe over and over again from the big horn speaker. With the kind of mechanical recording equipment that was available to the makers in those days, it was difficult to reproduce the sound of a full orchestra, so the best records were vocals and instrumental solos. My mother was very fond of Enrico Caruso and the violinist Efrem Zimbalist, as I recall. Whenever famous artists came to Nagoya, we always went to hear them. I remember hearing the great Russian basso, Feodor Chaliapin, and the German pianist Wilhelm Kempff, who was then a very young man. In those days one local record shop owner imported Victor Red Seal classical records, and each month when a new shipment arrived he would send one of each title to my mother on approval. I can still remember cranking the old mechanical player vigorously when I was just a small kid. Then, when I was in junior high school, an electric phonograph was imported to Japan from the United States and it was inevitable that we would get one.

My father thought that if you liked music you should have good sound. Besides, he told us later, he was worried that listening to that tinny-sounding Victrola would be bad for our ears and our musical appreciation. He didn't understand or appreciate music from an artistic or technical standpoint, but he wanted his family to have the best possible chance to hear the music as it was played. He felt that the only way a person could learn to appreciate good music and good sound was by listening to the best sound that was available. So when the first new phonographs arrived, he spent a lot of money to buy one of the first in Japan, or at least the first in our locality. I remember that the new machine, also a Victor, cost an incredible amount—six hundred yen. In those days you could buy a Japanese automobile for only fifteen hundred yen.

I will never forget the fantastic sound that came from the new electric machine—in comparison, of course, to the old mechanical machine. It was a completely different sound, and I was absolutely astounded. The first record we received after the new machine arrived was Ravel's "Bolero." I liked the "Bolero" because it conveyed pathos to me, and hearing it with this new, more realistic sound bowled me over. I listened to our records over and over again—Mozart, Bach, Beethoven, Brahms—full of excitement and wonder that an electrical device like the vacuum tube could take the same old scratchy, hissing records we knew so well and make them sound so marvelous.

I was obsessed with this new discovery and all the questions it raised in my mind. I had a relative who was an engineer, and when I heard that he had built an electric phonograph by himself I was eager to see it. I went to his house and he demonstrated it to me. It was in components, all wired together and strung out on the straw mat floor of his house. It seemed marvelous that things like this could be built by amateurs, not only by big factories. In fact, making radios was becoming a popular hobby, and some newspapers and magazines would run columns with diagrams and parts lists and instructions to show their readers how to do it. This was something I had to do.

I began to buy books about electronics, and I subscribed to Japanese and foreign magazines that contained all the latest information about sound reproduction and radio. Soon I was spending so much time on electronics that it was hurting my schoolwork. I was devoting nearly all my after-school hours to my new hobby, making electric devices from the diagrams in a Japanese magazine called *Wireless and Experiments*. My dream was to build an electric phonograph and make a recording of my own voice. I kept expanding my experiments as I learned more and more about the new technology. I had to teach myself because the subjects I was really interested in were not taught in my school in those days. But I managed to build a crude electric phonograph and a radio receiver on my own. I even made a crude recording of my voice and played it back on my electric phonograph.

In fact, I became so engrossed in my electronic tinkering that I almost flunked out of school. My mother was called to the school often for conferences about my poor academic performance. The principal was concerned and annoyed by my lack of interest in conventional studies. I remember that we used to be assigned desks in class according to our grades. There were two hundred and fifty in our class, divided into five groups of fifty each. The top student of each group was the head boy, and the seats were assigned from the back of the room in descending order of achievement. Although the class rankings changed every year, I was always seated up front under the eye of the teacher, with the slow learners.

I don't want to be too tough on myself here, so I will admit that I was good at mathematics, physics, and chemistry. But I would always get below-average grades in geography, history, and Japanese. I used to be called to the principal's office to be talked to about my uneven work. When it would get really bad, my parents would scold me and order me to put away my electronic toys. I would obey until my grades began to look a little better, and then I would go back to the things I liked best.

II

When I was in middle school, I read about magnetic recording for the first time in *Wireless and Experiments*. Up to then few people in Japan even had electric phonographs, which played poorly made records of shellac or aluminum with steel needles that gave bad sound and wore out the records fast. But then NHK, the Japan Broadcasting Company, imported a German steel-belt recorder. This machine was a brand-new design. It used a metal ribbon or belt as the recording medium, and it gave much better fidelity than the electric machines like our new Victor.

About that same time, it was announced that Dr. Kenzo Nagai of Tohoku University had produced a wire recorder. I was fascinated by the idea of recording my own voice and decided to build a wire recorder myself. I knew virtually nothing, but I had the reckless enthusiasm of the young, and so I went out and bought some piano wire and went to work. The first challenge, at least the most critical challenge, was to design and make a recording head. I worked for a whole year at it, trying one thing after another, but every attempt failed. I later learned why I failed: the head gap, the point where the sound is transferred to the wire in the form of an electronic signal, was too wide and so the signal just dissipated. I knew nothing of the importance of a bias current, which Dr. Nagai had perfected, or how to generate it. The books and magazines I had access to in those days had not explained it to me, and my own knowledge was primitive. And so, without knowing more than some basic principles and simple, practical methods, I struggled along. I was disappointed by my failures, and frustrated, but they did not discourage me.

When I entered the final year of middle school, I told my parents and teachers that I would take the science department examinations for the Eighth Higher School—in Japan in those days our school curriculum was very advanced, and higher school included what in the United States would be the first two years of college. My decision surprised them all, because even though my grades in the sciences and math were good, my overall grades were pretty terrible, and they reminded me that to get into the science department I would have to pass some tough examinations on subjects I had neglected. I knew it, but I was determined. And so I became a *ronin*. In ancient times a samurai who did not have a master or who had lost his fief was called a *ronin*, and a student who got off the track and had to spend time studying on his own for his next examinations after graduation is referred to this way even today. For one year I buckled down and studied harder than I had ever studied. I had private tutors to help me with English, advanced mathematics, and the Japanese and Chinese classics. I didn't do anything else that whole year but study. And I made it.

I'd like to say that because of my intense efforts that year I moved to the head of the class, but I can't. However, I earned another distinction: I became the lowest-ranking graduate of my school ever to be admitted to the science department of the Eighth Higher School. No student who had ranked one hundred and eightieth in his class as I did had ever been admitted to the science department before, but I made it because of my successful year of study and my determination. I have always been determined.

High school was not a snap, of course, and I discovered that even the science department curriculum was full of dull and uninteresting subjects—minerals and botany and other things I wasn't interested in—and I found myself in danger of failing for a time, but in my third year, when we are able to specialize, I chose physics, where I always got straight A's. I was in love with physics and I idolized my instructors.

But despite my optimism and enthusiasm, the year was 1940 and the future could not have looked bleaker. The world was in turmoil. In Europe France had surrendered to the German armies, England was being attacked by Luftwaffe bombers, and Winston Churchill was telling his people that they had nothing to look forward to but "blood, toil, tears, and sweat." Japan was on the road to disaster, although the news at home was reported favorably and censorship was in force. As students we didn't think much about global issues, or even domestic politics, but the military men who controlled the nation had announced a mobilization law in 1938, and about the time I began my college studies Japan dominated the map of Asia. At home all the old political parties were dissolved. Under the economic squeeze of the U.S. and the Allied powers, and the threat of a cutoff of the nation's raw materials and oil, the decision was being made to go to war with the United States, if necessary, for Japan's survival and its continued control of the nations it had forced into the so-called Greater East Asia Co-Prosperity Sphere. Important history was being made, but at the time I was interested only in physics.

One of my favorite teachers in high school, Gakujun Hattori, was very kind to me and was a big influence in my life. I was good at physics and Professor Hattori, who watched my progress with great satisfaction, knew my heart was set on continuing in the same field beyond higher school. When it was time for me to start thinking about university, I discussed the situation with him. I knew that the faculty at Osaka Imperial University's physics department included such famous researchers as Hidetsugu Yagi, who invented the Yagi antenna, which was so important in the development of modern radar. The department also had Professor K. Okabe, the inventor of the magnetron, the device that first made it possible to generate microwave frequency power.

One day Professor Hattori said to me, "Morita, a classmate of mine from Tokyo University is also teaching at Osaka now, a man named Tsunesaburo Asada. He is the most outstanding scientist in the field of applied physics. If that's what you want to study, Professor Asada is the man you should meet. Why don't you go see him during your summer holidays? I can arrange it for you." I jumped at the chance, and on my next vacation I went straight to Osaka and looked up Professor Asada.

I liked him the minute I walked into his cluttered office. The professor was a short, rotund fellow with a twinkle in his eye who spoke with the hard, nasal accents of Osaka. It was obvious that he liked to tell and to hear a joke, and although he was a master he did not play the role of the stern or pompous professor. He was a rarity in Japan, where teachers were accorded a great deal of respect, almost reverence, and generally seemed to take their exalted position seriously. Professor Asada didn't seem at all interested in the trappings of status. We hit it off right from the start. It was meeting this marvelous man that made me decide that Osaka was where I would study rather than the more famous Tokyo or Kyoto universities. Both Tokyo and Kyoto had good physics departments and were staffed with nationally known, but more doctrinaire or older, professors. At least I thought so at the time.

Professor Asada showed me around his laboratory and we talked quite a lot that day. He gave me a kind of oral examination—he wanted to know what I knew, what experiments I had done, what I had constructed, and what I was interested in. Then he told me about what kind of work was going on in his lab and that clinched it for me. Professor Asada was very serious about applied science, and among the things he was working on was light beam telephone transmission, using high pressure mercury lamps. He could demonstrate how very high intensity light beams could be modulated by audio frequency. I wanted to study with this brilliant, confident, and surprisingly relaxed and jovial scientist.

In the field of modern physics, Osaka Imperial University became the mecca for serious students and experimenters. It was the newest science department of any Japanese university, and therefore it had the most modern facilities. Also, since the university was new, many of the professors and instructors were younger people and not hidebound or wedded to old-fashioned ideas.

My father was disappointed that I did not choose to go into economics but chose science for my college career. From his point of view, even if I had gone into the science department I might have studied agricultural chemistry, which would have given me some courses relevant to the brewing industry, but I was pursuing instead the most basic of the sciences, physics. I wanted to know why things worked. He did not try to change my mind, but I am sure he still expected me to assume my role in the family business when the time came. He believed that physics would eventually be only a hobby for me and I sometimes feared that that's what would happen.

But, of course, when I entered university we were at war,

and Professor Asada's laboratory had been pressed into service as a naval research facility. I continued to experiment, but I skipped as many lectures as possible in order to get more lab time. I felt that most of the professors were boring as lecturers, and since they had all written books and papers I could always find out what they had to say by reading them. Because I was missing the lectures, I was able to spend more time in the lab than the other students. Professor Asada helped me more and more, and before long, I was able to help him in some small jobs for the navy, mainly electronics, which was closer to true physics than working with the old electrical circuits or the electromechanical ones.

At the university, Professor Asada was regarded as the expert in applied physics, and newspapers would often ask him to answer questions about science for them. Eventually he began to write a short weekly column elaborating on the latest developments in research and technology, at least those that were not secret. Readers of the newspaper would write to him to get his opinion of their scientific ideas. The column became quite lively and popular.

I often helped Professor Asada with his research, and occasionally when he was too busy I would write the column. I remember that in one of these columns I discussed the theory of atomic energy and I expressed the idea that, as I wrote it, "if atomic energy were treated appropriately, an extremely powerful weapon could be made." The idea of atomic energy or an atomic weapon seemed remote at the time. There were two cyclotrons in Japan, and progress toward creating an atomic reaction was being made very slowly. Japanese technology, then, to the best of my knowledge, would only permit the separation of a few milligrams of U-235 a day, and at that rate, I calculated that to accumulate enough to make a bomb would require twenty years. Of course, I did not know how far the scientific community in the United States and in Germany had come. And nobody in Japan knew about the Manhattan Project.

Some of Dr. Asada's work was research for the Imperial Japanese Navy, and I helped him with it. In doing so I came in contact with several naval officers from the Aviation Technology Center, which was located at Yokosuka, near Yokohama. I was nearing graduation and had not yet been drafted when one day an officer told me that physics graduates could apply for a short-term commission and become technical officers just by passing an examination. I wasn't too keen on the idea of becoming a naval officer at all, although I thought it might be wiser to volunteer and pick my assignment than be drafted into the army or navy and have no choice. Another officer, a captain, came to the lab one day and told me there was another possibility. The navy then had a program for assigning enlistees to universities. A second-year student could apply for a commission, and once accepted he would become an employee of the navy for life. That latter part in itself seemed very worrisome—I did not want to become a career naval officer—but I developed an interest in it quickly when he described the alternative. He said short-term commissioned officers with physics backgrounds were being assigned to ships of the line to operate the new radar sets that were coming into use then, and that meant war zone assignment and probably the end of my studies, if not my life. So the choice was to be drafted eventually and face a very uncertain assignment, to apply for a short-term commission and go to sea, or to sign up with the navy permanently and continue my studies.

He recommended that I take the test for a permanent navy position with a scholarship, so I could continue my work right there in the lab and get my degree. He said he didn't want to see dedicated researchers like me being sent to sea. It was his thought that after being accepted into the program I would only have to undergo basic training and then I could rejoin the research center. "That's the safest way for you," he told me. "You can keep up your research and we can continue to use you."

I didn't have to think it over too long. I decided that the lifetime service idea was preferable at the time—nobody knew what was going to happen—and so I took the examination and passed it. The navy gave me thirty yen a month and a gold-colored anchor insignia to wear on my collar. With that I became a navy man assigned to the university and my job was to continue to study physics. But this did not last long. In my third year the war intensified, and we physics students were put under direct military control like everyone else in the country; I was assigned to the Office of Aviation Technology at Yokosuka in early 1945.

But it wasn't what I expected. They billeted me in a workers' dormitory, and the first morning, instead of going into a laboratory as I anticipated, I was marched with the rest of the drafted workers into a factory. Somebody handed me a metal file and assigned me to the machine shop. Every day I would slave away in that shop, filing steel parts. After a few days, I began to think that if I didn't get out of there soon I would go crazy. All over Japan students were taken out of school and workers were taken off nonessential jobs to do war work, and now university science students seemed to be no exception.

Yoshiko Kamei, the woman who was to be my wife, was also assigned from her college classroom to a factory where she made wooden parts for the wings of a training aircraft called Red Dragonfly. She still knows how to use carpentry tools because of that work. When the airplane parts factory was bombed, she was assigned to a plant where they made hospital gowns for wounded soldiers, and later she was transferred to a printing shop where military scrip was printed for use in the occupied areas of Asia. Most schools could only hold one day of classes a week in the latter stages of the war, and some held no classes at all. There were few young men at home to do these jobs because Japan's military manpower was spread far and thin. Yoshiko and I did not meet until 1951 and we were married that year.

After several weeks of this factory drudgery, someone must have realized I was improperly assigned, because I was suddenly and without explanation transferred to the optics laboratory and I began to feel that I was getting back to the working world I knew best. There were officers there and workers who were graduates of photography schools, but I was the only university student majoring in physics, so they saved all the difficult technical problems for me to study. My first assignment was to try to find out how to prevent the damage to aerial photographs caused by jagged streaks of static electricity generated in the dry atmosphere at altitude. I needed access to a good library to research this job, and so I conceived a plan. Pretending that I had come directly from the navy, I called on a very famous professor at the Physics and Chemistry Research Institute in Tokyo, Professor Jiro Tsuji, to get his permission to use the institute's research library. He kindly offered me full assistance.

Then I made application with my unit to go to Tokyo every

day to do my research. I must have been very convincing, because I got permission almost immediately. But commuting on slow, crowded wartime trains from Yokohama to Tokyo, which took well over an hour, became very tiresome, so I moved into the home of a close friend and classmate from primary school who had been a law student at Tokyo University when he was drafted into the navy. On weekdays I would go to the research institute, and on Saturdays I would return to the workers' dormitory and spend the weekend with my fellow workers. I was learning how to be a military wheeler-dealer.

But I wasn't shirking work. I was trying to figure out how to prevent those static electric streaks. I know that when aerial pictures were taken by mapping cameras, which used very big spools of film, sparks were often caused by static electricity, which would ruin the picture. I began to get some ideas through my reading and experimenting. I moved into the darkroom, where plenty of film was available, and tried to simulate the sparks in the lab. I used various voltages across the camera parts and the film, and I switched polarity. In a short time I managed to come close to duplicating the phenomenon in the lab. In my first report I said that, although I had managed to simulate the phenomenon to a certain extent, I still had to find out precisely what caused it and how to remedy it, but I could not carry on with this experiment because the optics division did not have the proper facilities. Of course, the most suitable place with the best equipment was the laboratory of Professor Asada, and I asked to be assigned under temporary orders to the Asada lab.

I thought I would make it easier for my superiors to make the decision, so I told them that I didn't need any travel expenses, and since the lab was in my old university I knew where I could stay free of charge. All I would need from them was permission to study in the lab. Their only investment would be a large quantity of film, since film in those days was very scarce and I could not get it anywhere else. What their approval would mean for me, I hoped, would be the possibility of completing this assignment with the more advanced equipment at the university lab. And, as I hoped, I not only completed it but was able to use my formal research report to the navy as my senior thesis.

They saw it my way, authorizing a load of film, which I

packed into my rucksack before I returned to my university. So for a few months, while others were being given a hard time, I was staying at the old apartment my family had rented for me as a student, getting valuable advice from Professor Asada, and merely sending in a report on my research every week. It was the opportunity to do original work at my own pace that I liked, and of course I continued to learn from Professor Asada.

Forty years later, in 1985, I attended a reunion of the staff of the optics lab and I gave a speech confessing my motive for leaving. I said I had done a very selfish thing and apologized for any inconvenience my selfishness may have caused the other members of the lab. They all applauded, and then my former superior officer got up and said he also had a confession to make. He said the day I left for Osaka with my load of film and my freedom he reported to his superior officer, an admiral: "The admiral was furious! He scolded me severely and said that there was absolutely no precedent for what I had done." This dressing down went on for two hours, and my boss was dismissed with an order to go to Osaka and bring back Morita. The next morning he appeared before the admiral to announce his departure to bring me back when the admiral waved his hand impatiently and told him to forget it. And so I was allowed to remain in Osaka. But for forty years I was unaware of the trouble I had caused, and now I felt I had to apologize for it doubly. We all got a good laugh out of it, in retrospect.

With my graduation from university, I automatically became a professional naval officer, and this meant that I had to undergo some actual military training, so I was shipped off to a marine corps base at Hamamatsu, not far from Nagoya, where I went through the usual four-month officer's indoctrination and training course. I found it difficult, but proving myself physically was very rewarding.

At that time only students in the sciences, like me, could be exempted from the draft for a while. My brother Kazuaki, who was studying economics at Waseda University, could not qualify for a deferment and was drafted into the navy and given flight training in twin-engine bombers. And right after my graduation, when I was at the Hamamatsu base, he was at the navy's Toyohashi Air Base, which is very close by, and he was flying over my barracks on training missions every day. He was fortunate to be assigned to the twin-engine night bombing unit because the training took a long time and the war was over before he graduated. Some of his school classmates were assigned to fighters, which was a much shorter training course, and some became kamikaze pilots who flew suicide missions and, of course, never returned.

My younger brother, Masaaki, was in middle school, and the military was encouraging youngsters to volunteer. Entire classes were joining up. Japan at the time was full of war fervor and although a young man might not want to volunteer he would be ostracized if he did not. And so Masaaki was only fourteen or fifteen years old when his entire class decided they would join the navy. My parents were shocked and didn't want him to go, but he insisted, and I remember my mother's tears when he left the house. I took him to the train and I cried too. He went into naval flight training, and fortunately he was in the early stages of his training when the war ended. All three brothers at one time or another found themselves flying in naval planes. In my experiments I went on many night flights as a passenger to test the equipment we were using in our attempts to make a heat-seeking weapon, and my colleagues taught me how to pilot a plane, unofficially, of course. For a while three brothers were flying in the air and my mother thought there was no hope that we would survive the war. Fortunately, all three of us made it through unharmed.

The war with the United States was a tragedy and to most Japanese a surprise and a shock, despite all the propaganda about the Western countries ganging up on Japan. As a child, of course, I was not aware of all the political events that were taking place in the twenties and early thirties, but by the time I was thirteen, in 1934, we were being given military drill about two hours a week. All through those years we were brought up to consider the Soviets the potential enemy and were told that there was a possibility of war with the Soviet Union. We were taught that Communism was dangerous and that the reason Japan went into Manchuria was to secure a border and a buffer zone against the Communists for the protection of Japan.

Hotheaded ultranationalists, fascists, and some junior military officers had created several serious incidents at home and abroad for Japan in those days, and people like my father were worried about the future. In 1932, a group of these ultranationalists, together with forty-two young officers, attacked the so-called privileged classes, killing finance minister Jun-nosuke Inoue and a leading businessman, Baron Takuma Dan, who headed the giant Mitsui group of companies. Later that year, on May 15, they assassinated Prime Minister Tsuyoshi Inukai and attacked the home of the lord privy seal and also the offices of some of the giant holding companies. They also stormed the Nippon Bank and the Mitsubishi Bank.

People of our class were alarmed by these events. Although the rebels were aiming at the establishment of fascism, these events looked like parts of a Communist plot to many conservative people. Then, in 1936, the famous February 26 incident took place, when another band of army rebels occupied the prime minister's official residence and the war office and assassinated former prime minister Makoto Saito, who was lord keeper of the privy seal, a general who was in charge of military education, and a former finance minister. They wounded the grand chamberlain and brought the wrath of the emperor down on themselves. Military force was used to subdue the rebels, and fifteen officers and several of their civilian helpers were later executed.

Although the revolt failed, it became more and more evident that the upper-class politicians and businessmen had been intimidated by the attacks. The nation was in poor economic condition and the young fascist officers, though they were misguided, managed to arouse the sympathy of many people. In Japan there is a tradition of sympathy for those who strike out against overwhelming odds, even if their idealism or zeal is misplaced. Many of Japan's folk heroes are men who died trying to accomplish the impossible. From the middle thirties, the military increased its control over politics and the fascists began to dictate policy. In this atmosphere it was difficult forpeople to speak out. Even in the Diet, the Japanese parliament, few elected members had the courage to speak out against the militarists and those who did it once were not given a second chance to speak. And so the militarists took the upper hand.

Whenever my father and his friends would get together, they would talk of the dangers ahead. They were businessmen and they were more liberal in their thinking than the fascists, but they were unable to do anything but keep silent in public.

Young people in schools only knew what they were told, and at that time information was one-sided. The mission of the

Japanese forces that invaded China was glamourized. Some people had heard rumors of the attacks on Chinese cities, of what was happening in Nanking, and I assume my father heard more than he said, but the younger people didn't pay too much attention to such things. I knew that relations between the United States and Japan were getting worse, but I never expected war.

I had built a time clock, which was attached to my radio and was set to wake me up at six o'clock every morning. I remember very clearly the morning of December 8, 1941—it was still December 7 in the United States—when my timer turned on my radio and I heard the announcement that Japanese forces had attacked Pearl Harbor. I was shocked. Everyone in our house was stunned by this news, and I remember thinking that this was a dangerous thing. I had grown up believing the West was somewhat superior in technology. For example, at that time metal vacuum tubes could be bought only in America—we didn't have any such thing in Japan. I had bought RCA tubes for my experiments. And knowing about America's technology through movies and products such as cars and phonographs and from my uncle, I was concerned that a mistake had been made.

But in those weeks right after Pearl Harbor, our newspapers gave us a steady stream of good news of Japanese military victories—our forces sank the two British capital ships, *Prince of Wales* and *Repulse,* which were supposed to be invincible; they took the Philippines and Hong Kong, all in the month of December; and I began to think that perhaps we were stronger than I realized. Once the war started the general public, including my parents, believed that we had no alternative but to cooperate in the war effort. The newspapers were full of the news of the pressures the United States was putting on us, of the immigration laws that discriminated against Japanese, and the demands that we leave China and Manchuria, our buffer, we thought, against Communism. And that was the cry we all heard, that the Reds were a danger and threat to Japan and that only the fascists were going to protect us from them.

Everything the military-dominated government did was made to appear an order of the emperor, and they forced schoolchildren and adults alike to do incredible things. A school principal who made a mistake when he recited the Imperial Rescript on Education committed suicide to atone for it. Thought police and special police roamed the country arresting people on the slightest suspicion that they were not loyal or obedient enough or reverent enough. Conductors on the trolley cars that ran past the imperial palace grounds in Tokyo would announce the moment everybody was expected to bow. Schoolchildren bowed to the portable Shinto shrine that held the written words of the emperor. These were ways the military used to keep the nation in their power, and people like me and my parents went along. One might have dissent in his heart, and there were many who did, but it was difficult and dangerous to express it. Resisters were "reeducated" in special camps, and those who still resisted were thrown into the most menial jobs. All leftists and Communists were rounded up and jailed.

When my four-month period of military training was over, I received the rank of lieutenant and was ordered back to the optical division at Yokosuka. In short order, I was assigned to help supervise a special unit that had evacuated to the countryside to work on thermal guidance weapons and night-vision gunsights. We were to be based at a big old country house in Zushi, a small town south of Kamakura, looking out onto Sagami bay. Our unit was headed by a captain, and there were some other high-ranking officers, plus two or three lieutenants, like me, and a few ensigns. The senior lieutenant was the duty officer, a sort of general affairs manager. That was I. Aboard ship I would have been the deck officer. I had to handle all the details of our daily life, including providing food for the group, but I found the environment of the country house wonderful despite the responsibilities I had. The house was built on the Western style, faced with stucco, with a courtyard garden. Movie companies had used it frequently when they wanted a Western setting for a film. The house was built at the foot of a cliff just above the beach, and I took a room at the nearby Nagisa Hotel, which had also been taken over by the navy as an officers' residence, and commuted to work in the morning by walking along the beach from the hotel to the house. It seemed incongruous because sometimes it was as peaceful as any beach resort, yet we were right under the return path of the B-29's that were methodically hitting Tokyo and Kawasaki and Yokohama almost every day with incendiary bombs and high explosives.

Although I was very young, I had had plenty of management training at home already and I could take care of my entire group. There was a shortage of food in our unit, and we had to use our ingenuity to get enough to put on the table. A very clever ensign under me struck up a friendship with a fish shop owner from Zushi who used to show up on the beach frequently. As navy men we were entitled to a small sake ration and so we would exchange our sake, which was scarce, for a bit of fresh fish. But it still wasn't enough for young people to eat, so I hit upon another idea. I sent a letter to my family by military mail asking them to send me a barrel of soy sauce and a barrel of soybean paste marked "For Naval Use." At that time the Morita company was making dehydrated soy bean paste for the army—Japanese can do without almost anything but their soy bean soup—and alcohol products for the navy. This kind of shipment would not look unusual. Of course it was a naughty thing for me to do, but although I am sure it was a breach of regulations, we had to live by our wits in those days and I think I could have defended it successfully if I had been challenged. When the miso and the soy sauce arrived, we stored it in the basement, and whenever fish was available we would barter some of our precious hidden supply. That way our little unit stayed relatively well fed and happy under difficult circumstances.

I belonged to a special project group composed of researchers from the army, navy, and civilian sector, all working on heat-seeking devices. We were brainstorming the challenge, with the task of being original and audacious in our thinking. One of the civilian representatives in our group was a brilliant electronics engineer who was in charge of his own company in those days, a man who was destined to have a great deal of influence in my life. Masaru Ibuka is thirteen years my senior, but he was to become my very close friend, colleague, partner, and co-founder of the company we would create: the Sony Corporation.

Being part of this development group was quite heady stuff for me. I was young and cocky, but I was getting used to being in the company of superiors. We had all been thrown together on a project that was ahead of its time. Our small team spent days together, during which we got to know a great deal about each other, but we could not make much progress on the heat seeker. (The American Sidewinder missile, which is the sort of device we were trying to make, did not appear until many years after the war.) I was merely a recent university graduate, but in our joint meetings I found myself facing renowned professors and officers from the army who would lean across the table and demand, "What is the opinion of the navy on this point?" To which I had to reply, as seriously as I could, "Well, gentlemen, in the navy's view. . . ." I was grateful for my father's training in those moments.

Mr. Ibuka's contribution to this group was significant. He had devised a powerful amplifier at his company, the Japan Measuring Instrument Company, which was being used in a device that could detect a submarine thirty meters below the surface of the water by measuring any disturbance in the earth's magnetic flux. The unit was suspended from an airplane, and its key part was Ibuka's amplifier, which was powerful enough to detect and amplify a very small frequency of only one or two cycles per second to around six hundred cycles, where it could be noted. I have read that twenty-six enemy submarines were detected around Formosa with this device during its full-scale testing, but it was so late in the war that by the time the detector was ready to be deployed there weren't enough planes available to carry them. Japan was losing control of the air as American forces kept moving closer to Japan's main islands, with troops storming the island chain to the south and daily bombings destroying our aircraft factories.

As time went on the air raids became more frequent over Tokyo and all through the industrial and military area of Kawasaki and Yokohama, just north of our haven, which was on the Miura Peninsula. Whenever the raids began, the alarms would go off all around us, and although we were never bombed we were always alerted. It seemed to me that since we were at the bottom of the cliff it would be pretty difficult to be hit by a bomb, and besides, who would want to bomb us anyway? We were not an active military force, and I was sure the Americans didn't even know we existed. That was not military thinking, but it was logical. I felt if we got hit by a bomb it would be an accident. So I called everyone together to hear what I had in mind.

I put it as simply as possible. "Under naval regulations," I said, "we have to get up whenever the alarm sounds, put on our uniforms, and man the fire pumps. But since it seems almost impossible to get bombed in this location, I'm not going to wake you up even if the air raid alarms do go off." They seemed to like that.

"On the other hand," I warned them, "if a bomb does fall here there is nothing we could do about it. In that case it would be the end anyway." My colleagues accepted my reasoning with relief. And to show them that I meant what I said, I moved out of the hotel and very dramatically moved my gear into a second-floor room at our villa. It wasn't a brave thing to do at all. I realized that there would be no point in the Americans bombing a place like this. At the end, we weren't doing any really important research there anymore, and it seemed better to sleep during the night than to get up during each alert and drag through the next day suffering from lack of sleep.

III

In July and August of 1945, there were raids over the Tokyo-Yokohama area almost every day and every night. We could watch the big silver B-29's passing overhead after their bombing runs inland and an anti-aircraft battery nearby would open fire. Sometimes from our windows, we could see a B-29 being hit and falling into the sea. There were tracers crisscrossing the sky and spent shells all over the ground. During the raids, we could often feel the earth shaking, but we eventually slept through most of those raids. I guess I shouldn't admit that, but it has been many years and I think the statute of limitations must have run out by now.

The thing that concerned me a great deal then was that the military would not give up this war no matter how badly it was going and that the Miura Peninsula, where we were stationed, would become a bloody battleground, a last ditch battleground for the fanatical military, Japan's Bataan. We know now that there was an invasion plan, called "Olympic," that called for landings in our southernmost main island of Kyushu, but we all knew that the concentration of military targets in our area would be too important to bypass and that if worse came to worst, there would be a lot of fighting on the way to Tokyo. After the atomic bomb was dropped, I knew we were heading for the crisis. In the days following the bombing, many military people decided to take "official" trips to visit their families. But being duty officer I couldn't leave, even though

the situation was getting more and more worrisome and confused. One day I received orders to do some work in Nagoya,
and since my family home was nearby I asked for a day's leave
to visit my parents. My request was approved.

I remember that before leaving I announced to my fellow
officers that it was quite possible the war would end while I
was away. In that case, I said, no one could predict what would
happen to our station—the navy might even order us to commit
mass suicide. In that case, I said, I would not come back to
join them as they obeyed that final order. It was not much of
a joke, and I guess an officer of the Imperial Japanese Navy
should never have said such a thing to his superiors, but I just
had to say it. One lieutenant got very angry and yelled, "Lieutenant Morita, what are you talking about? If you do not come
back, you will be charged with desertion in the face of the
enemy!" It was the worst threat he could think of.

I turned to him and said calmly, "When this war ends,
Lieutenant, the crime of desertion in the face of the enemy will
no longer exist."

After taking care of my official business in Nagoya, I hurried back to our ancestral home in Kosugaya where my family
was then living again. The city of Nagoya and most of Aichi
Prefecture was targeted by the American Air Force because of
the industrial plants located there, which included aircraft factories—the famous Zero fighter was built in Nagoya—and anti-
aircraft artillery plants. By July the bombing had destroyed or
badly damaged half of the industrial buildings in Nagoya, and
statistics released sometime later said that 32 percent of the
population had been "dehoused" in the firebombing. It was
simply not safe for civilians, so many people who did not have
to be in the city moved away, like my parents. The bombing
caused millions of people to flee. Actually Nagoya suffered less
than Yokohama, where 69 percent of the population was home-
less, or Kobe, where the number was 58 percent, or Tokyo, with
46 percent. This put quite a burden on the people in the smaller
communities where the refugees sought shelter.

My future wife remained in Tokyo with her father and one
brother, and the rest of the family went to live with relatives
in the countryside. In Tokyo they survived the bombing in the
cramped backyard air raid shelter, but one night their fine old
house was destroyed by incendiaries, and they lived for weeks

in the shelter next to the rubble that was once their home. The house, which was brimming with books, smoldered so hotly for so long that Yoshiko actually cooked meals over the embers for many days.

It was the evening of August 14 when I found my family at home. We had a fine reunion, but my father looked worried. He was concerned about the end of the war. Like most Japanese then, he had sensed for a long time that the war was lost, but he had no idea how it would end and what would happen after. He confided to me that he was considering evacuating to some other, more remote place. I told him that there was no point in doing that, because from what I knew and could see, they were as safe where they were as anybody could be, considering the uncertainty of everyone's future. No one knew what to expect from the Americans. I told my father that I expected the war would not continue much longer. We talked until well past midnight, and then I fell asleep, exhausted.

I was shaken awake by my mother in the early morning—it seemed that I had hardly slept at all. Mother was agitated, and with great excitement she said that Emperor Hirohito was going to make an announcement on the radio at noon. It was August 15. Even the announcement that the emperor would speak to the nation was stunning. Something extraordinary was to come. The emperor's voice had never been heard by the Japanese people. In fact ordinary people were not allowed to look at him, and when he traveled by car or train, people along the route were required to face away. We all knew we were experiencing historic moments.

Because I was, after all, a naval officer, I put on my full uniform, including my sword, and I stood at attention while we listened to the broadcast. There was a lot of static on the radio and a lot of background noise, but the high, thin voice of His Majesty came through.

Although the people of Japan had never before heard his voice, we knew it was the emperor. He spoke in the highly mannered old-fashioned language of the court, and even though we couldn't follow the words exactly, we knew what the message was, what he was telling us, and we were frightened and yet relieved.

The war was over.

PEACE

Our New Life Begins

I

Suddenly our world was different. The emperor, who until now had never before spoken directly to his people, told us the immediate future would be grim. He said that we could "pave the way for a grand peace for all generations to come," but we had to do it "by enduring the unendurable and suffering what is insufferable." He urged Japan to look ahead. "Unite your total strength to be devoted to the construction for the future," he said. And he challenged the nation to "keep pace with the progress of the world."

I knew my duty was to go back to my station and do what would be required of me. Even though we all understood that the war was over, nobody knew what would happen next, and I was anticipating mass confusion. I could imagine the situation back at Zushi among the workers at our station, confused and uncertain about what had to be done. The civilians among them

35

were all very young and many of them were girls. They were my responsibility since I was the duty officer, and I felt it would be prudent to send them to their homes as soon as possible. We didn't know whether there would be a difficult occupation period or how the Japanese military would be treated. Would we all be arrested and thrown into jail?

I told my mother, "Whatever happens, I must go back," and I asked her to prepare some food for the road. She made a supply of cooked rice balls and wrapped them so I could carry them in my bag. I thought it might take me three days to get back to my base if the buses and trains were not running. I assumed that most local transport would be at a standstill and that I might have to hitch rides to get there. Food would be scarce on the way. I rode a borrowed bicycle about four miles to the local train station, and because I was an officer I had no trouble buying a ticket for the night train. I sat down and waited, expecting a long vigil, but to my surprise the train arrived precisely on time—very Japanese, I thought—and I got aboard expecting a difficult search for a seat, but I found the train had very few passengers. It was neat and clean and comfortable, so I had an easy trip back to Zushi and my station. And I still had most of a three-day supply of rice balls to eat.

My mission was turning out to be easier than I thought it would be—or at least different. Although I was not seeing it firsthand, there was confusion and fear all over Japan, and as I had expected there were some military attempts to prevent the surrender, one of them very close, at Atsugi, where Navy Captain Yasuna Kozono, an air group commander, gathered his men and told them that to surrender would be treason. Several air units in the area threatened to stage suicide attacks on the American fleet when it entered Tokyo Bay to accept the surrender, and the military affairs bureau immediately took the precaution of ordering all aircraft disarmed and fuel tanks emptied. There were other incidents, as I feared there would be. None, however, turned out to be the major last-ditch fight I expected from the navy. We were to learn much later that there had been attempts to prevent the emperor's message from being broadcast. Some young officers had planned to occupy the imperial palace to try to encourage the army to join in their rebellion against the surrender. A small band of rebels attacked the prime minister's official residence, and only by some quick thinking did the prime minister, Kantaro Suzuki, escape by using an emergency exit from his private residence. The rebels also searched for the lord privy seal, Marquis Kido, but he was safely inside the imperial palace. Some army and navy aviators even flew over the Tokyo area dropping leaflets calling on citizens to resist, saying the emperor's statement was invalid. Some army officers killed themselves to protest the surrender because technically the armies were still undefeated, although there had been grievous losses—no fewer than 2,750,000 Japanese soldiers, sailors, and airmen had died in the war. In the end even the military fanatics had to bow to the inevitable, "to endure the unendurable."

I was back on station by August 16, and some of my fellow officers reacted with surprise to see me—especially the officer I had taunted about not returning if suicide were ordered. He did not know me well, I thought. The officers all seemed to be in a kind of daze.

Many Japanese soldiers were soon on their way home from their bases around Japan and were beginning to crowd the trains and buses. It was difficult for some of them to understand the surrender. Although most of the Japanese army in the field was still unbeaten, it was stretched thin all across Asia. The string of horrendous losses at Leyte, Iwo Jima, Saipan, and Okinawa and America's superior air power against the home islands and the use of atomic weapons were evidence enough that the war could not be won. And then, of course, when the Soviet Union entered the war against Japan after the Hiroshima bomb, there was great fear that our old hypothetical enemy would take advantage of our weakened condition and try to occupy us. The Soviets seized the southern half of Sakhalin island and four islands just north of Hokkaido—the closest one is in sight of the Japanese mainland—and they still hold them today. The United States returned Okinawa, which they seized in 1945, to Japanese sovereignty in 1972.

In 1945 the Russians stormed into Manchuria—our buffer against them for so many years—when our forces were relatively small and weakened, unable to defend against massive Russian armor. There was chaos as Japanese civilians and soldiers tried to escape from the Russians, but in the end about five hundred thousand Japanese soldiers were taken prisoner and sent to labor camps in Siberia and other places in the

Soviet Union. Some of them remained prisoners and virtual slave laborers for as long as twelve years. Many families of Japanese in Manchuria were split in the confusion. Orphans were taken in by Chinese, and in some cases Japanese mothers and fathers unable to escape were able to persuade Chinese families to take their children in and protect them. Even today, four decades after the war, each year Chinese citizens who believe they are children separated from their parents in the confusion of defeat are brought to Japan and helped in the search for their long-lost relatives. Amazingly, some still manage to locate their aged parents or other kin, sometimes through telling what little they remember of their lives before the separation or by some scar or distinguishing mark. But, of course, as the years go by fewer and fewer of those parents are alive. There are those who say to this day that the emperor's decision to surrender was brought about almost as much by the fear of the Soviets—the fear that they might invade the home islands or partition the country, as had been done to Germany—as by the horrible events at Hiroshima and Nagasaki.

To most Japanese the end of the war was a great relief as well as a national tragedy. Japanese newspapers reported the beginning of the Occupation with breathless articles describing the Occupation and the occupiers in surprising ways. For example, the Domei news agency described a group of American navy fliers as being "very light-hearted and agreeable; they did not show any attitude, whether in speech or manner, of boasting of their victory. . . . The agreeable attitude shown by these pilots is something of which every Japanese must be ever mindful when coming into contact with the U.S. occupational forces from now on." Some Japanese even toasted the arrival of the Americans, but most looked at them with some fear and suspicion.

Meanwhile, we had no orders. We waited for days, with nothing to do but drink sake. The first order that came told us to burn our important documents, and I sometimes think we were much too diligent about it. I burned all my papers, including all my reports and all the data from our experiments. I had some personal notebooks and records, and I burned them, too, although I have often thought since then that they would be very interesting to have now and that I had been foolish to burn them. Later, we received a message ordering us to save some particular kinds of data, but it was too late—everything had gone up in smoke. Many people throughout Japan were burning their records in those days because no one knew how the Americans would treat us as a conquered people, whether they would look for incriminating evidence, or what. Newspapers burned their photographic archives; some companies did away with their records—all needlessly. Some people actually buried important papers and family records in their gardens. It was an example of just how confused things were throughout the country, not just at navy headquarters. We were also ordered to destroy any important machinery, but we didn't have any special machines; we didn't even have any weapons. Then finally an order came authorizing me to send the work staff home. It was the order I was waiting for, but carrying out the mission was more difficult than ordering it to be done. There was a lack of transport for ordinary workers. Some families of our staff were separated and living in evacuation areas far away from their normal homes. So I had to plan how I would get these people moved out, and quickly. How could we do it without transportation or food? The ensign who discovered the fish merchant who dealt with us for sake and bean paste came to me with a novel idea.

We realized that the office furniture and laboratory equipment we had was valuable, perhaps worth more than money in a time of war shortages. We had been told to destroy it. In some units, men were taking this property home and selling it on the black market. Taking a cue from the profiteers, we went to the biggest trucking company in the area and bargained the many storage batteries we had been using in our experiments for the shipment of luggage to the homes of our employees. The company was badly in need of the batteries for their trucks and was glad to make the swap. We threw in some of the office equipment, lockers, and desks for good measure. The National Railways stationmaster at Zushi was also very happy to get some used navy office furniture in exchange for most of the express train tickets and luggage transport we needed for our civilian staff.

I sent the high school students and the young women home first. There were rumors going around that we navy officers might be declared war criminals, and the civilians might be arrested. I thought that would be unlikely and illogical since we had never even fought against the Americans, but this kind of fear was typical in the confusion that existed, and I believed it was best to get our people home quickly just to play it safe. We didn't have any idea of what the behavior of the American troops would be so we wanted the women to be home. Because there was such a shortage of engineers during the war, our unit had been sent a group of third-year senior high school science students, about twenty of them, and these very young boys were also among the first ones I wanted to send home. But two of the boys didn't have a home to go back to, since their parents were living in Korea or Manchuria, I can't remember which, so I sent them to my parents. I gave them a letter to my mother, saying, "I cannot tell how long we will be kept here. We might even be killed by the Americans. So please take care of these two boys." Later my mother chided me, saying, "Why did you send us two big eaters at a time when there was no rice?"

We sat around doing nothing for many days before new orders came. After we had sent all the boys and girls home we didn't have anything to do. With an optical telescope we had, we would inspect the American ships that kept arriving in Sagami Bay before they went up to Tokyo Bay for the signing of the surrender document on the USS *Missouri*. It was a remarkable sight—it looked as though the entire U.S. Navy had steamed into the bay right in front of us. I was eager to get out of there, and when the time came I took the first train home. It was quite a reunion, because both of my brothers arrived back home about the same time, all of us safe and sound, to the great joy of my father and mother. We had managed to do our duty and had come home without physical scars. We had also avoided the fanaticism that seemed to grip so much of Japan's youth in those days, inculcated with worship of the emperor and the idea of glorious death. In Japan we often talk of a psychological climate or atmosphere that sometimes occurs and which seems to sweep people up into like-minded activity, as though everybody is breathing the same special kind of air. During the war the authorities took advantage of this trait by starting movements to volunteer—as happened in my younger brother's middle-school class. Many eager young Japanese were caught up in this atmosphere and volunteered, but many young kamikaze pilots who were frustrated by not being able to make their final flight later lived to be grateful that they did not have the opportunity. When the emperor spoke to the people and made a tour of the nation after the war as the nation's symbol, a kind of revered father figure instead of a god, a calming sense of normality began to return. To many people, now that the war was over, it was as though the country had suffered a gigantic natural disaster.

The new period of peace was strange. The bombers did not come anymore, but many cities looked as though there was nothing more to bomb. In the heart of cities such as Osaka, Nagoya, Yokohama, and Tokyo, only the sturdy concrete or stone buildings remained. Flimsy houses, shops, and factories made of wood and paper had burned like dry tinder under a shower of incendiary bombs dropped in huge clusters by the B-29's. The firebreaks cut through certain neighborhoods to contain the damage had been useless because the winds and flying embers easily leaped over them. In Tokyo, less than half of the prewar population of seven million remained in the city after the bombings started. Nearly four million had gone to the countryside or to smaller cities. The calamity was worse than the earthquake of 1923 for Tokyo, but the devastation by fire was similar, so some Tokyoites had seen their city destroyed twice in their lifetime.

At the end of the war, only 10 percent of the city's streetcars were running. There were only sixty buses in running condition and just a handful of automobiles and trucks. Most had been converted to run on charcoal and wood when liquid fuels ran out. Sickness was rampant and the tuberculosis rate was somewhere about 22 percent. Hospitals were short of everything, including bandages, cotton, and disinfectants. Department store shelves were empty or held a lot of useless unsold goods like violin bows and unstrung tennis rackets. Some movie theaters were still open and showing films, and they were crowded with people who had nothing to do and nowhere to go and wanted to divert their minds from their misery for a couple of hours.

The Morita family was fortunate because we had lost no one in the war and the company offices and factory in Nagoya, and even our home, survived with no serious bombing damage. After the first few days of reunion and relaxation, we began discussing the future, and particularly mine, as the eldest son. Father was still very healthy and robust and in charge of the business, and there really wasn't any need for me at the Morita company at the time. During the war the factory had continued to operate on war work, producing powdered miso and alcohol, and so the business was in working condition. I made some suggestions for improvements while I was home, but there was no direct need for me at the factory—it had enough managers with my father and his regular staff. Besides, I was only twenty-four and everybody agreed there would be plenty of time for me to move into the company later.

During my first few weeks at home, I received a letter from Professor Hattori, the physics teacher who had been such a good adviser to me in higher school. He said he had moved to the physics department at the Tokyo Institute of Technology, and he was helping to create a special school for demobilized students whose science education had been cut short by the war. His problem was a shortage of teachers, and he invited me—urged me strongly—to join the faculty. I thought it was a great idea because it would keep me in physics and would get me to Tokyo, where I hoped I could find other possibilities for interesting work now that the navy and the entire Japanese military establishment had been abolished. I got my parents' agreement to take the teaching job, and luckily, while I was still at home, I managed to reestablish contact again with Ibuka, the brilliant engineer I had worked with on the research project team. He was opening a new lab in Tokyo.

I had been in touch with Ibuka infrequently in those last few months of the war. As the war was coming to an end, it became more and more difficult for him to get to our villa because he had moved his factory to Nagano Prefecture, several hours northwest of Tokyo by train, because the Tokyo factory and lab were located in a target area where there were many small factories. He traveled to my lab in Zushi for meetings many times, but I had also made trips to the apple orchard in Nagano where his new factory was located. One day in Nagano I began talking to Ibuka about what we would do after the war when I realized we both knew from listening to shortwave radio that the war was lost.

Ibuka had other inside information. His father-in-law was Tamon Maeda, a right-hand man of Prince Fumimaro Konoe. Konoe had been prime minister of Japan several times and had fought against the military clique that eventually dominated the government and plunged Japan into war. Maeda was later picked as Japan's first postwar minister of education but was caught in one of the purges six months later and forced to resign because he had been associated with wartime government officials. Near the end of the war, Maeda lost his Tokyo home in the bombing and moved to the mountain resort town of Karuizawa, not too far from Nagano. Ibuka visited him there often. In those meetings he learned a lot about what was happening diplomatically and militarily.

The company that Ibuka ran was called Nihon Sokuteiki, or Japan Measuring Instrument Company, and its factory in Nagano Prefecture employed fifteen hundred people making small mechanical elements that controlled the frequency of radar devices. These devices had to oscillate at exactly one thousand cycles per second, and Ibuka had the ingenious idea of hiring music students, who had a fine sense of pitch, to check the accuracy of the elements against a simple one thousand–cycle tuning fork. I mention this as an example of the freshness and inventiveness of his mind, which so much impressed me and made me want to work with this man.

But Ibuka didn't feel professionally satisfied out there in the countryside, merely producing components in large quantity. Ibuka told Taiji Uemura, who was president of his company, that he wanted to move back to Tokyo, and Uemura reluctantly let him go and then offered to help set him up in business. Ibuka had another friend who owned what was left of a department store in Tokyo called Shirokiya, at Nihonbashi, which was literally in the bombed-out heart of Tokyo. The building had been a target because there was a vacuum tube factory underground.

In this empty and bare old building, set among the rubble and devastation, the burned-out homes and shops of the once-prosperous downtown area of Tokyo, Ibuka started Tokyo Tsushin Kenkyusho, or Tokyo Telecommunications Research Laboratories, with seven employees from the old Tokyo factory who had previously moved with him to Nagano. They squeezed into the old telephone operator's room on the third floor of the building and later used space on the seventh floor. Ibuka once told me that the rest of the employees who had moved from Tokyo originally didn't want to return because there were few places to live in Tokyo and food was scarce. They also knew that there was very little money in the company's coffers then and that there was, at best, a very uncertain future for the new company.

Ibuka's resources were all in his own pocket and in his head. (There was a trickle of cash coming in from the sale of voltmeters made by his old company.) The small group sat in conference in the depressing surroundings of the burned-out department store, and for weeks they tried to figure out what kind of business this new company could enter in order to make money to operate. In those days, only the black market prospered, and it was the only place to get certain components. The major old, established electronics companies were getting started and had little interest in selling parts to a competitor. Ibuka's idea was to build something new, but first the company had to establish a financial base. Many strange ideas were suggested in the early conferences. For example, one member of the team said that since most of central Tokyo had been burned out and was leveled, the company should lease some vacant land and open a miniature golf course. The people needed some entertainment, they reasoned. The movie theaters were crowded to capacity in those days. Everybody needed some escape. Another suggested that the food business was a sure money-earner and that perhaps sweet bean paste cakes would be a good line.

Actually, food was on everybody's mind, and so the group finally decided to work on a simple rice cooker, but they never perfected it, although they made many experimental models. The device was a simple wooden tub with spiral-shaped electrodes in the bottom. It depended on the conductivity of the wet rice to complete the electrical circuit and heat up the rice. The idea was that when the rice was cooked and began to dry, conductivity would be lost, the electrical circuit would automatically be cut, and the owner could sit down to dinner. But consistent results were never possible. Ibuka and his staff tried eating the stuff, but sometimes it would be overcooked and sometimes undercooked. They gave it up. They even thought of a bread-baking device based on the same principle of conductivity—the wet dough closing the circuit between the metal ends of a wooden box—but never really produced one. Finally, the wives were put to work helping to produce heating pads, stitching the wires to the cloth. The pads were popular in the street markets and brought in some badly needed cash to the families of the company employees.

But Ibuka hadn't made his move to Tokyo to go into the

entertainment or food business or to sell home-made heating pads. He had a more intriguing idea: since shortwave receivers were strictly prohibited during the war, a keen interest had developed in listening to shortwave broadcasts. Now that it was no longer illegal, perhaps the demand could be met. Ibuka figured out a way. Because the radio was very important for hearing air raid warnings and getting other information during the war, people had taken very good care of their radios, but they could only receive medium-wave band, regular AM broadcasts. So Ibuka designed a shortwave adapter unit consisting of a small wooden box and a simple radio circuit that required only one vacuum tube. This could be attached to any standard radio very simply and would convert the unit to shortwave reception. The employees had to scrounge through the black market to get the tubes, some of which were very expensive, but the product became very popular and it gave all the people at Tokyo Tsushin Kenkyusho a boost of confidence.

Maeda had a friend on Japan's biggest newspaper, the *Asahi Shimbun*, and this man, Ryuzo Kaji, wrote a regular column called, literally, "Blue Pencil." The *Asahi* newspaper in those days consisted of only one sheet because of the lack of newsprint, but the article on October 6, 1945, gave the new company some generous promotion:

> There is welcome news about how receivers some people may already have in their homes can be simply modified to pick up shortwave signals. Mr. Masaru Ibuka, a former lecturer at Waseda University's department of science and engineering and son-in-law of Minister of Education Tamon Maeda, recently put up a sign for the Tokyo Telecommunications Research Laboratory on the third floor of Shirokiya in Nihonbashi. From noncommercial motives, he has set out to spread the use of shortwave receivers by the conversion of regular receivers or by the use of an additional device. With the fairly high-class super heterodyne receiver, just a simple conversion allows you to turn it into a fine shortwave receiver. With sets one step above this, high frequency shortwave can be received with the implementation of an additional device.

The article went on to predict that eventually private broadcasts would be permitted by the Occupation authorities and that upgrading existing radios would be essential because of the expected "entanglement of wires" when the many new stations began broadcasting. It suggested that "by using an additional device, boundaries can be extended so that even these are rendered audible." By way of describing Ibuka, the writer said he "used to manage a weaponry company, but now he wants to make the technology he is so familiar with into something that can be put to good use. He is starting anew as the town's scholar. He says that he will accept any kind of questions including those regarding the repair of regular receivers."

As it turned out, Kaji got just some of it wrong—Ibuka had not been in the weaponry business, and he wasn't too keen on making repairs to old sets. And, of course, if the business turned out to be noncommercial it was not by choice; Ibuka really needed the money to keep paying his employees. I was fortunate enough to be reading the Nagoya edition of the paper on October 6 and was overjoyed to get the "welcome news" about my old friend Ibuka. I wrote to him immediately and said I would like to visit him in Tokyo. I said I wanted to help him in his new business and would support him any way I could. He wrote back immediately, inviting me to come see him and the new company, but told me that things were pretty tight and that he was paying his people out of his own pocket and was looking for funding.

I traveled up to Tokyo to take my new teaching job, and after settling myself in a friend's house on the western rim of Tokyo, where there had been less damage from the bombing than in the central city, I lost no time in looking up my friend Ibuka in Nihonbashi. Ibuka's new company headquarters in the almost gutted department store building looked pathetic. But there was enthusiasm on Ibuka's face, and he and his employees were happy to be working at a time when so few people knew what would become of them.

Because I knew Ibuka was having trouble meeting his payroll, I got the idea that I could work with this new company part-time and teach part-time. In this way, Ibuka would not have to pay me very much because I would have my teaching salary and we could both make ends meet. Ibuka and I talked for a long time about starting our own company—we had both been thinking about this since soon after we first met—and we finally decided in March 1946 that we would do it when we could get the details worked out. So there I was, a university instructor on the government payroll and a part-time researcher at Ibuka's new company with plans to form our own new company. We both realized that before we could actually form the new company there was the delicate question of my obligations to my family to be considered. So I joined Ibuka, and Maeda, who had resigned as minister of education, on the night train to Kosugaya in April 1946, where they intended to ask my father to help the new company by allowing me to join. They felt they wanted to demonstrate their courtesy toward my father because they knew what it meant to take a first son out of the family business.

In Japan it was considered a serious thing to take a son, especially a first son, out of his home and family environment and bring him permanently into a new atmosphere in the world of business. In some cases, it was almost as though an adoption were taking place. The practice of formally discussing such a plan with the parents is sometimes done today in some business circles, particularly in small enterprises. But even in large companies, family background and recommendations and unspoken pledges of sincerity on both sides are still indicated when a young man joins his business family. The commitments are genuine because they cover a working life, not just casual employment for a few years as in some countries where there is much more worker mobility. I was, indeed, taking on another family and another, different set of responsibilities.

Our journey had been uncomfortable. There were broken windows in the old railway coach and we had to sit in a blast of cold air, smoke, and soot all the way, but the welcome at the Morita house in Kosugaya was very warm. Ibuka said recently that he still remembers how well my family entertained him and Maeda, "even though it was only with bread—the Morita family owned a bakery and it was beautiful bread—and served with butter and jam and tea." Even these things were luxuries in the aftermath of the war. There were barely enough of the necessities. Japanese were feeding their smallest children their scarce rice a single grain at a time. Most people had difficulty even getting rice. During the war, people had become accustomed through necessity to mixing barley and even potato with the bit of rice they could get. The war had bankrupted and demoralized the nation and millions were struggling through those last days at a bare subsistence level.

After our socializing, Ibuka and Maeda told my father about the new venture and what they hoped to accomplish and they said that I was absolutely needed in the new business. When they had finished, we all waited tensely for a response. Father was obviously prepared for the moment. With very little hesitation, he said that he expected me to succeed him as head of the family and had also expected me to take over the family business. Then he turned to Maeda and Ibuka and said, "But if my son wants to do something else to develop himself or utilize his capabilities, he should do it." He looked at me and smiled. "You are going to do what you like best," he said. I was delighted. Ibuka was astounded. He told me later, "I thought it would be harder to get you." My younger brother, Kazuaki, who was then studying at Waseda University in Tokyo, volunteered to take over as the sake brewer of the Morita family when the time came for father to retire. There were smiles all around. Everyone was relieved and happy.

Back in Tokyo we pooled our resources for the establishment of our new company, Tokyo Tsushin Kogyo, or Tokyo Telecommunications Engineering Company—it came to about five hundred dollars. It was not a princely sum, or even an adequate one. We soon ran out of money, and in those days we turned often to my father for loans. He had faith in us and our new company, and he did not press for repayment. So I decided to give him stock in the company. It turned out to be a wise investment for him because his faith was well rewarded. The stock added up and he became a major shareholder in the company.

Although I appreciated having the separate income from my teaching job at Tokyo Institute of Technology, my heart was not in teaching. I was eager to get to work in our new company full-time. And so I was actually pleased to read in the paper one day that the Occupation authorities had decided to purge all teachers in Japanese schools who had been professional army or navy personnel. I figured that this meant me, because I was a professional technical officer, and according to my commission I had been committed to a lifetime in the now defunct Imperial Japanese Navy. The military purge ordered by the Allied Powers General Headquarters, which ran the Occupation (everybody called it GHQ for short), was based on the idea that professional military men, who had been the main culprits in the war and had controlled the government, should not be teaching and perhaps adversely influencing the impressionable schoolchildren of postwar Japan. The purge was good news for me, because I now had an excuse to be released from my commitment to the university and I could take up my job with the new company full-time.

I went to Professor Hattori and told him that while I appreciated the teaching job I could not continue because of this news. He went to the office to check, but was told there had been no formal advice from the Ministry of Education so they could not say what should be done. The school asked me to continue until the university received official notice, so I had to continue to lecture for a couple more months. I was eager to leave, but I felt obligated to continue helping my old mentor, Professor Hattori. I just couldn't quit. When still no notification had come, I got a bold idea. I showed the newspaper article to the dean, Koroku Wada, and expressed my concern that if I continued to teach and it were discovered, the university might be punished or penalized for not "cleaning house" on its own. I said, "According to this I should be purged, but your office said I should continue nevertheless. I am afraid that if I continue you might be in trouble and I do not want to be responsible for it." The dean considered this idea and finally said, "All right, you can stop teaching today." And so my formal teaching career ended then. I said a fond goodbye to Professor Hattori and went happily to the new company.

Months went by without any notice that I had been officially purged from my university job, and every month the school would call to tell me to come and pick up my pay, because for some reason I remained on the payroll. And even though I wasn't teaching, my salary increased every two or three months as adjustments were made for inflation. This went on until October of 1946, when the Ministry of Education finally got around to issuing my personal purge notice. I welcomed the subsidy while it lasted, because our new company was not setting any records for financial success in those days.

In August 1946, the Shirokiya department store was about to be renovated, and we were told there would be no room in it for us. We moved into other quarters for a while, in Kichijoji, one of the oldest sections of Tokyo, but they were not satisfactory. Finally, we settled down in a very cheap, dilapidated wooden shack on Gotenyama, a hill once famous for the beauty of its cherry trees in bloom, in Shinagawa near the southern edge of the city. Gotenyama had been fortified as part of the defenses of Tokyo Bay in 1853, but when we moved into our weatherbeaten old building on a cold day in January 1947, Gotenyama looked anything but fortified; the evidence of defeat was all around us. We could see bomb damage wherever we looked. There were leaks in the roof and we literally had to open umbrellas over our desks sometimes. But although we were far from the center of the city, we could be more independent here and had more room than at the department store.

In order to get to the rooms where Tokyo Tsushin Kogyo was located, you had to duck under some clotheslines on which the neighbors sometimes had their children's diapers drying in the breeze. When some of my relatives came to see me, they were so shocked by the shabby conditions that they thought I had become an anarchist and they said so to my mother. They could not understand how, if I was not a radical, I could choose to work in a place like that when I could have been in Nagoya, living as befitted my "station" as the son of the president of a long-established company.

II

During the search for a likely product to make, it was often suggested to Ibuka that we make a radio receiver—there was still a strong demand in Japan for radios, not just shortwave adapters—but Ibuka adamantly refused. His reasoning was that the major companies were likely to have a very fast recovery from the war and would make use of their own components in their own products first and sell parts to others later. Also, they would naturally keep their latest technology to themselves, trying to preserve their lead over their competitors as long as possible. Ibuka and I had often spoken of the concept of our new company as an innovator, a clever company that would make new high technology products in ingenious ways. Merely building radios was not our idea of the way to fulfill these ideals.

We took our own unscientific survey of Japan's surviving households. We had already sold quite a few shortwave radio adapters to enhance the medium-wave radios that many Japanese had carefully preserved through the war, and now we realized that there were a lot of phonographs out there as well. New motors and magnetic pickups were impossible to get during the war, and so it became obvious that there was a market for these items to be used to repair and upgrade the old wartime and prewar phonographs. The new, popular American swing and jazz music was arriving on records, and people were hungry for it. The Americans had brought their music with them, and a process was started during the Occupation of informing Japan about the United States and how the American people lived. The Occupation authorities had taken over control of the broadcasting stations and the English language could now be taught in the schools again and used on the air after being banned during the war years. Ideas of democracy and individual freedom and egalitarianism were being planted on very fertile soil after so many years of thought control and military dictatorship.

During the Occupation, everything was in short supply and the black market was the place everyone had to shop. Our new company—we formally incorporated Tokyo Tsushin Kogyo on May 7, 1946—managed to buy a small, very-much-used Datsun truck for the equivalent of about one hundred dollars. As it turned out, Ibuka and I, the two top officers of the company, were the only members who had driver's licenses, so we had to make the deliveries and go out and do the shopping and bring supplies and materials to the factory. We would do our "executive" work, help load the delivery goods in the truck, crank it to get it started, and make the deliveries or run the errands.

The street scene in Tokyo was chaotic, noisy, smoky, and smelly. Gasoline was very scarce and expensive, when you could find it. Many of the cars, trucks, and buses had been modified to run on waste oil, charcoal, or other solids that were burnable, including garbage and coal dust. They were still running after the war. Even an occasional donkey cart appeared in the streets. We always managed to get gasoline for our truck through legitimate and other means. But so many American soldiers were selling gasoline, siphoning it out of their jeeps and trucks and some actually selling it by the barrel, that the military authorities tried to stop it by putting a red dye in it. Random roadblocks were set up. The police would stop the traffic and an MP would put a long glass tube into your gas tank, stopper it with his finger, pull it out, and check the color. If it was red you had a lot of explaining to do. But they soon began to catch fewer and fewer people because some clever Japanese had discovered that you could filter out the pink color with charcoal and was doing a thriving business "legitimizing" black market gasoline.

We knew that the big electric companies were not interested in the replacement parts business; they were making and selling new phonographs. And while the parts business was certainly not the idealistic, high technology endeavor we were working toward, Ibuka knew what he was doing. The new motors and pickups we made were as good as people could get in those days, and they kept the company afloat financially. Money was very tight, and stringent controls against inflation created problems for us, because they froze a large part of the money in circulation. The authorities put limits on how much money an individual or a company could withdraw from the bank. This was the original reason for putting everybody to work making heating pads—to sell some things directly to the public to raise cash.

But Ibuka had his mind set on producing a completely new consumer product—not just an upgrading of what had been on the prewar market, but something entirely new for Japan, a wire recorder. We had seen examples of wire recorders made in Germany, and research was being done on special steel wire for these machines at Tohoku University in northern Japan. The researchers had already developed excellent new technology for magnetic steel in their laboratories.

Ibuka learned that Sumitomo Metals Corporation was capable of producing the kind of steel wire needed, a special wire with a diameter of exactly one-tenth of a millimeter, something very difficult to make. Ibuka made a trip to Osaka to talk with Sumitomo about producing wire for the new recorder, but the company was not interested in his order. He represented a small, new company asking for a very high-tech product that was expensive to produce and for which there would be only one customer. Other companies that had the capability to make the wire had the same reaction. But as it sometimes happens, the refusal turned out to be a blessing in disguise. We weren't able to make a wire recorder, which was a disappointment. But the bright side was that there was a recorder in our future, a much better product, the tape recorder, although we didn't know it at the time.

The Occupation forces had taken over the Japan Broadcasting Company, NHK, Japan's version of the BBC, and they needed new technical equipment such as mixing units and other studio and broadcasting equipment, with which Ibuka was familiar. Ibuka submitted a bid on a contract to build a large broadcast mixing unit for NHK, and the American officer in charge, a brigadier general, came around to our shack in Gotenyama to look over this unknown factory and its management and to discuss the specifications. Ibuka's friend Shigeo Shima was in charge of engineering reconstruction of war damage at NHK, and Shima had recommended that Ibuka get the contract. Shima came with the general on his inspection trip, but when the general saw our shop he was taken aback by how primitive it was, and he shook his head. He could not understand why the man from NHK was recommending this tiny, unknown company working in such primitive conditions. Ibuka's friend could only ask the general to trust his judgment, and the officer was finally persuaded to go along with the recommendation, but he was so concerned about our terrible building that he recommended we keep buckets of sand and water around the place in case of fire.

When the equipment was delivered to the NHK headquarters, then located only about a half mile from General MacArthur's headquarters in downtown Tokyo, everyone marveled at its quality, especially the skeptical officer, who was still puzzled by the fact that a small, new company in a makeshift factory could produce such a high-technology product. There were congratulations and smiles all around, and the general was very pleased. I think we were able to obtain further jobs from the American Forces Radio Service and the Far East Air Force because of the breakthrough in trust we made on that first job by demonstrating our quality.

While Ibuka was at NHK delivering the mixing unit and accepting congratulations, he spotted an American-made Wilcox-Gay tape recorder in one of the offices, the first tape recorder he had laid eyes on. After a brief examination of it, he made a decision. The wire recorder he had been trying to build couldn't match this tape recorder. There were some obvious drawbacks to a wire recorder, wonderful as the concept was. For one thing, in order to get decent fidelity, the wire had to pass over the recording and playback heads at a very fast speed, which meant you had to have a lot of wire on large spools. You could only store a limited amount of wire on the spools—or else you had to have too-thin wire, or enormous spools. Worse, it was not possible to edit the wire recording simply. Whatever you re-corded on it had to be perfect. If you wanted to change a part of something that was already recorded on the wire, you would have to rerecord it in perfect synchronization with what was already on the wire, something very difficult to do.

But it was obvious from just a glance at the new machine that tape was much easier to work with. Unlike the wire, tape could be spliced easily and simply, so that changes could be recorded separately and inserted wherever they were needed. You could get a lot of tape on a reasonably small spool. Best of all, the fidelity of the tape recordings was better than wire recorders could produce. We had read something about tape recording, which was invented in Germany. In fact, during the war the Germans were using tape for running many of their propaganda programs—they went on for hours and hours. Ampex in the United States was among the earliest companies in the hardware end of this new business right after the war, and the major tape producer was Minnesota Mining and Manufactur-ing Company, now called 3M Company. The technology was growing and improving. This kind of machine, not a wire re-corder, was what Ibuka now wanted our company to produce.

By this time, Ibuka had talked about so many different products as possibilities that his colleagues, and especially the accountant, were getting weary, and Ibuka knew he had a grow-ing credibility problem. He was determined to build a new tape recorder for Japan, and he had to convince his colleagues and our tightfisted comptroller that this was a viable idea. Ibuka talked to the American officer at NHK and asked per-mission to borrow the tape recorder for just a little while to show to his fellow workers. The officer was reluctant but finally agreed to bring the tape recorder to the company himself to demonstrate it. Everybody crowded around for the demonstration, and when it was over everybody was convinced that this would be a good project for the company to work on. Everybody, that is, except our accountant, Junichi Hasegawa, a man my father had sent to us from the family business to help us keep our little company financially sound.

Hasegawa and Shuzaburo Tachikawa, our company's general affairs manager, had both cast a cold and critical eye on everything we were doing and thought this new idea would be too expensive and held little promise. They did not think we should allocate money to do R&D on the project. Ibuka and I were so excited by the new concept of the tape recorder and so convinced it was right for us that we decided to gang up on Hasegawa and make him see the light. We invited him to dinner at a black market restaurant, where we had a magnificent feast complete with beer, which was a rare commodity then. We ate and drank long into the night. We told him all about the virtues of the tape recorder and how it would revolutionize an industry and how we could get in on this new field early, that we could beat all the slow-moving competition of the giant companies if we started immediately, but that we would have to be clever and fast on our feet. We must have done a terrific selling job on him because he approved our project on a full stomach right then and there and we were on our way.

Or so we thought. We soon realized that the main trouble we had was that we didn't know anything about how to make the crucial part of the system, the recording tape. Tape was the heart of the new project and the tape was a mystery to us. From our early work on wire recorders, we were pretty confident about building the mechanical and electronic components for a tape recorder. But the tape itself was a different problem. No one in Japan had any experience with magnetic recording tape, and there were no imports available to us, so we knew we would have to make our own tape. Our strategy from the beginning was not only to build a machine, but also to make and sell the recording tape, because we knew there would be a continuing market for tape from our customers who bought recorders. If we sold tape recorders and not tape, we would be handing good business to our eventual competitors.

Our first and most difficult problem was to get or produce the base material. We had no plastic. We had only cellophane, which we knew was inadequate, but we had to use what was on hand. Ibuka and I and a brilliant young engineer, Nobutoshi Kihara, worked as a team, cutting cellophane into long quarter-inch-wide strips and coating it with various experimental materials. It was soon obvious to us that this would not work because even the best and strongest grade of cellophane could only take one or two passes through the recording mechanism before it was stretched hopelessly out of shape, which distorted the sound. We hired chemists to figure out how to toughen cellophane, but that didn't work either. We tried thicker cellophane. No luck. Finally, I asked a cousin of mine, Goro Kodera, who worked for Honshu Paper Company, if he thought it would be possible to produce a very strong, very thin, and very smooth kraft paper that we might be able to use as a base for our tape. He said he thought it was worth a try, and in a little while he supplied us with some good quality paper and we went to work with our razor blades again.

Finding good magnetic material to coat our tape with was almost impossible in that time of shortages. It seems incredible even to me now, but Ibuka, Kihara, and I made those first tapes by hand. We would cut enough tape for a small reel and then we would lay out the long strip on the floor of our laboratory. Our first attempts to get a magnetic material were failures; the material was not right because the magnets we ground into powder were too powerful. We needed only a weak magnetic material for our tape. Kihara's research led him to oxalic ferrite, which becomes ferric oxide when burned. That was it! But where to get it? I grabbed Kihara and we went to the pharmaceutical wholesalers' district of Tokyo, and there, sure enough, we found the only store that handled the stuff. We bought two bottles of it and brought it back to the lab. We had no electric furnace to heat the chemical, so we borrowed a frying pan and, stirring the stuff with a wooden spoon, we cooked it until it turned brown and black; the brown stuff was ferric oxide and the black was ferrous tetraoxide. Kihara had the knack for checking the color of the powder and removing it from the frying pan at just the right color. We mixed this with a clear Japanese lacquer to get just the right consistency so we could airbrush it onto the strip. The airbrush technique didn't work, so we tried everything we could think of and ended up painting the coating on by hand with fine brushes made of the soft bristles from a raccoon's belly. To our surprise, we found this gave us the best results.

Those first paper tapes were terrible, of course. Ibuka said the quality was so bad you could hardly hear anyone say "moshi-moshi," the Japanese telephone greeting. But we were proud of it. At that time we had forty-five people working for us, and over a third of them were college graduates. We were top-heavy with brains, but we couldn't make the high-quality product we wanted to without plastic for our tape. When we were able to get plastic, we developed our own technology for using it. We had the technology ready and were on the market with tape early on. (Ibuka was so determined to get into the tape field that we put a lot of extra effort into it, and some years later, in November 1965, he got his satisfaction—as we all did—when IBM chose our magnetic recording tape for data storage in its computers. It was thrilling for all of us when our company began to provide the technology for making magnetic tape to IBM and set up the machinery and installed the technicians at the IBM facility in Boulder, Colorado.)

In those early days, the tape was the key to the future of our business. As for the hardware, we had the tape recorder mechanism perfected to the state of the art. The machine we produced in 1950 was bulky and heavy, but it worked beautifully, in our estimation, and I was absolutely convinced that after all this work we were finally on the road to great success. When our machine was ready for sale, we were confident that once customers saw it and heard it we would be swamped with orders.

We were in for a rude awakening. The tape recorder was so new to Japan that almost no one knew what a tape recorder was, and most of the people who did know could not see why they should buy one. It was not something people felt they needed. We could not sell it.

III

Looking back on it from today's vantage point, I can see pretty clearly what some of our other problems were. That first big boxy machine weighed thirty-five kilos (about seventy-five pounds) and we put a price of one hundred and seventy thousand yen on it. That was a lot of money in Japan during the Occupation period, when the new yen was officially exchanged at three hundred and sixty to the U.S. dollar. Few individuals in Japan had that much money to spend on something they didn't know they needed. (In those days, a university graduate working in industry earned less than ten thousand yen a month.) We made fifty of these recorders for a market that didn't seem to exist. Neither Ibuka nor I had had any real training in the consumer end of things or any real experience in making consumer products or selling them. Ibuka had made only products for the government or for broadcasting, except for his early shortwave adapters and phonograph replacement parts. I had never made anything for sale to anyone. And although I had had a lot of management training as a boy from my father, which I could put to use in the navy, I had no experience in merchandising or salesmanship. It never occurred to Ibuka or me that there was any need for this. Ibuka believed strongly that all we had to do was make good products and the orders would come. So did I. We both had a lesson to learn.

We were engineers and we had a big dream of success. We thought that in making a unique product, we would surely make a fortune. I was determined to make this tape recorder a success; when it was ready I demonstrated it every day, wherever I could find an audience. I took it to businesses, to the universities. I loaded it into the truck and took it to friends and recorded their voices talking and singing, every day. I was like an entertainer, setting up this machine and recording people's voices and playing them back to their delight and surprise. Everybody liked it, but nobody wanted to buy it. They all said, with variations, "This is fun, but the machine is too expensive for a toy."

I then realized that having unique technology and being able to make unique products are not enough to keep a business going. You have to sell the products, and to do that you have to show the potential buyer the real value of what you are selling. I was struck with the realization that I was going to have to be the merchandiser of our small company. We were fortunate in having a genius like Ibuka who could concentrate totally on innovative product design and production while I learned the merchandising end of the business.

A fortunate chance incident helped me to see the light. I was still trying to figure out what we were doing wrong in trying, but failing, to sell our tape recorders, when I happened to stroll by an antique shop not far from my home in Tokyo. I had no real interest in antiques and I didn't then appreciate their value. As I stood there looking at these old art objects and marveling at the high prices marked on them, I noticed a customer buying an old vase. Without hesitation, he took out his wallet and handed over a large number of bills to the antiques dealer. The price was higher than we were asking for our tape recorder! Why, I wondered, would someone pay so much money for an old object that had no practical value, while a new and important device such as our tape recorder could attract no customers. It seemed obvious to me that the value of the tape recorder was far greater than that of an antique because of its ability to enhance the lives of the many people who might come in contact with it. Few people could appreciate the fine lines of the vase, and something that expensive could hardly be handled by many people, for fear of breaking it. One tape recorder, on the other hand, could serve hundreds, or even thousands of people. It could entertain them, amuse them, educate them, help them improve themselves. To me there was no contest— the tape recorder was the better bargain—but I realized that the vase had perceived value to that collector of antiques, and he had his own valid reasons for investing that much money in such an object. Some of my ancestors had done the same, as I would do later. But at that moment, I knew that to sell our recorder we would have to identify the people and institutions that would be likely to recognize value in our product.

We noted, or rather Tamon Maeda did, that during that early postwar period there was an acute shortage of stenographers because so many people had been pushed out of school and into war work. Until that shortage could be corrected, the courts of Japan were trying to cope with a small, overworked corps of court stenographers. With Maeda's help, we were able to demonstrate our machine for the Japan Supreme Court, and we sold twenty machines almost instantly! Those people had no difficulty realizing how they could put our device to practical use; they saw the value in the tape recorder immediately; to them it was no toy.

It seemed to me a logical step to go from the courts into the schools of Japan. Ibuka pointed out to us in one of the many meetings we had on the subject of sales that Japanese education had traditionally been centered on reading, writing, and abacus skills. But when the Americans came at the end of the war, they felt that verbal communications and audio/visual training were very important, and the Japanese Education Ministry followed their lead. But there was little media available in Japan, only some sixteen-millimeter films with English language soundtracks, which were of very little use because English had been banned and its instruction prohibited during the years of war. As a consequence few, if any, instructors had the language facility to understand the audio portion of those films. And of course none of the students did. The idea of using tape recorders to play prerecorded language tapes and then to use them for practice was accepted quickly, and the idea soon spread to schools all across the country. Every prefecture, or state, in Japan had set up a film center, but all the materials were in English. Ways had to be found to do the instruction in Japanese. The tape recorder was the logical medium.

With this kind of instruction going on at the prefectural level, we felt that soon every school would need and want a tape recorder. Ibuka discovered that the schools had a budget for this kind of equipment, so we tried to design a smaller unit just for schools that we could price within the reach of an individual school. Our first success was a medium-sized machine, bigger than an attaché case but smaller than a small suitcase. We called it the H-type recorder. It was simple—only one tape speed of seven and a half inches per second—and sturdy. As a wedding present in 1951, the staff gave my bride Yoshiko and me the first production model of this recorder we called the H-type.

We began to make portable units of more attractive design and to gain confidence. Our company was beginning to expand and we moved into an adjacent and more substantial building on Gotenyama. New ideas were finally being accepted, perhaps some of them too eagerly, but Japan was building its new society—it was not rebuilding the old one.

As we matured, we were soon embroiled in a new kind of war that taught me a lot about the international business we were to develop. In order to get a high-quality recorded signal onto the tape of our recorders, we had been using Dr. Kenzo Nagai's patented high-frequency AC Bias system. This system demagnetized the tape before it reached the recording head, applied an alternating current to the recording signal, and produced a recording with much less noise and distortion than earlier, direct current (DC) biased systems. We were so dedicated to a future in recording technology that we wanted to buy the patent, which was then owned by Anritsu Electric, then, as now, a subsidiary of Nippon Electric Company, known as NEC. We couldn't afford to buy 100 percent of the patent, but we bought half of it in 1949, sharing the ownership with NEC. Dr. Nagai had registered the patent in Japan, and we learned later that he had also applied for a patent in the United States just before the war began, in December 1941—and had sent data on his invention to the Library of Congress and other places earlier that year. His patent was never registered in the United States, I guess because the timing couldn't have been worse, but his research was available to interested parties there.

When we bought the patent, we sent out letters to tape-recorder makers all over the world, informing them that we had the patent on the AC Bias system and offering to license it. We also told them that if they wanted to sell tape recorders using this system in Japan, they would have to have a license from us. We got back letters from several companies saying they had no intention of selling tape recorders in Japan and therefore didn't see any point in buying a license from us. We knew the system was being used abroad by makers who had not licensed it, but we saw no way to do anything about it. One day an officer from the patent department at GHQ called Ibuka and said he wanted to see him. In those days, if you were called by GHQ you had to worry about the possibility of going to prison for some infraction you might not know about or something that had happened in the past. Ibuka was so worried he even called his wife and told her of the summons just to prepare her. He took Maeda with him as interpreter. The officer wanted to know all about our claim to the patent. Ibuka had had the foresight to bring with him all the papers he could put together that pertained to our patent purchase. As the officer went through the papers, the tension mounted, and when he had examined everything he sat back and confirmed with a smile that the patent seemed to be complete. There were grins of relief all around, and the officer ended it happily by serving coffee.

Soon after that we learned that Balcom Trading Company of Tokyo was importing tape recorders from the United States, and we sent them our letter, warning them about our license on the recording system used in those machines. They ignored our letter, and so we considered going to court for an injunction against the trading company. It was an important decision for us because in the Japanese courts a plaintiff in a civil suit must pay a large and nonrefundable filing fee based on the amount of money for which he is suing. This is one way of discouraging frivolous lawsuits. If we decided to go ahead with a lawsuit, we would have to make a big investment in it. But we felt bold enough and sure enough of our case to file. Besides, our patent now had the approval of the Occupation, in a manner of speaking.

The court heard our plea and granted the injunction. We marched down to the customs warehouse with the proper officials and boldly put a court seal on the door, prohibiting Balcom from moving their tape recorders until the case was aired. The local newspapers thought it was a fine story and it made headlines. The papers saw it as a rare show of Japanese independence, a small Japanese company defiantly challenging big American manufacturers. The people at Balcom were furious, of course, because they reported our contention to the manufacturer in the States, and the maker of the tape recorders said they had licensed their system from Armour Research, which had its own patent on the AC Bias system.

Everybody got angry and Armour sent their lawyer, Donald Simpson, to Japan. It was the first time I had ever met an American lawyer and I was quite impressed with how tough a competitor he was. But we were able to prove that an English-language version of Dr. Nagai's work had been available to the public in the United States before the Armour patent was granted. If Dr. Nagai's technique could be considered general knowledge, then it would seem to put the AC Bias system in the U.S. into the public domain and perhaps make it no longer patent worthy. I threatened to go to the U.S. and invalidate the Armour patent. Actually I didn't know how I would go about doing that, but it must have seemed possible to them because when our case was presented they recognized the validity of Dr. Nagai's patent. The dispute dragged on for three years, but our victory in March 1954 meant that all tape recorders using the AC Bias system sold in Japan—even a big Ampex unit sold to a broadcasting station—would produce a royalty for us. I agreed in the settlement that we would not attack Armour. We got the right to use the Armour patent in the U.S., and therefore we could export to the United States without paying a license fee. Furthermore, we could sublicense the technology to other Japanese makers, and when they wanted to export to the U.S., we would get half the license fee. We held these rights for many years. It was my first negotiation with the Americans, and it ended so well I began to feel new encouragement about the future. Oh, yes, I also later hired Donald Simpson to work for us.

IV

The idea of an international market for Tokyo Tsushin Kogyo had been on our minds from early on, and it was inevitable that Ibuka and I would have to travel. In 1952 the tape recorder business was very good, and Ibuka thought he wanted to go to the United States to see what uses were being made of the tape recorder and to learn more about the manufacture of tape itself. He spoke virtually no English, but he managed to get around and observe things. He came away disappointed because, while he found some language laboratories using tape recorders, he saw that we were making wider use of them in our schools than they were in the U.S. Another disappointment for Ibuka was that none of the tape manufacturers would allow visitors into their plants. But the trip turned out to be of great benefit to us. In 1948, we had both read about the work of William Shockley and others at Bell Laboratories in the "Bell Laboratory Record," and we had been curious about their discoveries ever since. That year small articles began to appear in the American press and elsewhere about the device invented at Bell Labs called the transistor, and on Ibuka's trip he first learned that a license for this marvelous gadget might soon be available. He began to make plans.

This solid-state device was something completely new to our experience, and learning about it and deciding what we could do with it was a job for more than an electronics engineer or two. During one sleepless night in a noisy room in New York's old Taft Hotel near Times Square, it occurred to Ibuka that our company now had about one hundred and twenty employees, about a third of them graduate engineers—electronic, metallurgical, chemical, mechanical—and developing the transistor for our use would be a job that would challenge the skills of all of them. He didn't know then just what we would make with the transistor if we got the technology, but he was excited by the technological breakthrough it represented. Ibuka tried to get an interview with the Western Electric patent license manager the next day, as Western Electric was the patent holder for Bell Labs, but was told the man was too busy to see him, so he asked a friend of his, Shido Yamada, who lived in New York and had worked for a Japanese trading company, to make some inquiries. Then Ibuka went home.

I must make it clear that the transistor being made at that time wasn't something that we could license and produce and use right off the shelf. This miraculous device was a breakthrough in electronic technology, but it could only handle audio frequencies. In fact, when I finally signed the patent agreement a year later, the people at Western Electric told me that if we wanted to use the transistor in consumer items, the hearing aid was the only product we should expect to make with it. In those days there were no transistors made for use in radios. Of course we were not interested in the hearing aid market, which is very limited. We wanted to make something that could be used by everybody, and we had plans to put our research scientists and technicians to work developing our own high-frequency transistor for use in radios.

We started to consider what kind of radio we could make with transistors. At that time, the worldwide trend in the radio field was toward a new concept. The new phrase, "high fidelity," or hi-fi, was soon to be in vogue. People would be listening for purity of sound, for realistic reproduction, or at least for sonically exciting reproduction. Some early hi-fi fans were already buying records of locomotive noises, airplanes taking off, horses galloping, police sirens, old weapons being fired, and all kinds of other sound effects to show off their new systems. Speakers were getting bigger, sound was getting bigger, and the words "woofer," "tweeter," "distortion," and "feedback" were entering the language. Amplifiers using many vacuum tubes were thought to give the purest sound. We envisioned the transistor replacing the bulky, hot, and unreliable vacuum tube. It would give us a chance not only to miniaturize electronic products but also to lower the power consumption. If we could devise a transistor that could deliver a high enough frequency, we could make a very small radio powered by batteries. We hoped to get realistic sound using a minimum of power.

Miniaturization and compactness have always appealed to the Japanese. Our boxes have been made to nest; our fans fold; our art rolls into neat scrolls; screens that can artistically depict an entire city can be folded and tucked neatly away, or set up to delight, entertain, and educate, or merely to divide a room. And we set as our goal a radio small enough to fit into a shirt pocket. Not just portable, I said, but "pocketable." Even before the war RCA made a medium-size portable using tiny "peanut" vacuum tubes, but half the space was taken up by an expensive battery, which played for only about four hours. Transistors might be able to solve that power and size problem.

We were all eager to get to work on the transistor, and when word came that it would be possible to license the technology, I went to New York to finalize the deal in 1953. I also wanted to see what the world was like and where our new company could fit in, so I planned to visit Europe after my New York business was concluded. I was excited when I climbed aboard the Stratocruiser at Tokyo's Haneda Airport, a small suitcase in one hand and a bag slung over my shoulder.

I must admit now that I was initially discouraged by the very scale of the United States. Everything was so big, the distances were so great, the open spaces so vast, the regions so different. I thought it would be impossible to sell our products here. The place just overwhelmed me. The economy was booming, and the country seemed to have everything.

When I mailed Ibuka the license agreement with Western Electric, I had a surge of confidence. But in Japan exchange control was very strong at the time, and we needed approval from the Ministry of International Trade and Industry (MITI) to remit the initial transistor license fee of twenty-five thousand dollars out of the country. The transistor was so new, and foreign currency was so scarce in Japan, which was just then beginning to accelerate its recovery from the war, that the bureaucrats at MITI could not see the use for such a device and were not eager to grant permission. Besides, MITI thought that such a small company as Totsuko (as we were known) could not possibly undertake the enormous task of dealing with brand-new technologies. In fact, they were adamant against it at first. Ibuka was eloquent on the possible uses of this little-known device, but it took him six months to convince the bureaucrats. MITI has not been the great benefactor of the Japanese electronics industry that some critics seem to think it has.

While MITI was considering our request, I was traveling. I flew to Europe, where I visited many companies and factories and began to feel a little better about the future of our company and of Japan. I visited Volkswagen, Mercedes, and Siemens, and many smaller companies, some of which have disappeared in the years since then. And of course in the electronics field I wanted to visit Philips in Holland, an electronics company that was famous worldwide. It was my visit to Philips that gave me courage and a new insight.

I was a bit depressed when I left Germany. Conditions were improving very rapidly there despite the devastation Germany had also suffered in the war, and it made Japan's postwar progress seem slow. One day I ordered some ice cream in a restaurant on Koenigsstrasse in Düsseldorf, and the waiter served it with a miniature paper parasol stuck into it as a decoration. "This is from your country," he said, smiling and, I suppose, meaning it as a compliment. That was the extent of his knowledge of Japan and its capabilities, I thought, and maybe he was typical. What a long way we had to go.

I took the train from Düsseldorf to Eindhoven, and when I crossed the border from Germany to Holland I found a great difference. Germany, even so soon after the war, was becoming highly mechanized—Volkswagen was already producing seven hundred cars a day—and everybody seemed to be rebuilding and producing goods and new products very rapidly. But in Holland many people were riding bicycles. This was a purely agricultural country and a small one at that. You could see old-fashioned windmills everywhere, just as in old Dutch landscape paintings. Everything seemed so quaint. When I finally arrived at Eindhoven, I was surprised to see what a huge company Philips was, although I knew Philips was very successful with their electrical products in Southeast Asia and around the world. I don't know what I expected, but it was a surprise to find the great N. V. Philips enterprise of my imagination situated in a small town in a small corner of a small agricultural country.

I stared at the statue of Dr. Philips in front of the train station, and I thought of our own village of Kosugaya and the similar bronze statue of my father's great-grandfather that once stood there. I wandered around the town thinking about Dr. Philips, and when I visited the factory I was all the more taken with the thought that a man born in such a small, out-of-the-way place in an agricultural country could build such a huge, highly technical company with a fine worldwide reputation. Maybe, I thought, we could do the same thing in Japan. It was quite a dream, but I remember writing Ibuka a letter from Holland saying, "If Philips can do it, maybe we can, too." I spoke very little English in those days, and I just visited these factories as a tourist. I took no VIP tour, and I met none of the executives of the companies. I represented an unknown company then, but in the next four decades Sony and Philips, two companies from small and seemingly isolated places, cooperated in design standards and in joint development that has led to many technological advances, from the standard compact audio cassette to the newest watershed development in home sound reproduction, the compact disc (digital audio disc), where we combined our strength in pulse code modulation research with Philips's fine laser technology. There are still other joint developments in the R&D stage.

Soon after my return from Europe, the laborious work of creating a new type of transistor began in our research lab based on the Western Electric technology we had licensed. We had to raise the power of the transistor—otherwise, it could not be used in a radio. It was very complicated work, and our project team went through a long period of painstaking trial and error, using new, or at least different, materials to get the increased frequency we needed. They had to rebuild and virtually reinvent the transistor.

The early Bell Labs transistor used a slab of germanium to which indium was alloyed on each side. The germanium was the negative part and the indium was the positive. But we reasoned that since negative electrons move faster than positive ones, we could get higher frequency by reversing the polarity. That is, instead of a positive-negative-positive configuration, we would try to produce a negative-positive-negative one. We didn't seem to have the right materials to do this. Indium had too low a melting point for our purposes, for example, so we discarded the old materials and began experiments using gallium and antimony, but this didn't work well either. At one point everyone seemed stumped, and we thought of using phosphorus to replace antimony, but someone pointed out during one of our many brainstorming sessions that Bell Labs had already tried this and it hadn't worked.

The head of our research laboratories, Makoto Kikuchi, a leading expert in the semiconductor field, recalls that in those days the level of research and engineering in the United States was so high that "the voice of Bell Labs was like the voice of God." Nevertheless, one of our team kept trying what is called the phosphorus doping method, using more and more and more phosphorus in the process, and finally he thought he began to see results. He reported his findings at a meeting, cautiously. Nobody else was reporting any luck at all, and the head of the transistor development team, my late brother-in-law, Kazuo Iwama, who later become president of our company, was a scientist, and he knew the scientific mind. He said to the researcher, "Well, if it looks to you as though you are getting interesting results, why don't you just keep working and see what happens?" The phosphorus method eventually worked, and expanding on it we developed the high-frequency device at which we were aiming.

A year later we surprised the Bell Labs people who had invented the transistor by reporting how we made transistors by phosphorus doping, something that had been tried and discarded, obviously prematurely, by them. And it was also during our transistor research and particularly the heavy use of phosphorus that our researcher, physicist Leo Esaki, and our staff discovered and described the diode tunneling effect, how subatomic particles can move in waves through a seemingly impenetrable barrier. Esaki was awarded a Nobel Prize for this work in 1973.

Now that we had the transistor, getting and making the miniature parts for our small radio was another challenge. We had to redesign everything ourselves, or almost everything. Ibuka somehow managed to find a small company in Tokyo that made tiny tuning condensers, and we put that company to work producing their products mainly for our use. The project moved slowly while we continued our tape recorder and other business. We had to refine the transistor, learn how to mass-produce it, and design it into new products.

V

I had decided during my first trip abroad in 1953 that our full name—Tokyo Tsushin Kogyo Kabushiki Kaisha—was not a good name to put on a product. It was a tongue-twister. Even in Japan, we shortened it sometimes to Totsuko, but when I was in the United States I learned that nobody could pronounce either name. The English-language translation—Tokyo Tele-communications Engineering Company—was too clumsy. We tried Tokyo Teletech for a while, but then we learned there was an American company using the name Teletech.

It seemed to me that our company name didn't have a chance of being recognized unless we came up with something ingenious. I also thought that whatever new name we came up with should serve double duty—that is, it should be both our company name and our brand name. That way we would not have to pay double the advertising cost to make both well known.

We tried a symbol for a while, an inverted pyramid inside a thin circle with small wedges cut from the sides of the pyramid to give us a stylized letter "T." But for our first transistors and for our first transistor radio, we wanted a brand name that was special and clever and that people would remember. We decided our transistor radio would be the first consumer product available to the public with our new brand name on it.

I thought a lot about this when I was in the United States, where I noticed that many companies were using three letter logotypes, such as ABC, NBC, RCA, and AT&T. Some companies were also using just their full name as their logo. This looked like something new to me. When I was a boy, I had learned to recognize the names of imported automobiles by their symbols, the three-pointed star for Mercedes, the blue oval with Ford in it, the Cadillac crown, the Pierce Arrow arrow, the Winged Victory of Rolls-Royce. Later, many car companies began to use their names together with the symbol, like Chevrolet, Ford,

Buick, and others, and I could recognize their names even if I couldn't actually read them. I pondered every possibility.

Ibuka and I took a long time deciding on a name. We agreed we didn't want a symbol. The name would be the symbol, and therefore it should be short, no more than four or five characters. All Japanese companies have a company badge and a lapel pin, usually in the shape of the company symbol, but except for a prominent few, such as the three diamonds of Mitsubishi, for example, it would be impossible for an outsider to recognize them. Like the automobile companies that began relying less and less on symbols and more and more on their names, we felt we really needed a name to carry our message. Every day we would write down possibilities and discuss them whenever we had the time. We wanted a new name that could be recognized anywhere in the world, one that could be pronounced the same in any language. We made dozens and dozens of tries. Ibuka and I went through dictionaries looking for a bright name, and we came across the Latin word *sonus*, meaning "sound." The word itself seemed to have sound in it. Our business was full of sound, so we began to zero in on *sonus*. At that time in Japan borrowed English slang and nicknames were becoming popular and some people referred to bright young and cute boys as "sonny," or "sonny-boys," and, of course, "sunny" and "sonny" both had an optimistic and bright sound similar to the Latin root with which we were working. And we also thought of ourselves as "sonny-boys" in those days. Unfortunately, the single word "sonny" by itself would give us troubles in Japan because in the romanization of our language, the word "sonny" would be pronounced "sohn-nee," which means to lose money. That was no way to launch a new product. We pondered this problem for a little while and the answer struck me one day: why not just drop one of the letters and make it "Sony"? That was it!

The new name had the advantage of not meaning anything but "Sony" in any language; it was easy to remember, and it carried the connotations we wanted. Furthermore, as I reminded Ibuka, because it was written in roman letters, people in many countries could think of it as being in their own language. All over the world governments were spending money to teach people how to read English and use the roman alphabet, including Japan. And the more people who learned English and the roman alphabet, the more people would recognize our company and product name—at no cost to us.

We kept our old corporate name for some time after we began putting the Sony logotype on our products. For our first product logo, we used a tall, thin sloping initial letter inside a square box, but I soon realized that the best way to get name recognition would be to make the name as legible and simple as possible, so we moved to the more traditional and simple capital letters that remain today. The name itself is the logo.

We managed to produce our first transistorized radio in 1955 and our first tiny "pocketable" transistor radio in 1957. It was the world's smallest, but actually it was a bit bigger than a standard men's shirt pocket, and that gave us a problem for a while, even though we never said which pocket we had in mind when we said "pocketable." We liked the idea of a salesman being able to demonstrate how simple it would be to drop it into a shirt pocket. We came up with a simple solution— we had some shirts made for our salesmen with slightly larger than normal pockets, just big enough to slip the radio into.

The introduction of this proud achievement was tinged with disappointment that our first transistorized radio was not the very first one on the market. An American company called Regency, supported by Texas Instruments, and using TI transistors, put out a radio with the Regency brand name a few months before ours, but the company gave up without putting much effort into marketing it. As the first in the field, they might have capitalized on their position and created a tremendous market for their product, as we did. But they apparently judged mistakenly that there was no future in this business and gave it up.

Our fine little radio carried our company's new brand name, Sony, and we had big plans for the future of transistorized electronics and hopes that the success of our small "pocketable" radio would be a harbinger of successes to come.

In June 1957, we put up our first billboard carrying the Sony name opposite the entrance to Tokyo's Haneda International Airport, and at the end of the year we put up another in the heart of the Ginza district of Tokyo. In January 1958 we officially changed our company name to Sony Corporation and were listed on the Tokyo Stock Exchange that December.

We had registered the name Sony in one hundred and

seventy countries and territories and in various categories, not just electronics, in order to protect it from being used by others on products that would exploit the similarity. But we soon learned that we had failed to protect ourselves from some entrepreneurs right at home in Japan. One day we learned that somebody was selling "Sony" chocolate.

We were very proud of our new corporate name and I was really upset that someone would try to capitalize on it. The company that picked up our name had used a completely different name on their products before and only changed the name when ours became popular. They registered the name "Sony" for a line of chocolates and snack foods and even changed their company trade name to Sony Foods. In their logo they used the same type of letters we used.

In those days we sometimes used a small cartoon character called "Sonny Boy" in our advertising. The character was actually called "Atchan," and was created by cartoonist Fuyuhiko Okabe of the Japanese newspaper *Asahi Shimbun*. The bogus Sony chocolate merchants started using a similar cartoon. Seeing this stuff on sale in major department stores made me sick with anger. We took the imposters to court and brought famous people such as entertainers, newspapermen, and critics to confirm the damage that was being done to us. One witness said he thought the appearance of Sony chocolate meant that the Sony Corporation was in financial difficulty if it had to resort to selling chocolate instead of high-technology electronics. Another witness said she had the impression that since Sony was really a technical company, the chocolate must be some kind of synthetic. We were afraid that if these chocolates continued to fill the marketplace, it would completely destroy the trust people had in our company.

I have always believed that a trademark is the life of an enterprise and that it must be protected boldly. A trademark and a company name are not just clever gimmicks—they carry responsibility and guarantee the quality of the product. If someone tries to get a free ride on the reputation and the ability of another who has worked to build up public trust, it is nothing short of thievery. We were not flattered by this theft of our name.

Court cases take a long time in Japan, and the case dragged on for almost four years, but we won. And for the first time in

Japanese history, the court used the unfair competition law rather than patent or trademark registration laws in granting us relief. The chocolate people had registered the name, all right, but only after our name had become popular. In trying to prove that the name was open for anyone to use, their lawyers went to the major libraries of the country to show that the name was in the public domain, but they were in for a shock. They came away empty-handed because no matter what dictionaries they went to they could not find the word Sony. We knew they would discover that; we had done it ourselves long before. The name is unique, and it is ours.

On our thirty-fifth anniversary, we thought we should consider revising our trademark. Styles and fashions were changing in clothing, in product design, and in virtually everything, so we thought that perhaps we should consider changing the style of the letters of our name. We held an international competition, and we received hundreds of suggestions, along with hundreds of pleas from our dealers not to change. After reviewing all the suggestions, we decided not to make any changes. S O N Y still looked very good to us, and we decided, as they say today, that there was no point in fixing something that was far from broken.

SELLING
TO THE WORLD
My Learning Curve

I

Although our company was still small and we saw Japan as quite a large and potentially active market, it was the consensus among Japanese industrialists that a Japanese company must export goods in order to survive. With no natural resources except our people's energy, Japan had no alternative. And so it was natural for us to look to foreign markets. Besides, as business prospered, it became obvious to me that if we did not set our sights on marketing abroad, we would not grow to be the kind of company Ibuka and I had envisioned. We wanted to change the image of Japanese goods as poor in quality, and, we reasoned, if you are going to sell a high-quality, expensive product, you need an affluent market, and that means a rich, sophisticated country. Today, over 99 percent of all Japanese homes have color TV; more than 98 percent have electric refrigerators and washing machines; and the penetration rate for tape recorders and stereo systems is between 60 and 70 percent. But in 1958, the year after we produced our "pocketable" transistorized radio, only 1 percent of Japanese homes had a TV set, only 5 percent had a washing machine, and only two-tenths of 1 percent had an electric refrigerator. Fortunately, the Japanese economy began to grow vigorously from the mid-fifties onward. Double-digit increases in the gross national product and low inflation gave a great boost to consumer spending. Many people say Japan's true postwar era really began in 1955, the year we introduced the first transistorized radio in Japan. The country's GNP grew, amazingly, by 10.8 percent. Japanese households needed everything, and because of the high savings rate, which in those days was over 20 percent, the people could afford to buy. So with good and growing markets at home and potential markets abroad, the world was beginning to look bright to us.

As a new company, we had to carve out our own niche in the Japanese market. The old established firms were coming back into production with familiar brand names. We had to make our name familiar. We did it with new products—we even coined new names for some of them, such as "Tapecorder," but found that there was a downside even to this kind of innovation. The tape recorder was virtually unknown in Japan when we introduced the first one. Since we obviously could not register the name "tape recorder" as our own, we came up with "Tapecorder." The name Tapecorder became generic almost overnight, because we had the only machine on the market, but later, when our competitors began making tape recorders, it became a doubtful blessing because the public referred to any maker's tape recorder as a "tapecorder." From then on, we made it a point to display our company name prominently on our products, even if we also gave the products invented names, such as Walkman, so that the brand, company, and product names were all clear.

Despite rising affluence in Japan in the late fifties, we had a great deal of difficulty raising money and had to rely on friends and introductions by friends to people who might become investors. In this regard, we were lucky to have a board of advisers who had real stature. They could get us introductions to potential investors that we could not arrange on our own. Our chairman from 1953 to 1959 was Junshiro Mandai, former chairman of Mitsui Bank, and our advisers included Ibuka's father-in-law, Tamon Maeda, the former cabinet minister; Michiji Tajima, who became director general of the Imperial Household Agency; Rin Matsutani, the man who hired Ibuka at Photo Chemical Laboratory, Ibuka's first big job; and, of course, my father, Kyuzaemon Morita.

One of the businessmen our advisers recommended as a possible investor was Taizo Ishizaka, who later became head of the Keidanren, Japan's Federation of Economic Organizations. Ibuka and I called on him and persuaded him to invest in our company, but a few months later, the Mitsui Bank asked him to become president of Tokyo Shibaura Electric Company (Toshiba), because it was having financial and labor troubles. The postwar antitrust laws were in effect then, and so he felt that even though Toshiba was a giant corporation and Sony was very small, he could not hold shares in another company that made some of the same types of goods. He gave his shares to his daughter, Tomoko. After Toshiba came out with its own small transistor radio—much later than our company—he advised his daughter to sell the shares. He told her no small company could compete with the giants of Japan's electrical industry now that these companies had started to make the same things. Ishizaka's daughter is a good friend of mine who lives near me. She used to say jokingly, "My father is a successful businessman and a big shot in Keidanren, but he doesn't know how to make money for himself." Like a dutiful daughter she had sold her Sony stock as her father recommended—and lost the opportunity to get rich on it.

Mandai, our chairman, was one of Japan's great bankers. He had been the head of Mitsui Bank before the war and was still regarded almost as a deity by the staff. Like many others connected with the old giant financial combines, the *zaibatsu*, he had been purged by the Occupation authorities. We felt very lucky to have him with us. Ibuka and I had been having a difficult time borrowing more money from Mitsui Bank, which had been helping us from the beginning. One day Mandai took Ibuka and me to the bank to talk to some of the bank officers about our company. We had been trying to sell shares, and we hoped that Mandai just might mention the fact at the bank. To our surprise, as we made calls Mandai told everyone in authoritative tones, "My company has decided to increase shares, and I just might be able to arrange for you to buy some." It was almost a command, coming from such a great figure. Several bank executives later told me how hard they struggled to get enough money to buy the shares; they felt they had to buy because Mandai had virtually ordered it. I don't know anyone who complained, though. Several became quite rich on those early purchases, and I know at least one man who very quickly built a house on his early dividends.

We were doing well, although we still had tough competition getting our name known in Japan, where brand consciousness and brand loyalty are very high. Overseas we were all on an even footing. And perhaps we were in a better position abroad than anybody. Quality Japanese consumer goods were virtually unknown before the war. The image of anything marked "Made in Japan" that had been shipped abroad before the war was very low. Most people in the United States and Europe, I learned, associated Japan with paper umbrellas, kimonos, toys, and cheap trinkets. In choosing our name we did not purposely try to hide our national identity—after all, international rules require you to state the country of origin on your product—but we certainly did not want to emphasize it and run the risk of being rejected before we could demonstrate the quality of our products. But I must confess that in the early days we printed the line "Made in Japan" as small as possible, once too small for U.S. Customs, which made us make it bigger on one product.

I came to realize from my earliest experience in trying to sell the tape recorder that marketing is really a form of communication. In the traditional Japanese system for distributing consumer products, the manufacturers are kept at arm's length from the consumer. Communication is all but impossible. There are primary, secondary, and even tertiary wholesalers dealing with some goods before they reach a retailer, layer after layer of middlemen in between the maker and the ultimate user of the product. This distribution system has some social value—it provides plenty of jobs—but it is costly and inefficient. At each layer the price has to go up, even though some of the middlemen may not even come in contact with the goods. The system is adequate for commodities and low-technology items, perhaps, but we realized from the beginning that it could not serve the needs of our company and its new, advanced technology products. Third or fourth parties simply could not have the same interest in or enthusiasm for our products and our ideas that we had. We had to educate our customers to the uses of our products. To do so we had to set up our own outlets and establish our own ways of getting goods into the market.

We were bringing out some products that had never been marketed before—never made before, actually, such as transistorized radios and solid-state personal television sets—and were beginning to get a reputation as a pioneer. In fact some people called us the "guinea pig" of the electronics industry. We would produce a new product; the giants of the industry would wait to see if our product was successful; and then, if it was, they would rush a similar one onto the market to take advantage of our efforts. This is the way it has developed over the years; we have always had to be out in front. We have seen this in most of our major product developments, from small solid-state radios and transistorized TV sets (we built the very first one) up to today's portable stereo player, Walkman; our small hand-held flat television, Watchman; and our compact disc player, Discman. We introduced stereo into Japan. We built the world's very first video cassette recorder for home use; invented the Trinitron system, a new method of projecting a color image onto the TV tube; and we innovated the 3.5-inch computer floppy disk, which now has the highest storage capacity in the world for its size. We revolutionized television news gathering and broadcasting worldwide with our hand-held video cameras and small videotape players. We pioneered the filmless camera, Mavica, the compact disc system, and invented eight-millimeter video. That's only to name a few of the more easily recognizable things we have done.

In the beginning, when our track record for success was not established, our competitors would take a very cautious wait-and-see attitude while we marketed and developed a new product. In the early days, we would often have the market to ourselves for a year or more before the other companies would be convinced that the product would be a success. And we made a lot of money, having the market all to ourselves. But as we became more successful and our track record became clearer, the others waited a shorter and shorter time before jumping in. Now we barely get a three-month head start on some products before the others enter the market to compete with us with their own version of the product we innovated. (We were fortunate to get a whole year's lead on the portable compact disc player, Discman, and almost six months with the Walkman.) It is flattering in a way, but it is expensive. We have to keep a premium on innovation. For many years now we have put well over 6 percent of sales into research and development, and some years as much as 10 percent. Our plan is to lead the public with new products rather than ask them what kind of products they want. The public does not know what is possible, but we do. So instead of doing a lot of market research, we refine our thinking on a product and its use and try to create a market for it by educating and communicating with the public. Sometimes a product idea strikes me as a natural.

As an example, I can cite a product surely everybody knows of, the Walkman. The idea took shape when Ibuka came into my office one day with one of our portable stereo tape recorders and a pair of our standard-size headphones. He looked unhappy and complained about the weight of the system. I asked him what was on his mind and then he explained, "I like to listen to music, but I don't want to disturb others. I can't sit there by my stereo all day. This is my solution—I take the music with me. But it's too heavy."

I had been mulling an idea over in my mind for a while, and now it was coming into focus as Ibuka talked. I knew from my own experience at home that young people cannot seem to live without music. Almost everybody has stereo at home and in the car. In New York, even in Tokyo, I had seen people with big tape players and radios perched on their shoulders blaring out music. I remembered that one time when my daughter, Naoko, came home from a trip she ran upstairs before even greeting her mother and first put a cassette in her stereo. Ibuka's complaint set me into motion. I ordered our engineers to take one of our reliable small cassette tape recorders we called Pressman, strip out the recording circuit and the speaker, and replace them with a stereo amplifier. I outlined the other details I wanted, which included very lightweight headphones that turned out to be one of the most difficult parts of the Walkman project.

Everybody gave me a hard time. It seemed as though nobody liked the idea. At one of our product planning meetings, one of the engineers said, "It sounds like a good idea, but will people buy it if it doesn't have recording capability? I don't think so."

I said, "Millions of people have bought car stereo without recording capability and I think millions will buy this machine."

Nobody openly laughed at me, but I didn't seem to be convincing my own project team, although they reluctantly went along. I even dictated the selling price to suit a young person's pocketbook, even before we made the first machine. The Pressman monaural tape recorder was a relatively expensive unit, selling for forty-nine-thousand yen in Japan, and I said I wanted the first models of our new stereo experiment to retail for no more than thirty thousand yen. The accountants protested but I persisted. I told them I was confident we would be making our new product in very large numbers and our cost would come down as volume climbed. They thought we should start from a cheaper base than the Pressman, but I chose the basic configuration of the Pressman because many parts for the Pressman were available worldwide at our service centers, and we knew the unit was reliable. Therefore we could start out without worrying that the thing would turn out to be a mechanical failure.

In a short time the first experimental unit with new, miniature headphones was delivered to me, and I was delighted with the small size of it and the high-quality sound the headphones produced. In conventional stereo with large loudspeakers, most of the energy used to produce the sound is wasted, because only a fraction of it goes to the listeners' ears. The rest of the sound vibrates off the walls and the windows. Our tiny unit needed only a small trickle of battery power to the amplifier to drive the tiny lightweight headphones. The fidelity that came through the small headphones was as good or better than I expected. I rushed home with the first Walkman and was trying it out with different music when I noticed that my experiment was annoying my wife, who felt shut out. All right, I decided, we needed to make provision for two sets of headphones. The next week the production staff had produced another model with two headphone jacks.

A few days later I invited my golfing partner, the novelist Kaoru Shoji, for a game of golf, and as we settled down in the car for the ride to my club I handed him a set of headphones and started playing a tape. I put on the other set and watched his expression. He was surprised and delighted to hear his wife, Hiroko Nakamura, a concert pianist, playing the Grieg piano concerto. He smiled broadly and wanted to say something, but he couldn't because we were both hooked up to headsets. I recognized this as a potential problem. My solution was to have my staff add a button-activated microphone to the machine so the two people could talk to each other, over the music, on the "hot line."

I thought we had produced a terrific item, and I was full of enthusiasm for it, but our marketing people were unenthusiastic. They said it wouldn't sell, and it embarrassed me to be so excited about a product most others thought would be a dud. But I was so confident the product was viable that I said I would take personal responsibility for the project. I never had reason to regret it. The idea took hold and from the very beginning the Walkman was a runaway success. I never really liked the name Walkman, but it seems to have caught on everywhere. I was away on a trip when the name was chosen by some young people in our company, and when I got back I ordered them to change the name to something like Walking Stereo, or anything a bit more grammatical, but they said it was too late: the advertising had already been prepared and the units were being made with that name. Sony America and Sony U.K. feared they couldn't sell a product with an ungrammatical name like Walkman but we were stuck with it. We later tried other names overseas—Stow Away, in England, and Sound About in the United States—but they never caught on. Walkman did. And eventually, I called up Sony America and Sony U.K. and said, "This is an order: the name is Walkman!" Now I'm told it is a great name.

Soon we could hardly keep pace with the demand and had to design new automated machinery to handle the flood of orders. Of course, we helped stimulate sales by advertising heavily, and in Japan we hired young couples to stroll through the Tokyo Ginza "Pedestrian Paradise" on Sundays listening to their Walkmans and showing them off. Although I originally thought it would be considered rude for one person to be listening to his music in isolation, buyers began to see their little portable stereo sets as very personal. And while I expected people to share their Walkmans, we found that everybody seemed to want his or her own, so we took out the "hot line" and later did away with one of the two headphone jacks on most models. I had been convinced the Walkman would be a popular product, but even I was not prepared for the response. I posed with my once-skeptical project team at the five million mark and I predicted they had only seen the beginning. Since the first Walkman went on sale, we have sold more than twenty million in more than seventy different models—we've even made waterproof and sandproof models—and there are more versions to come.

It is interesting that what has happened with Walkman is that something that began by taking away features from a full-scale recording and playback unit has now come almost full circle. We have put back—or made available with add-on devices like tiny speakers—all the features we removed in the first place, and even added some new ones, like the capability of copying from one tape to another.

My point in digressing to tell this story is simple: I do not believe that any amount of market research could have told us that the Sony Walkman would be successful, not to say a sensational hit that would spawn many imitators. And yet this small item has literally changed the music-listening habits of millions of people all around the world. Many of my friends in the music world, such as conductors Herbert von Karajan, Zubin Mehta, and Lorin Maazel, and virtuosos like Isaac Stern, have contacted me for more and more Walkmans, a very rewarding confirmation of the excellence of the idea and the product itself. As a result of developing small, lightweight options for the Walkman series, we have been able to miniaturize and improve the quality of our standard headphones and introduce dozens of new models, and so we have become one of the world's largest makers of headphones. We have almost 50 percent of the market in Japan.

It was this kind of innovation that Ibuka had in mind when we wrote a kind of prospectus and philosophical statement for our company in the very beginning: "If it were possible to establish conditions where persons could become united with a firm spirit of teamwork and exercise to their hearts' desire their technological capacity," he wrote, "then such an organization could bring untold pleasure and untold benefits."

He was thinking about industrial creativity, something

that is done with teamwork to create new and worthwhile products. Machines and computers cannot be creative in themselves, because creativity requires something more than the processing of existing information. It requires human thought, spontaneous intuition, and a lot of courage, and we had plenty of that in our early days and still do.

And so we set out to build our own sales and distribution network, as a way of getting our message directly to the consumer. We used the old distribution system where it was useful, but we set up our own outlets and dealt directly with our dealers where we could. That way we could get to know them personally and make them understand the value of our products and the uses to which they could be put. Our salesmen became communicators and encouraged the retailers to do the same.

II

Our first transistor radio of 1955 was small and practical—not as small as some of our later efforts, but we were very proud of it. I saw the United States as a natural market; business was booming, employment was high, the people were progressive and eager for new things, and international travel was becoming easier.

I took my little $29.95 radio to New York and made the rounds of possible retailers. Many of them were unimpressed. They said, "Why are you making such a tiny radio? Everybody in America wants big radios. We have big houses, plenty of room. Who needs these tiny things?"

I explained what I had learned in looking around me in the United States. "There are more than twenty radio stations in New York City alone," I said, "and, yes, the houses are big— even big enough for every family member to have his or her own room where he or she could turn on this tiny radio and listen to whatever pleases him or her without disturbing or bothering anybody else. Of course the fidelity isn't as good as a large unit, but it is excellent for its size." Many people saw the logic of this argument, and I was happy to be offered some tempting deals, but I was cautious and more than once I turned down what looked like a chance to make big profits. The buyers thought I was crazy, but even though our company was young and I was inexperienced, time has shown that I made the right decisions.

The people at Bulova liked the radio very much and their purchasing officer said very casually, "We definitely want some of these. We will take one hundred thousand units." One hundred thousand units! I was stunned. It was an incredible order, worth several times the total capital of our company. We began to talk details, my mind working very fast, when he told me that there was one condition: we would have to put the Bulova name on the radios.

That stopped me. I had vowed that we would not be an original equipment maker for other companies. We wanted to make a name for our company on the strength of our own products. I told him I would check with my company, and in fact I did send a message back to Tokyo outlining the deal. The reply was, "Take the order." I didn't like the idea, and I didn't like the reply. After thinking it over and over, I decided I had to say no, we would not produce radios under another name. When I returned to call on the man from Bulova he didn't seem to take me seriously at first. How could I turn down such an order? He was convinced I would accept. When I would not budge, he got short with me.

"Our company name is a famous brand name that has taken over fifty years to establish," he said. "Nobody has ever heard of your brand name. Why not take advantage of ours?"

I understood what he was saying, but I had my own view. "Fifty years ago," I said, "your brand name must have been just as unknown as our name is today. I am here with a new product, and I am now taking the first step for the next fifty years of my company. Fifty years from now I promise you that our name will be just as famous as your company name is today."

I never regretted the decision not to take what is called an original equipment maker (OEM) order because the decision gave me added confidence and pride, although when I told Ibuka and the other executives back in Tokyo what I had done some of them thought I was foolish. But I said then and I have said it often since: it was the best decision I ever made.

While making the rounds I came across another American

buyer who looked at the radio and said he liked it very much. He said his chain had about one hundred and fifty stores and he would need large quantities. That pleased me, and fortunately he did not ask me to put the chain's name on the product. He only asked me to give him a price quotation on quantities of five thousand, ten thousand, thirty thousand, fifty thousand and one hundred thousand radios. What an invitation! Now I could recoup what I had lost in refusing the OEM order. But back in my hotel room, I began pondering the possible impact of such grand orders on our small facilities in Tokyo. We had expanded our plant a lot since we outgrew the unpainted, leaky shack on Gotenyama. We had moved into bigger, sturdier buildings adjacent to the original site and had our eye on some more property. But we did not have the capacity to produce one hundred thousand transistor radios a year and also make the other things in our small product line. Our capacity was less than ten thousand radios a month. If we got an order for one hundred thousand, we would have to hire and train new employees and expand our facilities even more. This would mean a major investment, a major expansion, and a gamble.

I was inexperienced and still a little naive, but I had my wits about me. I considered all the consequences I could think of, and then I sat down and drew a curve that looked something like a lopsided letter U. The price for five thousand would be our regular price. That would be the beginning of the curve. For ten thousand there would be a discount, and that was at the bottom of the curve. For thirty thousand the price would begin to climb. For fifty thousand the price per unit would be higher than for five thousand, and for one hundred thousand units the price would have to be much more per unit than for the first five thousand.

I know this sounds strange, but my reasoning was that if we had to double our production capacity to complete an order for one hundred thousand and if we could not get a repeat order the following year we would be in big trouble, perhaps bankrupt, because how could we employ all the added staff and pay for all the new and unused facilities in that case? It was a conservative and cautious approach, but I was convinced that if we took a huge order we should make enough profit on it to pay for the new facilities during the life of the order. Expanding is not such a simple thing—getting fresh money would be difficult—and I didn't think this kind of expansion was a good idea on the strength of one order. In Japan we cannot just hire people and fire them whenever our orders go up or down. We have a long-term commitment to our employees and they have a commitment to us.

Of course I was also a bit worried that if I quoted a very low price for one hundred thousand units, the buyer might say he would take one hundred thousand but would initially order only ten thousand at the one hundred thousand unit price as a test, and then maybe he wouldn't order any more.

I returned the next day with my quotation. The buyer looked at it and blinked as though he couldn't believe his eyes. He put down the paper and said, patiently, "Mr. Morita, I have been working as a purchasing agent for nearly thirty years, and you are the first person who has ever come in here and told me that the more I buy the higher the unit price will be. It's illogical!" I explained my reasoning to him, and he listened carefully to what I had to say. When he got over his shock, he paused for a moment, smiled, and then placed an order for ten thousand radios—at the ten thousand unit price—which was just right for him and for us.

I was lucky in those days. I didn't have much experience in business and I didn't have a boss looking over my shoulder, so when I decided to come up with that quotation nobody could say no to me in the company. I made company policy as I went along. Later we certainly welcomed such large orders.

I was not the only Japanese doing business in New York in the middle fifties. Many, if not most of them, relied on the giant Japanese trading companies that understood foreign markets and had established offices overseas. That wasn't good enough for me, because none of the trading houses knew my products and my business philosophy.

I think it is ironic that American businessmen now complain about our complex Japanese distribution system, because when I was first planning to export to the United States I was astonished and frustrated by the complexity of marketing in America. It always comes as a surprise to American businessmen when I tell this to them. But the accepted way of getting Japanese goods into the U.S. in those days was to hand over your goods to an experienced Japanese trading company with offices in the States. The trading company would ship the goods to an American port, where their agent would clear customs, then move them to a distribution company, and then to the wholesalers, and then to the retailers. The time consumed in shipping and the demands for servicing in such a big country staggered me. But I never considered the size of America or the English (or French or German) language to be a nontariff barrier.

I can understand the frustration of American and other foreign businessmen facing the Japanese distribution system and the complex Japanese language because it must seem as complex to them as the American system and language did to me several decades ago, but many of them have successfully figured out ways to work outside the traditional established system; that was what I felt I had to do in the United States. We needed a distribution route in which the message of our new technology and its benefits could be more easily and directly passed on to the consumer. It took us a long time to find the way. We also had to learn some hard lessons.

I was lucky enough to be introduced to Adolph Gross by my old Japanese friend, Shido Yamada. Gross was a manufacturers' representative, and he had a company called Agrod Company, located at 514 Broadway. When I told Gross about my company and what we were trying to do, he said he liked the sound of it and he immediately agreed to represent us. He even offered me some desk space in his office, and the relationship grew into a personal one as well as a business one; he was a good friend and a teacher to me. I was fortunate to find several good teachers in the United States. One of them I met in Tokyo, a Hawaiian-born Japanese-American named Yoshinobu "Doc" Kagawa, an American citizen who came to Japan as a lawyer with the economic section of the Occupation forces. When the Occupation was over in 1952, he opted to stay on in Japan and represented some Japanese companies, including the Toho movie company. I asked him to advise my company, and when I came to the States on some of my early trips he came with me. So I had good teachers, Adolph Gross, "Doc" Kagawa, and then probably my best teacher, Edward Rosiny, who was Gross's lawyer and became mine.

Adolph Gross and I became very close, although he was in his late fifties and I was only in my thirties. He was a kind, intelligent, unpretentious, soft-spoken man who liked a good joke and was full of integrity. He was interested in international business, and in fact he was already importing some high-quality European electronic goods, including the fine German-made ELAC turntable, which was popular with early hi-fi enthusiasts. He talked to me for a long time the day we first were introduced; he wanted to know everything about me and my company and its philosophy. In a short time I learned a lot about American business practices from him. He explained America and America's business world to me, including some very practical information about the image and character of the different stores and the best ways to do business in America. He also kept trying to Americanize me or at least to give me some worldly polish and sophistication.

One day he asked me casually if I wanted to see *My Fair Lady*, which had just opened on Broadway and was already the hit show of the season. I said, "Certainly I'd like to see it, Adolph, but I'm sure I couldn't get a ticket—the show is a sellout!" He said, "Never mind that," and in no time he had a pair of tickets. They must have cost him one hundred dollars each, a lot of money for a theater seat any time, but a fortune to me, at least, in 1957. We worked late the night of the show and went directly to the Mark Hellinger Theater. It was a new and exciting experience for me to be with that audience at the biggest show of the season. Adolph was blasé about it. As soon as the lights dimmed and the orchestra struck up the overture, Adolph turned to me and said, "Akio, goodnight." He slept all through this marvelous show in his hundred-dollar seat.

When Adolph Gross died suddenly of a heart attack in London in 1958, we were all devastated. I have always felt my debt to him strongly and think of him as my American father. Mrs. Gross is still very close to our Sony family, and we always ask her to all the anniversary functions of Sony America.

I didn't meet Edward Rosiny, Gross's lawyer, until after we lost Gross, and I also then met Irving Sagor, who was the accountant for the Gross business. I learned about American business accounting and law from these fine men. I needed someone I could trust when I began to think of establishing Sony America, and these two men were the finest teachers and helpers to me. Since Sagor was a CPA, he was able to see that my tax affairs were being properly handled. Eddie Rosiny and I became like brothers, working together, eating together, playing golf (he got me into his country club in Spring Valley, N.Y.), handling business problems together. Among other things, Eddie taught me about American business contracts, something almost unknown in Japan.

In the early days I would come to New York and take a cheap hotel room, and because my English was not good and because I had little money I would eat in the automat or a cafeteria, where I didn't have to speak to anybody, fumbling around in English. When I first brought Doc Kagawa with me to the States and began taking him to the automats and booking us into inexpensive hotels, he let me know this would not do, that for our own pride and the dignity and prestige of the company name we had to operate at a higher level. He showed me that it was better to stay in the cheapest room in the best hotel than to stay in the best room in the cheapest hotel. He insisted that I eat in good restaurants and learn to appreciate the differences in food and service. When we would travel around the U.S. on our meager budget, we would sometimes have to share one room, but we always stayed in the better hotels. In New York I stopped eating at Horn & Hardart's and moved up to Stouffer's. The 666 building on Fifth Avenue in midtown was new then and Stouffer's was on the top floor. (When we lived in New York when my daughter was a child, Naoko got to love this restaurant and its view of New York. Just a few years ago when I took an apartment on the forty-eighth floor of the Museum Tower, the first thing she noticed from our windows was the 666 building where she once had so many good meals. She remarked how from our tower apartment now she could look down at it but when she was a child it seemed to be up in the clouds with all of New York below her.)

The value of having fine teachers like Doc Kagawa is beyond estimation. Most Japanese businessmen who visited the United States in those days tended to be clannish and learned about the country from the other Japanese businessmen who had preceded them. But it doesn't take much analysis to see the inadvisability of this approach. Despite a couple of years of living in a foreign country, these Japanese businessmen were still strangers; following their advice was like the blind leading the blind. I was learning about America from people who were right at home in America and had twenty-twenty vision.

As executive vice president of my company in Tokyo, I had

many things to do and the job of selling our products in the United States was more than I could take on as a one-man show. I had discussed the problem with Gross, and on his advice I appointed Delmonico International as the distributor of our radios. The relationship with Delmonico was fine for a while, but it wasn't long before I began to worry about it. As our name became better known and sales increased, the people at Delmonico seemed more interested in low price than in quality. It got to the point where we would find ourselves haggling over the cost of the imitation leather case and whether we could make it a few cents cheaper. They frequently asked us to produce some inexpensive radios that they could sell at high volume at big discounts. That was not my style, and I said so. We were not interested in producing low-quality goods just to make money.

When we announced to the world that we had succeeded in making the world's first transistorized television set at the end of 1959, Delmonico, without even consulting with us, began advertising that they were going to be handling it. I was alarmed by this, because I did not like the way things had been going, and I could see disaster ahead if our relationship continued. Before the ink was dry on their ad campaign, I told Delmonico that I had no intention of marketing television sets through them. I was afraid our great new TV sets, the first of their kind in the world, would be merchandised cheaply or even discounted. What I had in mind for my product line was an image of class and high quality, which really represented the products.

We had quite a fight over this. Thanks to Ed Rosiny, we avoided a long, drawn-out court battle, but we did have to negotiate for a long time and it cost a lot of money. We pointed out to Delmonico that we had signed a contract with them for radios at a time when we knew television would follow—we were actually working on TV at the time but we didn't know when we would be able to come out with it—but we had not specifically mentioned TV to them. I had known that one day we would get into the TV business, so I cited the patent filing date to prove my point. That meant we were not giving Delmonico the right to our TV sets, and in fact were exempting or omitting TV purposely from the Delmonico sales contract.

The people at Delmonico didn't like that, and we decided the only way to resolve the difficulty was to end our relationship. They wanted a big settlement—three hundred thousand dollars to break the contract—and as we resisted they gradually came down a bit in their demand. At more than one point I was ready to settle. I thought they would not go lower. But Ed Rosiny was not ready to settle, and I went along with his judgment. He said, "Give me one more day and I'll get it down to one hundred thousand dollars." Sure enough, he managed to bring the settlement down to seventy-five thousand dollars. I asked him how much his fee was and he said, "Twenty-five thousand. I'll take my fee out of their money!" I got to like him even more. It was a lot of money for us to pay then, but the principle was important to me, and I was gratified to see that my American teachers felt the same way I did, that we had to get out of that deal even if it cost us heavily. In the end, we found ourselves buying back Delmonico's complete inventory of our radios, about thirty thousand units, as part of the settlement.

When you talk about production figures and annual shipments and sales on paper, thirty thousand doesn't sound like very much of anything in the consumer electronics business. But in the bitter cold of February in New York City in 1960, the small staff of what was soon to be Sony Corporation of America was faced with several truckloads of radios, each radio packaged in its attractive display carton, of course, increasing the bulk. The thirty thousand looked like a million to us. We hadn't considered the actual work involved, and we hadn't hired anybody to help us.

Irving Sagor had offered us the Agrod warehouse for storing the radios, and when the trucks arrived on a freezing February morning, there was nothing for us to do but put on work jackets and start lugging the goods into the warehouse. About five of us worked from midmorning until about four o'clock the next morning. We were exhausted by the time our thirty thousand radios had been neatly stacked on skids, and we shuffled into the office for some instant coffee. Our warehouseman, Charlie Farr, who is still with us, turned down the offer of coffee and went home to Brooklyn to get some rest. One of our group decided he wanted to check the stacks of boxes again and went back into the warehouse from the office. When he had done his recounting, he came back into the office side, but as he opened the door he inadvertently set off the burglar alarm.

The security guards came bursting in and caught us red-handed, sipping coffee, a soiled and weary looking band of Japanese and one American. It was hardly the burglary scene they expected, but it looked suspicious to them nevertheless. Irving Sagor was one of our crew of executive laborers, and since he was the only American in the crowd he tried to explain to the security guards that we were the management of the company. The guards cast a wary eye on our dirty work clothes and weren't buying it. We couldn't reach Farr, who knew the code numbers for the burglar alarm system, because he was still on his way home, so we sat around staring at each other until Sagor got the idea of opening the safe. That idea bothered our captors for a minute until Sagor showed them he actually knew the combination. He opened the safe and showed them the company papers that identified himself and our operation. The guards accepted the proof grudgingly and left, shaking their heads, but the experience made us all begin to feel more like members of a family.

III

I was soon virtually commuting between Tokyo and New York. As executive vice president, I couldn't afford to be away from Tokyo for long, but as the man who was establishing our company in the United States, I couldn't afford to spend too much time in Tokyo either. I began to feel that to establish our company more firmly in the U.S. I had to get to know the country better, and even though I had many good friends in America I felt I needed to know more about how Americans lived and how they thought. To make the company name more common in the U.S. was one thing; to understand Americans would be more difficult. But I realized that my future and the future of my company would depend a lot on the United States and on other international business. Slightly over half of our production was going abroad already, and I was struck with the idea that our company had to become a citizen of the world, and a good citizen in each country where we did business. We had to know more than the market statistics and sales data.

I decided to found a company called Sony Corporation of America. Back in Tokyo, Ibuka and Kazuo Iwama, who was later to become president, were skeptical, not to mention the small cadre of Sony employees and executives we had assembled in New York. I was convinced it was the right thing to do, and nobody could come up with very good reasons why we shouldn't do it. We would be able to set up our own sales network, be our own distributor, and develop our own expertise in marketing. My colleagues in Tokyo decided that since I knew the American scene best they would leave it up to me. It seemed a long-range project, in any case, and so we decided to do it when the proper time came. As things turned out I didn't have long to wait.

We had been requesting permission from the Ministry of Finance to remit five hundred thousand dollars to the United States for future use, but we didn't know when and if the ministry would authorize it. Unexpectedly, the permission came through just at the time when we were considering establishing the American company. So we officially established the Sony Corporation of America in February 1960, with capital of five hundred thousand dollars; sixteen months later, we offered two million shares of Sony common stock in the U.S. market as American Depository Receipts (ADR). It was a profound learning experience for me. Although Tokyo Electric Power Company had issued bonds in the U.S. market before the war, we were the first Japanese company to offer its stock in the United States and it was made possible by the then-new system of ADR. Under the ADR system, the shares of stock are held in the country where they are issued, but the receipts for an offering of shares are deposited with an American financial institution, and they can be traded in the U.S., just like regular domestic shares.

Our bank and Nomura Securities, whose executives knew us well, and the American firm of Smith Barney and its president Burnett Walker thought we should be in the American market, and we were intrigued by the possibility of raising capital with a stock offering in the U.S. We discussed it in the fall of 1960 in Tokyo, and Smith Barney agreed to be the co-managing underwriter, with Nomura Securities.

The work may have been the hardest I ever had to do. We had to comply with the Japanese commercial code, the rules of the Japanese Ministry of Finance, and the American Securities and Exchange Commission. It was all new and very strange and complicated. Fortunately, Prime Minister Hayato Ikeda was pleased with the idea, because he was an internationalist and this would be a first for Japan, a first postwar capital liberalization. His positive attitude had a lot to do with convincing the conservative, traditional thinkers at the finance ministry that they should approve our request. We had to work fast. We put together a good team: myself and our staff at Sony; Ernest Schwartzenbach of Smith Barney, who represented the underwriters; John Stevenson of the law firm of Sullivan and Cromwell, which he now heads; Yoshio Terasawa of Nomura Securities, who had just returned from his honeymoon in February 1961 (and, as things worked out, was so busy with this project that he didn't see his bride for the next four months!).

We were working on the "red herring," the preliminary prospectus, and we had a difficult time explaining our way of doing business to the satisfaction of the SEC. We had to do a lot of things that were new to me. For example, we had to change our accounting methods to comply with the consolidation system used in the West and therefore consolidate our figures for the first time. After seeing how it worked, I had to agree with one of our American colleagues, who asked, "How can you possibly know the health of your company if you don't consolidate?" We are much better off for having learned to consolidate, and after our experience, consolidation became the standard reporting method in Japan.

We had to translate all of our contracts into English and explain the company on paper in minute detail. The first thing that puzzled the lawyers and accountants was that many of our contracts specified that if, during the life of the contract, conditions changed in a way that affected the ability of either side to comply with the terms, both sides would sit down and discuss the new situation. This kind of clause is common in Japanese contracts, and many companies do much or even most of their business without any contracts at all. However, it looked alarming to people who did not understand the way business is conducted in Japan. I guess this was the first real perception gap we came up against. The American side could not understand how we could sit down together and talk in good faith if the two parties were having a major disagreement.

More serious in the eyes of our underwriters was our method of finance through the traditional Japanese system of short-term loans. It is customary in Japan for a company to operate on a large number of renewable ninety-day loans. Someone said, "How can you run a business on so many short-term loans? If the bank calls them, you are out of business." We explained that the bank would not call them, that this is the traditional way to get the cheapest money. It gave Japanese firms a lot of flexibility; you can renew if you need to, or can pay off the loan if you no longer need the money. The banks pay very close attention to the companies they are supporting and are careful about making the loans in the first place. But our American colleagues wanted to see guarantees in writing from the bank that the loans would be renewed. I explained that there is trust between the bank and the company, but they said they would prefer to see the trust replaced with something in writing. Eventually they came to understand and accept the way we did things. We learned a lot, too.

After three months of day and night work, when we thought we had everything solved on the home office side in Tokyo, we moved to New York for the final details leading up to registration. The Tokyo Stock Exchange closed at 3 P.M., which was 2 A.M. in New York. We had to keep a close eye on the Tokyo stock market because if the stock price fluctuated too much we might have difficulty with the SEC, so every night we worked up to at least 2 A.M. at the Nomura Securities New York office, where the last thing we would do is talk to Tokyo and check on the market. I would then take the subway back to the apartment hotel where I was staying, which happened to be on East Fifty-sixth across the street from the Gaslight Club, and every night when I came home about 2:30 or so, worn-out and weary, I would find the front door locked and would have to ring the bell for the doorman. As my stay lengthened into weeks, he began marveling at my stamina and looking at me with a kind of sly admiration every morning as I dragged myself home. Finally he said to me one night, with a chuckle, "I sure don't understand where you get the strength to spend every night 'til two-thirty in the Gaslight Club."

We were so tired by the time it was over we could hardly stand. Finally the day came when we had to decide the price. This meant we had to get the final closing price at Tokyo, which was at 2 A.M. in New York, get the approval of the underwriters, actually Ernie Schwartzenbach, put the price into the prospectus, and have it printed immediately. Then a lawyer had to take the 6 A.M. train to Washington (there was no very early morning air shuttle in those days) to file it with the SEC at 9 A.M. Then if it was filed and approved, the lawyer had to get on the public phone at the SEC and call New York, and we could release the ADRs to the market. But by late on the final day Ernie Schwartzenbach was dead on his feet. Since only the price was yet to be decided, and the formula for doing that was already set, he decided to go home and get some rest. "Why don't you call me when you get the price," he suggested. "I can give my approval from home instead of waiting around here."

It sounded like a good idea. Schwartzenbach went home and lay down on his couch with the telephone beside him and immediately went to sleep. But when we called him he was sleeping so soundly we couldn't wake him up. We rang and rang and rang. No answer. Time was running out. Nomura, Tokyo, and I had all agreed on the issuing price—I'll never forget that it was $17.50 for one ADR, which consisted of ten shares—but we had to have Schwartzenbach's approval. The phone kept ringing, he kept sleeping in his living room in Great Neck, and we were all looking at our watches, trying to think what to do. Sam Hartwell, Ernie's assistant, got the idea that since Schwartzenbach was also the mayor of Great Neck, we could call the Great Neck police and have a patrol car go to the house and wake him up. Great idea, we thought. But it happened that only the week before some nut in Great Neck had been harassing the mayor and the police chief with crank phone calls, and so when Hartwell called, he got a cool response. In fact, at first they laughed at Sam's plea. It took a long time to explain what had happened, and finally they believed him and dispatched a policeman to wake up the mayor.

I was worn out when it was all over, but I was pleasantly shocked to see the result: a check for four million dollars from our first overseas stock offering. I had never seen such a big check. When I finally got home, for almost two weeks I was so tired I could hardly get out of bed. Later we published a very detailed book as a kind of bible or text for Japanese companies that wanted to issue shares on the American market, and it became quite popular. When Schwartzenbach retired from Smith Barney in 1966, I jumped at the chance to hire him as Sony America's president, replacing me, while I moved up to chairman. He knew about as much about Sony as I did after going through our stock offering experience, and he held the post until he died in 1968.

IV

Back in 1960 I had opened a showroom in the Ginza district of Tokyo where potential customers could handle and try out our products with no salesman around to try to sell them anything, and it was becoming quite a popular place. Its advertising value was enormous. Because we were new we had to introduce our company to the Japanese just as we would have to introduce ourselves to Americans and later to Europeans.

To have a showroom in New York became a goal. I surveyed the city and realized that if the people I wanted to reach were people who had money and could afford to buy our rather high-priced products, Fifth Avenue was the place to find them. I strolled up and down Fifth Avenue in mid-Manhattan looking at the people and the shops. It was very impressive: Tiffany, Cartier, Sak's Fifth Avenue, Bergdorf-Goodman. I narrowed down my search to the east side of Fifth Avenue between about Forty-fifth and Fifty-sixth because it then seemed the most elegant part of the street.

While I was searching for a suitable ground-floor spot to rent, I noticed that flags of many nations were on display, but not the Japanese flag. I decided that when we opened our showroom we would be the first to fly the Japanese flag on Fifth Avenue.

It took me two years to find a really suitable place, and we had to settle for rather small quarters, but I drew the original design myself and mirrored one wall to make it look bigger. Working on that showroom and trying to absorb the rhythm of American life, it struck me that if I were really to understand what life was like in America, and if we were going to be successful as a company in the giant American market, we would have to do more than establish our company on American soil. I would have to move my family to the United States and experience the life of an American. When I was alone in New York, I received many invitations and got to know many people, but I knew that as a family man in America I would enrich that experience because wherever I went, to the country club and to weekend parties or dinners, American families were together. Many invitations came to Mr. and Mrs. Morita, and I learned that a single male is often a problem for the hostess. If we lived in the U.S. as a family, we would get to understand the people as visiting foreigners cannot.

I kept this thought to myself, but as time went on, I became more and more convinced that I had to do it. The United States was open and progressive, and New York had become the international crossroads of the world. I brought my wife Yoshiko to New York for the opening of the showroom in October 1962, and at the height of the excitement during our opening I realized that this was the time, and I said bluntly, "Yoshiko, we are moving to New York." She knows me very well and she didn't even act very surprised. I knew that as a city person born in Tokyo, she could handle the move to another big city and the change in life-style, although she spoke practically no English. She determined she would make the best of my plan, and she actually did things that amazed everyone, even establishing a business of her own as a result of the move. I knew she could handle it because I had left her alone a great deal in Tokyo during my business travels, and she not only took care of the house and the children but acted as my confidante and business liaison when I was out of town. I would often call her with news and messages to be delivered at the office and elsewhere, and I frequently consulted with her.

In the United States many things would be different, but I knew that her personality and her determination would help her make a success of it; she has many friends abroad now because she turned out to have an exceptional gift for adapting to new people and places and a knack for being an unofficial international diplomat. It is all the more admirable, I believe, because Yoshiko grew up without any real interest in foreign countries and had no great desire to travel, although she was good at cooking French food. She came from a samurai family that went into the bookselling and publishing business at the end of the Tokugawa era and expanded into a large chain of bookstores. The company, Sanseido, today publishes the popular "Concise" line of foreign language dictionaries, an idea that originated with her father. The Concise dictionaries are also the most popular line with high school and college students.

Yoshiko's life as a young girl was full of activity; her Tokyo household was not too different from mine in Nagoya, that is, with servants and relatives bustling around, and sisters and a brother having their good times and spats. There was talk of business in the house all the time, she recalls, just as there was in my home. As a child, she had only twice been as far west as the resort area of Hakone, near Mount Fuji, and after we were introduced, back in 1951, she confided that she thought my hometown, Nagoya, which is even farther west, was really out in the boondocks. But her father wore Western clothes and was something of an internationalist. He liked to take the family out to dine. One of their favorites was the New Grand restaurant in the Ginza. My parents had taken me to the same restaurant, and later Yoshiko and I discovered we both remembered from childhood the impressive big blue and red neon sign on top of the building.

Our two boys, Hideo and Masao, and our daughter, Naoko, would find the new life-style in America difficult, we knew, but they were young and adaptable. Hideo was ten, Masao was eight, and little Naoko was only six. I felt that it would be a good experience for them, even though it would be difficult for everybody in the beginning.

Back in Tokyo, Ibuka was skeptical. His main objection was that he didn't like the idea of his executive vice president being so far away, but I proposed that I commute every two months and spend a week or so in Tokyo each time. I also was a great advocate of the telephone, and still am, and explained that we could really be in touch at any time. He agreed, as I knew he would, and I put my plan into motion. My travels across the Pacific would not diminish much, I knew. (I stopped counting my trans-Pacific trips at one hundred and thirty-five, a long time ago.)

In New York I already had our office people searching for an apartment for my family, and in no time they came across the perfect apartment for us. Nathan Milstein, the great concert violinist, lived in a third-floor apartment at 1010 Fifth Avenue, across from the Metropolitan Museum of Art at Eighty-second Street. He had decided to move to Paris for two years, and the apartment was for rent, completely furnished. The rent was rather high, or at least so it seemed to our Japanese pocketbooks in those days, twelve hundred dollars a month, but everything was right about the apartment: the location had prestige and we did not have to move a lot of furniture to New York or even do any decorating. Maestro Milstein's taste would be good enough for us. We could move right in. The place had twelve rooms— to us, accustomed to very small quarters in Japan, it was palatial. It had at least four bedrooms, plus servants' quarters, a huge living room, a separate dining room, and a den, all very spacious and tastefully and comfortably furnished. At night the lights of the museum would turn on, flooding the façade, and we could imagine it was Paris, though New York was very glamorous to us. I moved in in April, but because the children were still in school the family couldn't come until June. I was alone, but I had a lot of work to do. I commuted to the office by bus every day, mingling with New Yorkers, listening to them talk, observing their habits almost like a sociologist. I was also selling our products, making calls on clients, and when I could break away I visited schools in Manhattan to try to find places for the children.

Sam Hartwell, of Smith Barney, was my biggest helper in the school search. He had children in school in the city, and he knew the territory. He gave me invaluable advice and even set up interviews and sometimes went along with me. I must have had interviews at twenty schools, trying to find a suitable one that would take three young Japanese who had no English-language ability at all. I wanted a school that would accept them for at least two years, because that was how long I originally intended to stay. There wasn't a lot of interest among the schools. Most of them had established a European-influenced tradition, but finally the headmaster at St. Bernard's said he was interested in making his school more broadly international and he agreed to accept the boys. I found the Nightingale-Bamford School for Naoko, and with the school problem solved, I began to feel more comfortable with the idea of the family move to America.

Next we had to break the news to the children, and so I flew back to Tokyo and took the whole family to the new Palace Hotel, where I rented a suite for the weekend. It was 1963, and the city was getting ready for the 1964 Summer Olympics, building an entire expressway system and many new hotels and public facilities. It was a treat for the family to stay in one of Tokyo's newest hotels at this exciting time. The boys remember that suite very well because it was their first visit to a Western-style hotel, and Hideo was impressed that he didn't have to take his shoes off at the door of the room. That Saturday night, we had a big dinner in the elegant top-floor Crown Restaurant overlooking the grounds of the imperial palace, and later back in our suite I broke the news about going to the United States. I promised them a trip to Disneyland on the way. The children didn't know what they were getting into, but Masao, who was eight, was eager. He said later that since all the Western movies on TV were dubbed into Japanese, he thought everyone in America spoke Japanese. Hideo, who was older, wasn't as enthusiastic about the move, as he was reluctant to leave his friends. But we did go to Disneyland and we stayed in a hotel right at the park and gave the children the full tour before we moved on to New York. We all still remember the trip happily.

I realized what a disruption this move would be for the family, but I am a believer in the total immersion theory, and so one week after we arrived in New York, and before we could get settled, we enrolled the boys at Camp Winona in Maine. I figured that there would be no quicker way of getting them into the swing of life in America. Camp rules were that we could not visit them for the first two weeks, so they would really be on their own and would have to make an adjustment to this new life quickly.

Once we had settled the boys in camp, I suggested that Yoshiko get an American driver's license because, I told her, in America everybody had to drive. And besides, there might be some business driving for her to do. Also, with the boys in Maine (we found a day camp for Naoko in Manhattan) and because I would have to travel, it would be important for her to be able to get around on her own. I felt we ought to be able to see friends in the suburbs and take weekend trips. Preparing for the written test, she was so worried about her limited English-speaking ability that she just memorized all the test material, including the one hundred possible test questions, although she didn't understand much of it. She passed with a perfect score and had no trouble passing the driving test, but we had to borrow a stick-shift Volkswagen for her because the Cadillac

I bought was automatic and she didn't feel comfortable yet
driving an automatic car.

Yoshiko likes to recall that one of the first things I demanded of her after we were married in 1951 was that she get
a driving license, which was unusual for a woman in Japan
then, but she did it and was a very experienced driver by the
time we needed her in New York. While we were developing
our company we had a steady stream of Tokyo engineers and
others visiting New York, and Yoshiko was invaluable to them.
Sometimes one of our visiting Japanese would get ill or have
a problem with the strange food or need help because he couldn't
understand what was taking place. Yoshiko would cook for
them and counsel them.

Our den became an electronics lab where the engineers
would examine and test competitors' TV sets. There were TV
sets and components and tools all over the den, and Japanese
were going to and fro all day long. When Tokyo executives
arrived, Yoshiko would be assigned to drive out to meet them
at Kennedy Airport, then called Idlewild. Sometimes in bad
weather or for some other reason, an incoming flight would be
diverted to Newark, and so Yoshiko would have to drive all
the way from Idlewild to New Jersey to meet the flight. In
Manhattan she would chauffeur us to our meetings downtown,
to Wall Street, or elsewhere. And sometimes she would drive
an engineer all over the suburban area while he checked to see
how sensitive our FM radios were, that is, how far away from
the Empire State Building he could go in every direction before
the signal began to fade.

For the boys, life at summer camp was tough at first. There
were no other Japanese children there, and they were assigned
to different groups, and slept in different tents. The camp director bought an English-Japanese dictionary so he could learn
a few words of Japanese to use with them so they wouldn't feel
completely cut off. We heard later that the boys cried a little
at night, and that's understandable. We had given them a note
that read "Please call my father" and told them to use it in
case they had trouble and didn't know what to do, but they
didn't use it. I felt terrible, in a way, but I thought this experience was for their own good. When we left them that first
day, both Yoshiko and I were fighting back tears.

Masao said he spent his days doing what everybody else

did, at first not realizing or understanding why he was doing it. At Camp Winona there was a lot of personal choice, which is very different from Japanese summer camp, where everybody follows the same curriculum. Masao just did what the majority did. Because of their age difference, Hideo was in intermediate camp and Masao was in junior camp, and so they only saw each other at lunchtime, two Japanese boys with no English, learning how to play baseball, swimming and climbing rocks with American kids who spoke a third language, American slang. But they got along well with the other campers, and my wife and I visited on weekends as often as possible. Hideo, a hearty eater, was thrilled with the big portions, the variety of ice cream, and the large servings of melon and fruit juice. Masao wasn't as happy with the camp, but when it was time to return the next summer he was eager to go, and when he had to leave he was upset.

The children were learning independence and American style, and it was all very healthy for them. They saw the differences between Americans and Japanese and came to understand the feeling of pride in your country and the symbolism of the national flag. They felt it was great to sing the American national anthem and to hoist the flag every morning. Later, when we built a new house in Tokyo, we had a flagpole installed, and every morning until the boys again went overseas to school they would hoist the Japanese flag. All of our Sony factories today fly the Japanese flag, the Sony flag, and the flag of the host country they are in. Like Olympic athletes, we are, after all, in a concrete way representing Japan and should wear the symbol of our country proudly.

Naoko was too young to send to camp that year, so we sent her to Beachwood day camp in the city, and she grew accustomed to the new life with the adaptability very small children seem to have. After a year of first grade in New York, she seemed ready for summer camp, and she thought she was, too, after hearing her brothers talk about Camp Winona. When we made our first visit to see her after two weeks the next year, she took us down to the lake and rowed us around in a row boat all by herself, proud of her accomplishment. When I asked her about her feelings later, she confessed that she got very lonely at night when the lights went out and would cry. To make herself feel more secure, she would turn on her flashlight under the covers. The flashlight story explained the small mystery of her dwindling allowance. She was spending all the money we gave her to buy flashlight batteries at the camp store.

The boys returned from Maine after that first summer full of fresh air and vitality. The first thing they noticed about New York—and complained about—was the smell of exhaust fumes and the smog of the city. As the school term began, the other students at St. Bernard's accepted the boys with curiosity at first. They had trouble pronouncing their names. Hideo remembers that most of his classmates called him "High-dee." Later, at boarding school in England, they called him Joe, which was an abbreviation for Tojo, the only Japanese name his classmates had ever heard, apparently. Masao remembers how frustrating it was with his very limited English vocabulary to understand what was going on in French class. He was trying to learn English as a second language, and now he was expected to learn a third language by using the second language he was only beginning to understand.

Yoshiko's English was terrible in the beginning, but she made up her mind to use it and study and listen, and she made friends quickly. While I traveled, and when she didn't have heavy company duties, she would take the kids skiing in the Catskills or visit our friends in the suburbs of New York. On weekends when I was in New York, we would sometimes go on picnics, Yoshiko driving and me with a map in my lap, acting as navigator. She also became very good at entertaining, giving dinner and cocktail parties, with only one Japanese helper, a maid we brought with us. During our New York stay, we entertained more than four hundred people in our apartment, and Yoshiko became so good at it that when we returned to Japan she wrote a book titled *My Thoughts on Home Entertaining*, which was an instant hit and is still used as a reference on the subject by Japanese who are having foreign guests or visiting in foreign homes. It is still uncommon today for Japanese to entertain in their homes, although those who have international experience and live in something better than the average apartment are inviting foreigners home more frequently these days.

Yoshiko had a difficult time at first because she would often be invited to luncheons by wives of American businessmen and others, but we only had one interpreter in New York at the time, a man, and Yoshiko felt it wouldn't be proper to bring him to a ladies' luncheon. Also, in Japan husbands never take their wives along on business entertainment outings, and on other occasions when two or more couples are together, husbands and wives sit side by side. But of course in the West it is customary for the host to have the female guest of honor on his right, often far away from her husband, so the pressure was really on Yoshiko to learn how to communicate.

In her book, Yoshiko told how encouraged she was, as a poorly traveled Japanese with almost no English-language fluency, to go to parties in New York and find French and Spanish women whose English was no better. She gave a lot of practical advice. For example, she cautioned Japanese women against wearing kimono at the wrong times: "A party is held so that those who are invited can enjoy themselves equally over a meal and conversation with each other. When everyone wears the same kind of outfit, harmony is enhanced. If there is even one person wearing prominently splendid clothing, it makes everyone uncomfortable and the whole party lacks warmth." She learned how to entertain elegantly and simply and how to make people feel relaxed. In Japan, she realized, some foreign guests were apprehensive about the possibility of being served a Japanese meal with chopsticks, even though we have a modern, Western-style home. When we have such a guest, she will open our dining room doors early while we are having cocktails so that the guests can see that the table is set with silverware in the Western style. She kept lists of the people who visited our home, when they came, and what they liked. For example, her lists note that the German baritone Dietrich Fischer-Dieskau likes only simple grilled meat; pianist Andre Watts's mother doesn't like fish; conductor Leonard Bernstein likes sushi and sashimi, and so on.

Her outgoing manner pleased the Americans she met and sometimes confused the Japanese, as I myself have done, being rather outspoken for a Japanese. One day in New York, my friend the fashion designer Issey Miyake told me that he was upset that Yoshiko and Diana Vreeland, the fashion editor, who was also his friend, had had "a terrible fight." In no time Diana was on the phone asking for Yoshi, as everyone called her. What about the fight? There was no fight, just a difference of opinion that is natural among Westerners, but which most Japanese try to avoid. It is very difficult to fight in the Japanese language because of the character and structure of the language, and the fact that it is very indirect and nonconfrontational forces politeness on you unless you want to get very rough. Most Japanese, hearing any Western argument, tend to overreact to such exchanges.

Yoshiko has always been interested in fashion, and through the friends she made in New York she began to bring the fashion news to Japan. Using our newest U-Matic video tape recorder, she has interviewed fashion designers such as Bill Blass, Oscar de la Renta, the late Perry Ellis, and others and has videotaped their fashions. When we moved back to Japan, she did a television show on fashion for about ten years, traveling to the fashion centers abroad and bringing back interviews and introducing new ideas to Japan, which was then behind the times in fashion awareness and not the fashion leader it is today.

Although we had planned to stay two years in New York, our visit was cut short by the unexpected death of my father. He had relieved me of the responsibility for the family business after the war, but I remained the eldest son and now I was the head of the Morita family and its fortunes, and so I had to be back in Tokyo. I left New York immediately, and Yoshiko cleared out the apartment in one day, rushed up to Camp Winona and brought the children back to New York, tied up all the loose ends, sent the baggage ahead, and was back in Japan within a week. The children were not happy to be leaving camp or the United States; they said they were just getting to enjoy it and to feel at home. The children took up their education for a time back in Japan, but then we found schools for them abroad, Hideo and Masao in England and Naoko in Switzerland.

A death in the family makes you examine your life and the future of the family. Where my children were concerned, I felt very strongly that the new postwar educational system in Japan lacked discipline. The teachers, with some important exceptions, did not have the dignity they once had and were not given the status they should have in society. The leftist teachers' union and pressure from PTA groups had watered down the quality of education, and study for examinations was nothing but rote application.

When I attended middle school, discipline was very strict, and this included our physical as well as our mental training.

Our classrooms were very cold in winter; we didn't even have a heater; and we were not allowed to wear extra clothes. In the navy, I had hard training, even though I only had to undergo four months of it in boot camp, but every morning we had to run a long way before breakfast. In those days I did not think of myself as a physically strong person, and yet under such strict training I found I was not so weak after all, and the knowledge of my own ability gave me confidence in myself that I did not have before. It is the same with mental discipline; unless you are forced to use your mind, you become mentally lazy and you will never fulfill your potential.

When I was traveling abroad, I realized that in Britain some of those traditional schools still existed. Most American schools seemed much too permissive to me. In my own case, I had a hard time learning English, and I knew that in the future the world would become smaller and smaller as airplanes became faster and as communications improved, so I wanted all my children to speak English and learn how to work under strong self-discipline.

I had been thinking about this since my very first trip to the U.S. and Europe eleven years before. When I left the United States for the European part of the trip, I was very hesitant to use my English, but when I got to the Continent I realized that many other travelers from America and other countries could not speak the languages of the European countries they were visiting, and so I was emboldened to speak some English. I met many people on trains who spoke none of the local languages, or even less than I knew of English, and I realized that not speaking fluent German, for example, put all of us in the same boat.

So I started to use my junior high school English and the bits I knew of German and French, and I discovered I could communicate. Suddenly a group of travelers on a train found everybody had the same problems. We had English in common though, and even though mine was rudimentary, it was good enough to be understood and it was accepted. When I returned to New York after that trip to Europe, I surprised everybody by speaking English. My Japanese friend Shido Yamada, who had done the interpreting for me while I was closing the transistor licensing deal prior to leaving for Europe, was astounded. Before I left the States, I spoke only Japanese with him and during all the negotiations. Now, a month later, I was speaking English! He thought for a while that I had learned English during my month-long visit to non-English-speaking countries in Europe. Actually, I explained to him, it was just a matter of gaining enough confidence, and the European trip gave me that confidence.

During my search for schools, many of my British friends told me about the prep school at Atlantic College, and I wanted to send my oldest son, Hideo, there, but it didn't work out because he was already a year too old for the prep school. When the children came home from America, we decided to put them back one grade in Japan to make certain they got all the essentials, Japanese language and history, and so on.

My wife and I spent a lot of time in Britain looking for a school for Hideo, who was in his second year of high school then. Yoshiko made quite a science of it, traveling all around Britain with a friend, the wife of one of our executives based in London, Midori Namiki, a famous TV personality for quite a while in Japan when she was the first hostess of the Japanese version of the children's program "Romper Room."

(It was ironic that we had Midori and her husband, Masa Namiki, with us on our school search in Britain. You see, when we were developing Chromatron color TV, "Romper Room" was the only daytime program on Japanese television that was broadcast in color. No matter what we were doing in those days, when someone would yell, "Hey, it's ten o'clock!" we would all rush to the lab to see how our experimental sets were performing. Getting genuine, natural color, especially the flesh tones, was crucial, and so I would check the colors very carefully. In fact I had scrutinized Mrs. Namiki's face to the smallest detail, and I have joked with her husband that maybe I have looked at her more closely than he, at least when she was on TV.)

I think Yoshiko and Midori visited more than a dozen boarding schools in Britain before she found the school she was looking for, a two-year boarding school that took only fifty students. Hideo found it very difficult, but he applied himself, and in the second year he was named Head Boy. He took A and O levels and was accepted at two British universities. But because of his weakness in subjects like European history and literature, they accepted him only in science, and he didn't want that. "I don't want to compete with my father," he said. He was more interested in economics.

Masao jokes that he was forced into going to Atlantic College. The headmaster, Admiral Hall, was visiting Japan and had been referred to me while he was looking for funding. It happened that Masao had a day off from school and was visiting me in the office when Admiral Hall was there. "I was trapped," Masao says now. He was interviewed and tested on the spot and given an acceptance.

Atlantic College is an interesting place, located in a one-hundred-and-thirty-five-room castle on a small estate at St. Donat's in southern Glamorganshire County, Wales, about fifty miles from Cardiff. It was built in the eleventh century, and its owners kept adding to it. The American press magnate, William Randolph Hearst, bought the castle about 1934 and added tennis courts and a huge swimming pool. The movie actress Marion Davies, Hearst's mistress, once said that when she and W. R., as she referred to him, would arrive for one of their rare visits, about forty Welsh singers wearing high silk hats and lace dresses would line up on the lawn to sing a welcome for them. In 1938 Hearst put it up for sale, but the British Army requisitioned it for officer training during the war. In 1960 it was bought by a rich donor and given to the school. Masao spent two years there, graduated, and was accepted at Georgetown University in Washington, D.C. Hideo came back to college in Japan. For a time I considered starting a cattle ranch in Brazil, and Hideo was interested in managing it, so he transferred to the University of California at Davis, where he studied agricultural economics for two years before returning to graduate from Ashiya University here in Japan. I never did buy the ranch, though.

Naoko had a more complicated schooling than the boys. At first she said she didn't want to go to college, which was partially my fault because I had written a book called *Never Mind School Records*, a kind of tract against overemphasis on college ties in the business world in Japan. I established a policy at my company of disregarding school records once an employee was hired so that nobody would be tempted to judge a person on his academic background rather than on his proven ability and performance or what his potential seemed to be. This is because so much emphasis—too much—

is placed on the mere name of the university you attend in Japan.

Naoko studied French in high school and then we found a finishing school in Lausanne, Switzerland, for her. But although she was very successful academically (she also won an award as an outstanding volleyball and basketball player), she felt the French language as spoken by the Swiss was not the pure Parisian dialect she wanted to speak, so we sent her to Paris, where she stayed a year and acquired the accent she wanted. English was next, and so she came to Washington and enrolled in language classes at Georgetown, where Masao was studying at the time. She later studied fashion design in Los Angeles, and when she came home she was completely cosmopolitan. When she went away, Naoko was very shy, and when she came back to us she was full of cheer, lively and confident. She and her husband, a sales engineer for Kyoto Ceramics (Kyocera), have recently been transferred from California back to Tokyo.

I have learned a lot from my children's education, too, mainly that the exposure to other cultures teaches an insular Japanese that he is Japanese and in the minority in the world. He learns to appreciate his Japanese-ness, but also to understand that he must fit into the world, and not the other way around. Yoshiko says that one of the important things to be learned is that "foreigners" are individually different, have different ideas, different religions, different backgrounds. And so our excursion abroad opened the minds of the Morita family, and we can feel comfortable anywhere in the world, though Japan is our true home.

V

I was traveling more than ever during the middle sixties. At Sony we had been deeply involved in video even before I took up residence in the United States. The idea of video tape recorders for home use had been in our minds and on our drawing boards for a couple of years. Television, still black and white, was booming everywhere and we were selling as many sets as we could make. Ampex in America was making large video tape recorders for broadcast use, and it had struck Ibuka and me that there should be no reason why people would not want to have a video recorder at home just as they had audio tape recorders for home, personal use. We were supported in this belief by some very progressive young staffers and associates. One of them was Norio Ohga, who had been a vocal arts student at the Tokyo University of Arts when he saw our first audio tape recorder back in 1950. I had had my eye on him for all those years because of his bold criticism of our first machine. He was a great champion of the tape recorder, but he was severe with us because he didn't think our early machine was good enough. It had too much wow and flutter, he said. He was right, of course; our first machine was rather primitive. We invited him to be a paid critic even while he was still in school. His ideas were very challenging. He said then, "A ballet dancer needs a mirror to perfect her style, her technique. A singer needs the same—an aural mirror." (Ohga is now the president of Sony.) The idea of a mirror is very apt. We had one kind of mirror in the audio tape recorder, and with video we had an even better mirror than the mere audio tape. If only we could perfect it.

The first Ampex video tape units for broadcasting stations were huge, almost filling a room, and they cost one hundred thousand dollars and more. They used two-inch-wide tape in open reels, and that was really cumbersome. We had to design a small system that people could install in their homes and we knew it would take a long time. We built several models, each one smaller than the last, starting with two-inch tape in an open reel machine, which we put into Pan Am and American Airlines planes for passenger entertainment back in the early sixties. Then we brought the tape size down to three-quarters of an inch and built a cassette to handle the tape, like an audio cassette but much bigger. We called it U-Matic, and since we introduced it in 1969 it has become the standard all over the world, replacing the big two-inch units in broadcasting stations.

The U-Matic machine also became an industrial machine. Ford Motor Company bought five thousand units for use in their agencies, to train mechanics and salesmen. Many thousands of these units were put into use by other companies for the training of technicians and sales personnel and are still being manufactured, sold, and used today, all over the world. It is the most popular machine of its kind in broadcasting. We were actually a bit surprised at the speed with which our videotape cameras and U-Matic systems replaced sixteen-millimeter film in broadcasting stations. Electronic news gathering, ENG as it came to be known, came about because the machinery was so practical. The cameras are small and easy to handle; with videotape there is no lost time between shooting and editing; and no high costs were needed to build and maintain film processing labs.

But Ibuka was not satisfied. This machine would never be a home unit because it was still expensive and much too big. Using half-inch tape, we produced the world's first all-transistor video tape recorder for home use, and we kept adding models, but Ibuka was never satisfied. He wanted a truly small unit with a very handy cassette. He returned to the office one day from a trip to the United States, and he called together the video development group. He emphasized that the home video tape recorder was the most important project at hand and that the size of the unit was crucial. He reached into his pocket, took out a paperback book he had bought at the airport in New York, and placed it on the table. "This is the size I need for the cassette," he said. "This is your target. I want at least one hour of program time on a cassette that size." That was the challenge that created the original Betamax system.

In television, color was the thing. We had a lot of experience with black and white, but color was quite a new story for us. In the early sixties, there was a lot of development going on in the color field, and although the RCA shadow mask system became the standard picked by the FCC, Ibuka thought we ought to reinvent color TV ourselves. We were behind many of our competitors with color, but we wanted something new, something better. Ibuka wanted to study TV from the basic principles. We did not like CBS's rotating filter design or the RCA shadow mask design. There was another system, invented by Professor Ernest O. Lawrence of the University of California, that looked intriguing. Lawrence was the physicist who had invented the cyclotron. His color picture tube was called Chromatron, and it differed considerably from the other designs. The concept was technically very interesting, if complex, and when the system was adjusted properly it was extremely bright and efficient. We committed ourselves to it very early by buying a license in 1962 from Paramount Pictures, which held the patent, although we knew that production costs for the picture tube would be high and that there would be many technical problems. We only made thirteen thousand Chromatron sets, all of them sold in Japan, before we gave up. Meanwhile, we had been working on our own tube, a new idea that we finally called Trinitron.

Our competitors were using a system in which three separate electron guns at the back of the picture tube emitted the TV picture in the form of a series of red, green, and blue electron beams focused by lenses at the shadow mask, a plate with many holes located behind the face of the picture tube. The electron beams had to be focused on the holes in the mask, and they had to pass to the face of the picture tube, where they created the picture as they activated the colored phosphor on the inside of the face of the tube. The Chromatron system used one gun instead of three to generate the three electron beams, and a set of thin wires instead of a shadow mask permitted more of the electron beams to reach the face of the picture tube, where, instead of dots, strips of colored phosphor were used. This system gave a much brighter picture than any of the others, but there were many technical problems. High voltage, switching on and off, had to be applied to the wires, and we had trouble getting it to work reliably from the beginning. But while we were trying to fix it, we were working feverishly on our own new system. Ibuka never wanted to settle for somebody else's design, and even as we tried to make Chromatron work, he spent long hours in the lab working side by side with the engineers on Chromatron and also on the new system we were trying to develop.

We revised the three-gun "delta" system, packaging all three into one that emitted three electron beams as in the Chromatron tube, but we focused them with one large lens instead of a series of lenses. We were going for compactness and efficiency. Instead of a grille composed of a complicated set of wires or the shadow mask, we produced a simple, low-cost metal grille, actually a plate with long slots etched in it.

Our system gave us 30 percent more transparency—in our system more of the beams struck the face of the tube than in the shadow mask system. Our system was twice as bright and used less power. We began to make twelve-inch and seven-inch Trinitron sets, and of course they were expensive. It was our policy to charge a premium for our products. At an annual meeting of RCA, President Robert Sarnoff was asked about our new competitive tube design and he said that only the RCA shadow mask design "has passed the crucial test of mass production on an economic basis." When I was asked about this comment I couldn't help smiling. "The situation is normal," I told a reporter for *Business Week* magazine. "They laughed when we introduced both the transistor radio and the small TV set."

We had no competition making small color TV sets. It was possible to buy a twenty-three-inch black and white television set in the United States in a big cabinet for the same four hundred dollars we charged for our personal color set then. I predicted at the time that by the end of the year (it was 1968), there would be ten million households in America with color sets, most of them in the living room. But I believed, and rightly, as it turned out, that people would want a personalized set they could take into the kitchen or the bedroom, or even outdoors in the daytime. To go out onto the American patio for a lunchtime barbecue or a rest in the hammock with your TV set, you need portability and a very bright picture, and we had both. Our strategy of making small sets was not new. Our first transistorized black and white set made in 1959 was bucking what many said was the market trend for bigger sets. When we began making integrated circuits for our products, we produced a little three-ounce radio you could carry on the end of a key chain, and we even put a radio in a watch, but that was just to show that it could be done. And, of course, new technology for TV now enables us to make a television set you can carry in your pocket. Oh, yes, as for our efforts in devising our own color TV system, we were very pleased in 1972 when, in the U.S., the National Academy of Television Arts and Sciences awarded Sony an Emmy for the development of Trinitron. It was the first time an Emmy had been given for a product. Sony received a second Emmy, in 1976, for the U-Matic video tape recording system.

VI

Our business at home and overseas was booming. We had begun to make desktop calculators in 1964, and I thought this would be a good addition to our product line. We demonstrated what we considered to be the world's first solid-state desktop calculator at the New York World's Fair in March of 1964. I went there to demonstrate it, something I have always enjoyed doing. (In fact, one day in New York I was demonstrating our video camera to a reporter from *The New York Times* when I heard fire engines outside. I looked out the window and saw smoke coming from our own basement, so I grabbed the camera and filmed the scene as the fire fighters arrived, then played it back for the reporter immediately. It was the most convincing demonstration I could have given.)

We later marketed a special calculator model we called SOBAX, which stood for "solid state abacus." But I soon realized that several dozen Japanese companies had jumped into the business of making calculators, and I knew the shakeout would come sooner or later through a very brutal price war. That is the way it is on the Japanese market, and it was just the kind of thing we have always wanted to avoid. When it became obvious that others would be discounting dangerously to get a share of the market, we gave up the calculator business.

My prediction was right. Many calculator makers went bankrupt and others just got out of the market, taking a big loss. Today there are only three major makers of calculators, and in a way I have been vindicated. There was still much to be done in audio, television, and video to keep us challenged, and we were always looking for new applications.

But I must say here that, on reflection, I was probably too hasty in making the decision to get out of calculators. I confess that today I think it showed a lack of technical foresight on my part, just the thing I think we have been good at. Had we stayed with calculators, we might have developed early expertise in digital technology, for use later in personal computers and audio and video applications, and we could have had the jump on our competition. As things developed, we had to acquire this technology later, even though we once had the basis for it right in-house. So from a business viewpoint we were right in the short term, but in the long term we made a mistake. Fortunately, I haven't made too many of those wrong short-term decisions.

In 1964, business was so good that we had to open a new television assembly plant to meet the demand for color sets because Japan was hosting the Summer Olympic Games that year and it seemed as though every family in the country had to have a color TV set on which to watch the games. The televised wedding of Crown Prince Akihito and Princess Michiko had stimulated black and white TV sales a few years before. In fact the excitement about the Olympics gave the entire nation a kind of unified national goal. The Olympics galvanized the country into making many important and needed improvements. Tokyo's expressway system and the high-speed bullet train were needed long before the Olympic games were scheduled, but when Japan bid for the games and was awarded the honor, it was obvious that the road system could not handle the coming traffic, and the sight of Japan's legendary traffic jams, which stretched for miles through city streets, and sometimes remained gridlocked for hours, would have been too humiliating for Japan to tolerate on international television, and so the expressway system was built in record time.

Our planners also realized that the influx of tourists during the Olympics and afterward would include thousands who were visiting Japan for the first time and would want to see the ancient capital of Kyoto, the commercial center of Osaka, and other places along the Pacific corridor west of Tokyo to Hiroshima and the southern island of Kyushu. These people would badly strain the existing rail system, which needed improvement anyway, and so the latest technology was blended to produce the computerized high-speed rail system called Shinkansen. Today the so-called bullet trains on that original line leave Tokyo Station every twenty minutes. Visitors still marvel at the smooth one-hundred-and-fifty-five-miles-per-hour ride they get on the bullet train, although that system has been in service for more than twenty years. New lines have been opened to the northern parts of the country, while the next generation of high-speed trains is being readied, a train floating magnetically and propelled by a linear motor at twice the speed of the bullet trains—and considerably faster than France's high-speed TGV.

Also in that pre-Olympic campaign for improvements, Tokyo's Haneda Airport was modernized and expanded, new hotels were built, new landscaping helped to beautify the city, and many private citizens and Japanese companies developed projects and new products keyed to the Olympics. The authorities recognized that the noisy blowing of automobile and truck horns was a bad pollution problem that would be embarrassing for Japan as well, and so they took this national drive for change and improvement as an opportunity to quiet the city by outlawing needless horn blowing.

This kind of modernization drive keyed to a national event is not unique to Japan, but it worked exceptionally well. In 1972 when the capital city of Sapporo in Hokkaido was host to the Olympic winter games, the city went through a similar major modernization program, including the construction of its first subway system, and visitors to the city during the Olympics marveled at the changes that had taken place. With the physical modernization also came an increased sense of civic pride in a city that had caught up with the modern era, leaving much of its provincial past behind. Sapporo citizens became more sophisticated and began to take a broader outlook toward the rest of the nation and the world outside.

For me, it was becoming more and more important to keep traveling abroad through the late sixties and visiting our growing network of production and research facilities in Japan. There didn't seem to be enough hours in the day, and so it seemed logical for our company to have a company plane and later a helicopter. This is in itself a rarity in Japan, even today, where general aviation lags far behind that of the United States. But I soon had the advantage of being able to decide, for the sake of efficiency, whether to travel by road or air. Today I have a comfortable blue Mercedes 380 SEL in Tokyo and Sony has Aerospatiale 350 and 355 helicopters. (We are the sales agents for Aerospatiale in Japan.) Or I can take the Falcon jet, as I have, to China or elsewhere, although I almost always fly commercially overseas. (We are also the sales agents for Falcon in Japan. When I am in the States I sometimes fly a Falcon 50 or Falcon 100.)

Although I stopped counting my trips over the Pacific a long time ago, lengthy flights are not as tiring to me as to many others. I sleep wonderfully on planes; in fact, I sometimes get better rest in the air than I can in a hotel room. I bring a small box of sushi on board with me, just simple vinegared rice and raw fish, and I drink one small bottle of sake. I then wrap myself in a blanket, tell the stewardess not to wake me for meals or drinks or movies, and I go off to sleep immediately, almost like Adolph Gross at *My Fair Lady*.

I usually leave Tokyo in the early evening, arriving in New York the same evening (it is the same day because of the international date line, even though the flight time is about twelve hours). After I arrive in New York, I try to play about an hour and a half of tennis, then I sleep again until about 4 A.M., when I wake up and begin reading my business papers so that I will be ready for the day's work at the opening of business. I am always partially jet-lagged, so I try to sleep as much as I can, because I can never really catch up with the lag before I must make another trip.

I thought my activities as chairman of the Electrical Industries Association of Japan (EIAJ) would slow down my travels a bit in 1985, but I still managed to cram some really rapid globe-hopping trips into the schedule. A trip, for example, from Tokyo to New York, to London, from London to Los Angeles and then to Hawaii, and from Hawaii to Los Angeles to Paris and back to Tokyo in less than two weeks is not unusual for me.

Traveling like that I had to devise ways to cope with my work load. With half our business abroad and with our own corporate style as a product innovator, there was no model I could follow, so I just had to come up with a system that suited me and with which I could live. Now with communication systems improving all the time, it is possible to be in touch wherever you are, and I have been called a phone freak because I spend so much time on the telephone. Since our business is worldwide, when I am in New York, say, awake in my hotel room at 4 A.M., it is in the midst of some Sony person's business day somewhere in the world, and I can always call.

I am a person who loves his work, but I enjoy play also— I took up tennis at age fifty-five and downhill skiing at sixty, and at sixty-four I went back to water skiing, but I find it very hard on the thighs. I have played golf for almost forty years, and I still enjoy the game with a sixteen handicap. Every Tuesday morning we have an executive committee meeting in Tokyo, and if I am in Japan I make it a point to attend, but first I play several sets of tennis from seven to nine o'clock in the morning at the indoor courts near the office. My brother, Masaaki, who is deputy president of Sony, is also fond of the game, and so I play with him sometimes and with other Sony executives. I like to play sports with young people because I get ideas from them and they give me a fresh slant on almost everything. I think it is good for my spirit, too, to be with young people who are enthusiastic.

Since I have been playing tennis, I notice my reflexes are improving, and this pleases me, because when you start to age, the reflexes and reactions tend to slow down. It may mean the mind is going, also, although I hope not. When I began to play I missed the ball a lot, but now I find I can return very fast serves. Of course I don't play singles anymore. I noticed when I began to ski that my balance wasn't too good, but it has improved also. Every executive should be aware of the need for this kind of vigorous exercise, not only for the heart but also for the mind and the sense of confidence it gives you. It is important to maintain confidence in yourself.

Flying is a case in point for me. On one of my first rides in the company helicopter, I noted that the pilot was older than I was, and it occurred to me that if anything happened to him while we were flying we would crash. It would be silly for me to sit there in the back seat and worry, I thought. So I took out a learner's permit, climbed into the copilot's seat, and learned how to fly a helicopter, just in case. As long as I fly with a pilot who is also a licensed instructor in helicopters or fixed-wing aircraft, I can legally handle the controls of either without having to get my pilot's license, so all our pilots are instructor-rated. I keep my license renewed each year, not because I intend to fly the helicopter on any trips, but just in case I have to take over; I do not want to be helpless. I feel good with the confidence that comes with knowing I can land the thing.

One time when I was flying by helicopter from Geneva in an Aerospatiale 350, I said to the pilot, "This is the same helicopter as ours," and he said, "I saw you at the airport in Paris and I thought you were a pilot as well as an executive. Here, you take it." I didn't want to take off from Geneva airport by myself so I asked him to take off, and then I took over for a while. I like helicopters a lot; they are more difficult to fly than a fixed-wing plane as far as balance and stability is concerned, but it's really fun because of the maneuverability advantage the helicopter has over a fixed-wing plane.

Every day I am given homework by my secretaries. I have two fiberboard boxes with me always—one is black, the other reddish. The black one contains all the domestic material I must deal with and the reddish one is all international. I have four secretaries, two working on international and two on domestic matters. In the daytime I have no time to read any papers, because I receive and make so many phone calls and talk to visitors and have conferences—some people say the main thing Japanese executives do is hold meetings. The papers and letters keep coming whether I can keep up with them or not, so before I can go home I have to work my way through both those boxes each day. The black box may contain papers about Sony business, production, and sales reports, or queries, or have something to do with my EIAJ work, or other activities in the Keidanren, or Federation of Economic Organizations, such as the international investment and technical committees, which I chair. My international box may include invitations to speak in the United States or Europe or somewhere else, some details of problems or new plans for marketing or advertising, or tentative schedules for a new trip, and letters from friends and business associates overseas.

Also, we have a section at Sony called the Outside Liaison Section, which works almost exclusively for me. In this section, we have specialists in each of the areas I am involved in such as the EIAJ, the Keidanren, the Japan–U.S. Businessmen's Conference, and the various councils I belong to. One is full-time in charge of my Keidanren affairs, another with EIAJ, and still another with government liaison. I also have an assistant to help me draft speeches, although I rarely speak from a text. My boxes also have memos from my staff, even newspaper clippings. My secretaries know how to reach me wherever I am anywhere in the world. My New York secretary and my Tokyo secretary can always find me. One time I was skiing in the mountains near Karuizawa in Japan, trying to take three consecutive days off, but it didn't work out. I was paged on the slopes. (Usually my staff people try to solve problems without me; they did this only because they couldn't answer for me.)

I sometimes get calls from the United States about congressional matters that might affect Sony, and all sorts of personal calls as well. I have five telephone lines in my home, two of them exclusively for my use. I also have my own special phones at our apartment in Hawaii, at our apartment in Museum Tower in New York, and at our country house at Lake Ashi near Mount Fuji.

The need for the special phone lines originally came about when we had a couple of teenagers at home, but we still keep the extra phones because it won't be too long before our grandchildren will be using them. Having two lines exclusively for me is essential because I can use the second line to get information I might need while I am holding a caller on the first line. I just had a second line installed in my car. I also insist that every company executive when he takes office gets a special twenty-four-hour hot line installed in his home so that he is always reachable.

Even though I am constantly busy with work, I try to take short vacations when I can. In the winter I ski every weekend, and I play tennis on summer weekends. During the New Year holidays I usually spend seven or eight days in Hawaii playing golf and tennis. We often go to the Easter music festival at Salzburg, and the Wagner festival at Bayreuth, and I usually rent a Mercedes in Munich and drive there. It's about one hundred and fifty-five miles, and sometimes my wife spells me at the wheel. We don't get all that much chance to drive in Japan, and certainly no chance to drive as fast as you can in Germany, but I have a very responsive Toyota Soarer that we often use to drive to our weekend cottage in the mountains.

I like to travel fast, although I don't consider myself a speed demon. One time when Yoshiko and I were in Bayreuth for the Wagner festival, the opera singer Peter Hoffman showed me his pride and joy, a twelve-hundred-cc Honda motorcycle. This huge and powerful machine is not available in Japan, but is much in demand in Germany where they have no speed limits on the autobahn. He invited me to drive it, but I declined, saying I would prefer to ride with him, and off we went for a spin. At one hundred and forty miles an hour I could hardly hold on, even though I had my arms locked around him, but it was exciting.

When we got back and dismounted, he asked me if I would

like to ride in an aerobatic plane. Of course I said yes—it was something I had not done before. We all climbed into the car and drove out to the airport, where we met his friend who was a German aerobatics champion. He invited me to go up with him, and I of course jumped at the chance. When I was settled in the cockpit he said, "I'll watch you and if you get sick we will land." I've never been sick in a plane, so I just nodded.

As soon as we took off, he handed the controls to me and told me to climb to four thousand feet, which I did. When I leveled off, he took over and without any warning went into his program—inside and outside loops, snap rolls, barrel rolls, stalls, spins, all of it. It seemed to go on for hours, and I was constantly involuntarily reaching for my seat belt to have something to hold on to. I have a very strong stomach, but I was happy when he signaled we were going down. As we turned into what I thought was our final approach, I could see Yoshiko and Peter Hoffman waiting for us on the tarmac, smiling and waving.

But just as we came over the edge of the runway, he rolled the plane upside down at about fifty feet and gunned it. We were so low I felt like my head was almost scraping the runway. My wife said she could see my hair hanging straight down as we whizzed by. I get a kick out of roller coasters and such things, which last about three minutes. Yoshiko and I both rode the stand-up roller coaster at Science Expo '85 in Japan. But thirty minutes of aerobatics was the longest thrill I have had, a little too long. I must confess my legs were very shaky when I finally climbed out of the little stunt plane, and my thank you may have sounded a bit hollow.

I enjoy being in Europe, especially for the music and the great musicians, many of whom I have come to know very well through our products and through mutual friends in business as well as in the arts. In 1966, when Maestro Herbert von Karajan was conducting in Tokyo, we became close friends. He did not remember meeting me before, but on my trip to Europe in 1953 I called on him when I visited Vienna. At that time Vienna was still under occupation by the Allied Powers, and I had to get special permission in London to go there.

I had just seen the film *The Third Man*, which takes place in Vienna, and I found it very thrilling to be going to that town of intrigue and mystery. I had booked a hotel through the travel agent in New York, and I arrived in the city at night and made my way to the hotel. In the morning when I came down for breakfast I saw red flags on almost all the tables in the dining room. I hadn't realized it the night before but now it was clear that I was in the Soviet sector and this hotel was mainly for Russian officers. My friend, a Japanese composer named Shinji Toyama, was studying in Vienna at the time and he came to see me at the hotel. He had a worried expression on his face. "Why are you staying in the Russian sector?" he whispered, looking around nervously. I shrugged and stuck it out for a couple of days. My travel agent had booked the hotel and I didn't know anything about how to go about changing it. The maître d'hôtel assigned me to a corner table in the dining room, which suited me fine at the time; I didn't have to talk to anybody, just observe.

I went to the Vienna Philharmonic and there I met the great von Karajan, who was already a famous conductor, of course, and he asked me, "What do you do, Mr. Morita?" I told him in very broken English that I was in the electronics business and that I was making tape recorders. "Good," he said. "Do you know Max Grundig? You should visit him." Well, no, I told him, I didn't know Max Grundig but I had visited the famous Grundig electronics factory in Germany before I came to Vienna, and I had had no introduction to the great man of German radio. Unfortunately I was not going back that way on my trip, but I met Grundig some years later. Von Karajan comes often and is a frequent guest in our home.

VII

The popularity of the Tokyo and New York Sony showrooms convinced me that we needed a real permanent presence in Tokyo's central district, because our offices and factories were far from where crowds of people move. So we bought a corner in the Ginza district, at one of the busiest intersections in the city, and we put up an eight-story building, which was as high as we were allowed to go under the building code. Although we couldn't go up any higher, there was no hindrance to going down six stories, which we did. We built a shopping center and utility floors, and with all that space I decided we could make some special use of a couple of those basement floors. We were getting a lot of visitors in Tokyo, and it struck me that having our own restaurant in the building to entertain these guests would be impressive, and we also might make some money at it because of the way Japanese like to eat out and entertain in restaurants. It took quite a while to decide just what kind of restaurant we should have.

I ruled out a Japanese-style restaurant, although that might have seemed logical. I had just taken a trip to Korea and was treated to Korean food night after night, and I realized that a traveling person might like the local food occasionally, but not every night. Besides, it would be difficult to compete with the really great old Japanese restaurants. Chinese was also not such a good idea, I thought, since there were so many other Chinese restaurants in Tokyo and the chefs change jobs too often. There were very few French-style restaurants then, and none of them was really authentic.

I had traveled to France frequently and I knew Maxim's de Paris and its owner, Louis Vaudable, and I also knew that he catered the first-class meals for Pan Am in those days, so he might be interested in doing something innovative. I approached him with the idea of opening a replica of Maxim's in Tokyo, with authentic decor, French chefs, and the same menu, wines, table service, and style as in Paris. He thought it was a fine idea, and so I sent my architect to Paris, and we took two basement-level floors of the Sony building and re-created Maxim's, which remains as popular today as when we opened it. I like to think we stimulated the high interest in French food among restaurateurs in Tokyo by showing it can be done. In 1984 La Tour d'Argent opened a branch in a Tokyo hotel, and the number of French restaurants and small bistros in Tokyo is great and growing. Visitors from France are amazed to find such good French cuisine here. There is even a Japanese bakery that has a branch in Paris, selling French bread to the French.

I decided we needed a showroom in Paris, and to my mind it had to be on the Champs Elysées, which I think is probably the most famous street in the world, even better known, and even busier at night, than Fifth Avenue. Late at night Fifth Avenue is deserted except for a few bookshops. But the Champs Elysées seems to be full of strollers at almost any hour.

We had established Sony Overseas, S.A. (SOSA, we call it) the year after we founded Sony America, and we based it in Zug, Switzerland, on the advice of a friend who pointed out that the tax situation in Zug was very favorable. We became the first Japanese company based in Zug at a time when quite a number of American firms were already there. In London and Paris we had local agents to handle our goods, but with the confidence we gained doing our own sales and marketing in the United States we decided we should do the same in Europe. Easier said than done. Negotiating ourselves out of those agreements was very time-consuming and difficult. Changing the arrangement with our London agent was relatively easy, although we lost money there for a long time. My colleague at one point jokingly suggested we might make some money by starting a Japanese bathhouse for tourists, because we were getting free hot water and doing little business. But when we got to France, I began to realize that Japan Inc., as many Americans and Europeans call our government-business relationship, is second-rate compared to the French government-business relationship, or the English one for that matter.

For one thing, I have never heard a Japanese head of state or head of government try to sell foreign companies on moving there or doing business, as Prime Minister Margaret Thatcher did. Whenever she had a chance, even during summit meetings, she would promote England, asking when Nissan Motors or some other company was going to build a factory in Britain. In our case, even the Prince of Wales was involved in the promotion. He came to Expo '70, and I had been asked by the British ambassador to put Sony TV sets in the living room of his suite at the British embassy in Tokyo. Later, when I was introduced to the prince at a reception in the embassy residence, he thanked me for providing the TV sets and then asked me if we had any intention of building a plant in the United Kingdom. We didn't have any such plans yet, I told him, and he said with a smile, "Well, if you should decide to put a plant in the U.K., don't forget my territory."

When we did go into the U.K., it seemed reasonable to take a look at Wales, but we looked at many other areas as well, covering all the possibilities. We finally did decide on Wales on the basis of our needs for location, convenience, environment, and so forth, and we set up a manufacturing operation at Bridgend. And when we were ready for the dedication in 1974, I contacted the ambassador, who was then back in Britain, and asked him to approach the Prince of Wales to see if he would accept an invitation to be present at the opening.

The prince accepted and came, so we put a big plaque at the entrance of our factory to commemorate the occasion, in English and Welsh, but not Japanese. In my remarks at the opening ceremony, I reminded him of our conversation at Expo '70. "This factory represents a major step in the international policy that our company has followed since its inception," I said. "Sony's ideal is to be of service internationally through its unique technology and through internationally shared efforts, such as this one, where the work force, engineers, and suppliers in this locality can work together with us to turn out products of high quality for an exacting market." I went on to say that I hoped the factory would eventually become a supplier not only to the British market but also to continental Europe, which it indeed has. The prince later gave an interview to *The South Wales Echo* and told of our meeting in Tokyo. "Nobody could be more suprised than myself," the paper quoted him as saying, "when two years later the smile on the face of the inscrutable Japanese chairman turned into an actual factory in South Wales." I never thought I was inscrutable, but I wouldn't dispute it with a prince.

Afterward, Queen Elizabeth made an official visit to Japan and I had the honor of being presented to her at the reception at the British embassy. She asked me whether the story about Prince Charles's recommendation for the plant's site was true. I said it was a true story and she was very pleased. When I visited London for the official opening of the Japan Style exhibition at the Victoria and Albert Museum a few years later, I met the queen again and had a chance to report on our progress. We later were given the Queen's Award for our work. We were exporting about half of our U.K. production to the Continent and Africa, and it represented about 30 percent of total British color TV exports.

In 1981, when we expanded our plant at Bridgend to add a picture tube factory, we invited the prince again. He said his schedule was too full, but he would send Diana, the Princess of Wales. She was then pregnant with Prince William, and we were thrilled that she would come. Since the factory had glass under pressure, everyone who visits is required to wear a hard hat and protective eyeglasses. We even sent the hat and glasses to London for approval, and when the princess arrived she toured the plant wearing this hat with Sony on it in big letters, while all the photographers took pictures of her. I admit I was a little embarrassed by the commercial look of it, but nobody else seemed to be, least of all Diana. She was charming, good-natured, cooperative, friendly, and very warm. Of course, we put up another plaque to commemorate the occasion.

I am not complaining that the royal family of Britain is interested in the progress of my company, far from it. I am extremely pleased and flattered. I cite this experience to make the point that it is natural and healthy for a government to be interested in business and in helping a nation increase its employment situation. The idea that seems to linger in the United States is that somehow people in government should be the enemies of business, or at least neutral. But I like the sense of involvement of the British.

The British have been very good to me in many ways. In 1982 I went to London to receive the Albert Medal of the Royal Society of Arts "for outstanding contributions to technological and industrial innovation and management, industrial design, industrial relations and video systems, and the growth of world trade relations." I was humbled to realize that the Albert Medal had been given to such renowned scientists as Thomas Alva Edison, Madame Marie Curie, and Louis Pasteur. In a lighter vein, the members of the society even gave me a certificate for my English-speaking ability, which may set a new record for generosity. It happened this way: after the Albert Medal ceremony at the Royal Society, I gave a reception for my hosts. When I welcomed them, I said that Sony and I have always been innovators and that I have not only innovated products but even made innovations in the English language. As proof of this contention, I reminded them of the name "Walkman" and our unique corporate name. They gave me a big round of applause, and the officers wrote out an Honorary Certificate in Advanced Spoken English and presented it to me.

Our experience with France Inc. was quite different. It took several years of negotiating to cancel our contract with our agent in France so that we could establish Sony France. As it turned out, our agent was both a close friend of the minister of finance and an avid hunter who had his own airplane. He would often take the minister off on hunting trips. When we tried to cancel our agreement with the agent and establish a wholly owned subsidiary, the ministry of finance would not give us approval. We worked on it for a long time through our lawyers, and finally the government reluctantly gave us approval, but only to establish a fifty-fifty joint venture. We accepted it and chose a bank, Banque de Suez, to be our partner until we could eventually get permission to buy out the partner. But we still keep a representative of the bank on our board.

Our German subsidiary was easy to establish, compared to the French saga, but since I didn't want our company and its employees to be involved in the Japanese community, which was concentrated in Düsseldorf, we set up our company, Sony GmbH., in Cologne, within easy reach by the autobahn, but far enough away that the staff would be spending most of its time with Germans, not expatriate Japanese. I have always stressed that our people should concentrate their time and effort on the people of the host country. I made the same rule in my family when we moved to the United States. We went there to learn about America and Americans. I told Yoshiko that she must avoid the Japanese community; she already knew all about Japan. So while it would be easy to move in the home country circles, I have insisted that our company and our family must become truly internationalized.

We opened our Sony showroom in Paris finally in 1971, on the Champs Elysées, where I wanted it, and by then we had also established Sony Hawaii, Sony Panama, Sony U.K. We also negotiated and set up CBS-Sony Records and established a new research center in Japan. I was invited to become a member of the international council of the Morgan Guaranty Trust Company in 1969, which was the despository of our ADR shares in the United States.

When we decided that it was time for us to open a factory in the U.S., it was not a move to be taken lightly. Back in 1963, when I moved to the United States, a Japanese chemical company had decided to open a factory in the U.S., and I had a recorded dialogue with the president of that company that was published in an influential monthly magazine in Tokyo, *Bungei Shunju*. My contention in that interview was that it was a mistake to open a factory overseas without first having a sales and marketing system established and knowing the market very well. My view was that you must first learn the market, learn how to sell to it, and build up your corporate confidence before you commit yourself. And when you have confidence, you should commit yourself wholeheartedly. In a few years the chemical company, Sekisu, withdrew from the U.S. They couldn't sell their product satisfactorily and found the competition severe. They were premature.

I always had an eye on producing in the United States, but I felt that we should do it only when we had a really big market, knew how to sell in it, and could service what we sold. When all that was in hand, we could then benefit from having a source of supply close to home. That time came in 1971. Our sales volume was high, and we were now shipping bigger sets to the U.S. It dawned on me that you pay by volume in shipping and that the biggest part of a TV set is the picture tube, which is a glass envelope containing a vacuum. So we were paying good money to ship vacuums across the Pacific, which, if you looked at it that way, didn't make sense.

Besides, the other advantages of being onshore in a big market are pretty obvious: we could fine-tune production depending on the market trends, and we could more easily adapt our designs to market needs in a hurry. At that time, my brother-in-law Kazuo Iwama was promoting the idea. He was then president of Sony America, living in New York, and he had scouted out locations, including the one we finally chose, in Rancho Bernardo, an industrial park in San Diego. We started out with an assembly operation of components shipped from our factories in Japan, but now just about the only things we send from Japan are the electron gun and some special integrated circuits. To get maximum U.S. input into our sets, we have always bought as much as possible in the U.S., and as a result our sets are more completely American than some famous U.S. brand sets that are actually built in the Far East by American companies and their subcontractors and shipped to the United States. One of the ironies of the situation today is that almost any "American" television set is about 80 percent Japanese inside, but ours is more truly American than theirs.

ON MANAGEMENT

It's All in the Family

I

There is no secret ingredient or hidden formula responsible for the success of the best Japanese companies. No theory or plan or government policy will make a business a success; that can only be done by people. The most important mission for a Japanese manager is to develop a healthy relationship with his employees, to create a familylike feeling within the corporation, a feeling that employees and managers share the same fate. Those companies that are most successful in Japan are those that have managed to create a shared sense of fate among all employees, what Americans call labor and management, and the shareholders.

I have not found this simple management system applied anywhere else in the world, and yet we have demonstrated convincingly, I believe, that it works. For others to adopt the Japanese system may not be possible because they may be too tradition-bound, or too timid. The emphasis on people must

130

be genuine and sometimes very bold and daring, and it can even be quite risky. But in the long run—and I emphasize this—no matter how good or successful you are or how clever or crafty, your business and its future are in the hands of the people you hire. To put it a bit more dramatically, the fate of your business is actually in the hands of the youngest recruit on the staff.

That is why I make it a point personally to address all of our incoming college graduates each year. The Japanese school year ends in March, and companies recruit employees in their last semester, so that before the end of the school year they know where they are going. They take up their new jobs in April. I always gather these new recruits together at headquarters in Tokyo, where we have an introductory or orientation ceremony. This year I looked out at more than seven hundred young, eager faces and gave them a lecture, as I have been doing for almost forty years.

"First," I told them, "you should understand the difference between the school and a company. When you go to school, you pay tuition tp the school, but now this company is paying tuition to you, and while you are learning your job you are a burden and a load on the company.

"Second, in school if you do well on an exam and score one hundred percent, that is fine, but if you don't write anything at all on your examination paper, you get a zero. In the world of business, you face an examination each day, and you can gain not one hundred points but thousands of points, or only fifty points. But in business, if you make a mistake you do not get a simple zero. If you make a mistake, it is always minus something, and there is no limit to how far down you can go, so this could be a danger to the company."

The new employees are getting their first direct and sobering view of what it will be like in the business world. I tell them what I think is important for them to know about the company and about themselves. I put it this way to the last class of entering employees:

"We did not draft you. This is not the army, so that means you have voluntarily chosen Sony. This is your responsibility, and normally if you join this company we expect that you will stay for the next twenty or thirty years.

"Nobody can live twice, and the next twenty or thirty years is the brightest period of your life. You only get it once.

"When you leave the company thirty years from now or when your life is finished, I do not want you to regret that you spent all those years here. That would be a tragedy. I cannot stress the point too much that this is your responsibility to yourself. So I say to you, the most important thing in the next few months is for you to decide whether you will be happy or unhappy here. So even though we recruited you, we cannot, as management, or a third party, make other people happy; happiness must be created yourself."

The idea of an employee spending all of his working life with a single company is not a Japanese invention. It was, ironically, forced upon us. To give a simplified view of history the Japanese system of so-called lifetime employment, or at least long-term employment, was actually imposed on us by the labor laws instituted by the Occupation, when a lot of liberal, left-wing economic technicians were sent from the United States to Japan with the goal of demilitarizing the country and making it a democracy. One of the first targets was the basic structure of what was left of the industrial complex. In prewar Japan, a handful of giant holding companies virtually controlled the Japanese economy. Together, the four biggest of these groups held as much as 25 percent of the paid-up capital of the entire nation. Family-owned conglomerates such as Mitsui, Sumitomo, and Mitsubishi each had as many as three hundred companies in their control.

Because of their tremendous economic power, the *zaibatsu*, as they were known, had political power: they could support a politician of their choice with money and election manpower and whatever else was needed. But actually once the *zaibatsu* gave their support to the military-men-turned-politicians, when they took control of the government, the tail began to wag the dog; the *zaibatsu* thought they had hired a watchman, but pretty soon the watchman was giving orders to the *zaibatsu*, and they became, in a way, captives of the system they thought they were controlling.

When the war was over, the Occupation authorities declared that the country could not be democratized so long as the *zaibatsu* system of interlocking companies and enormous holdings in land continued. Almost immediately, fifteen of the *zaibatsu* were disbanded by the Holding Company Liquidation Commission. Their assets were frozen, and in the end the shareholdings of eighty-three holding companies were transferred.

Another forty-five hundred companies were declared "restricted concerns." These companies were not allowed to own stock in any of the other companies, and their employees were forbidden to work for another company in the old group.

One of the figures involved in the planning of the *zaibatsu* dissolution, economist Eleanor Hadley, said recently in a seminar on the Occupation period in Tokyo that the program "did not go forward coherently and elegantly. We were woefully ignorant of Japanese economics and society. But even the Japanese didn't have a good idea of how the *zaibatsu* operated because of the great secrecy they had always maintained."

The attempt to crush the interlocking relationship of the *zaibatsu* was effective, but it caused some unusual situations. For instance, it was impossible to open a company branch or new division of a restricted concern, and that is the reason the sales arm of Toyota Motor Company, Toyota Motor Sales Company, which was established in 1950, was operated with complete managerial independence from Toyota Motor Company, which made the cars. Actually, the two companies did not merge into one until 1984, thirty-five years later.

Wealth and power were also taken away from the richest families. Compensation was limited. New banking laws were imposed, and controls were needed because inflation was high, soaring to 150 percent in 1947. The new constitution (still the law of the land in Japan) was written by GHQ, in English, and was translated into Japanese and quickly approved by the Diet. The document gave equal rights to women and minorities, established the basis for divorce and marriage laws and the rights of individuals. The nobility was deposed and their ranking system abolished. But land reform may be the most significant single reason for change in the social structure after the war. Many families who owned a lot of land, which was used to farm and to give employment to local people, were dispossessed, as in the case of my family. Landowners were only allowed to keep their homes and their forest land, and some of the richest people in Japan today, consequently, are those who had a great deal of forest land at that time, which did not fall under the land reform program.

The American New Deal economic and social technicians also made it virtually impossible to fire anybody; they enabled—they actually encouraged—labor organizing, which was banished during the war years except for a government-sponsored nationwide company-type union. Before, loyalty to the *zaibatsu* company was the main goal of any worker's organization. The designers of the labor laws knew that there would be a problem with the Communists, who would be sure to move into the labor organizations now that the party was no longer outlawed. The American labor experts knew there was a risk, but they thought whatever troubles might be caused would be part of Japan's education in democracy. In a way the Occupation authorities' attitude showed a lot of faith in the basic conservative nature of the Japanese people. But what an education it turned out to be!

As soon as the new labor laws were passed, as many as twenty-five thousand labor unions sprang up and five million Japanese workers joined. It was a heady time for the long-suppressed liberals, socialists, and Communists, and they wasted no time getting organized. Many of the unions came under the domination of the Japan Communist Party (JCP), and on May Day 1946, they paraded in front of the palace with red banners and flags and placards. The parade turned into a full-scale riot with some of the marchers attempting to storm the palace. The nation was shocked. There was a flurry of strikes over workers' rights and many protests to the government over wages. When the Communist-controlled unions threatened to call a nationwide general strike to demand the resignation of Prime Minister Shigeru Yoshida and to get a big increase in pay, the prime minister and GHQ finally came down hard on them.

Yoshida, who was always suspicious of the Communists and their motives and who was against legalizing the JCP, wrote in his 1957 memoirs, *Random Thoughts from Oiso* (his country home was in the town of Oiso), that "immediately after the war's end, the Soviet Union as an Allied Power set up its mission in Tokyo, which was manned by more than five hundred trained propagandists and secret agents who guided and directed the activities of the Japan Communist Party, who abetted labor strikes, incited riots of Koreans, and created all manner of disturbances throughout the country."

With the support of the Supreme Commander Allied Powers, General Douglas MacArthur, Yoshida introduced a bill into the Diet banning strikes of public employees. It put the Communists on warning, and they backed down from their threatened general strike. But the new social legislation, which included social security and other welfare benefits, in addition to the new labor laws, was with us to stay.

The effect of three things—the new laws, the revision of the tax system, and the elimination of the *zaibatsu* conglomerates—was to make Japan an egalitarian society for the first time. There was an opportunity for lower-income people to improve their life-styles, and even today if you come to Japan you can see that there is virtually no poverty as it is known elsewhere in the world. You will find a kind of egalitarian society rare in the world, which the Japanese people prize.

Off and on for centuries, the people had to deal with privation and even famine. Poverty in the city and in the countryside was common. In fact, for generations of Japanese of the lower classes, life was little more than a bitter struggle for survival. Today if we have no poverty, we also do not have family wealth as it was once known. Every year the prime minister's office takes a survey of people's attitudes, and for more than ten years the number of people who consider themselves to be in the middle class has been over 90 percent.

Today's Japanese do not think in terms of privilege. Although some of our trains have first-class cars, we had no first-class section on our domestic airliners for many years. I am reminded of how Konosuke Matsushita, the grand old man of the Japanese electronics industry, even in his nineties, gets on the commercial flight from his headquarters city of Osaka to Tokyo together with hundreds of simple salarymen. Nobody thinks twice about it. Very few companies have private planes or helicopters, as Sony has, but these companies that have them do not use them to ferry executives on thinly veiled private junkets as is done in some countries; they are devoted to business travel and efficiency.

Japan's postwar success has made many people rich, of course, but today there is no such thing as the great wealth of the landed families of Britain or the Continent, wealth that seems to survive upheaval, change of government, even war. Some years ago I was visiting Paris, and at a party I admired the diamond necklace being worn by a lovely Rothschild lady. Her husband immediately and very generously offered to give me the name of his jeweler so that I could have him craft a similar fabulous thing for Yoshiko. I thanked him, but I told him I could never afford such an expensive object.

He raised his eyebrows. "But you are rich," he said. "You can afford it, I am sure."

"There is a major difference between you and me," I told him. "Yes, I am rich. But you are wealthy. And that is why you can buy such jewelry and why I cannot." Japan has no wealthy families as in the old days, families with vast holdings and untold riches. Confiscatory inheritance taxes have helped to destroy real personal wealth, just as the peerage was abolished after the war. Today the idea of wealth seems somehow badly out of place to most Japanese, and in reality, the acquisition of vast amounts of land and control of many large companies is simply not possible, and that was the basis of the family wealth that once existed in Japan.

Before the war, families like mine were very rich. We lived a completely different kind of life from what anybody lives in Japan today. All of our neighbors were the richest—the wealthiest—people in Nagoya when I was growing up. We had tennis courts, a real luxury in land-poor Japan, maids and butlers, and private cars with chauffeurs. My family had all of this, foreign cars and everything we wanted, and it was all paid for by my father, who had a substantial income. Taxes were low, and so no one ever thought of having a company-paid car or company-paid entertainment. The Japanese teahouses, where the business entertaining took place, would send the bill once every six months or once a year, and rich people like my father would write their own personal check, not a company check, to cover it.

After the war, the situation completely changed because with the new laws, if you had to pay 85 percent of your income in taxes, it was difficult to afford a car and hire a driver and pay other business expenses. That is why it became the custom, gradually, for companies to pay these expenses for their executives.

My family was lucky that despite the heavy bombing of Nagoya our business and home properties were not damaged at all, and, in fact, we were almost an exception. But after the war, we no longer had a maid or a butler, and my mother had to start to do her own housework. She said it was good for her health, and I am sure it was. We had to pay a huge wealth tax, and we lost a lot of our property in the land reform. Almost all of our land was being rented to farmers who grew rice to sell to the Morita family business. So we lost almost everything, but that was all right; we were grateful that the three sons had come out of the war uninjured and that we still had the basic business. But it was a big change. My father had to ride a bicycle to work during the war, and now there was no chance of having a chauffeured car. It is a common saying in Japan today that inherited wealth will not last three generations unless a family works and adds to it, because the inheritance taxes are so high.

GHQ wrote new laws aimed at making the worker and the employee more powerful and at seeing that the wealthy people would not rise again. Their view was that the wealthy families, especially the dozen or so main *zaibatsu* families involved with the industrial war machine and those of their kind, had to be weakened because they had collaborated with the military. Somehow they must have thought that all people of wealth were responsible for the war, which was wrong, of course. Many people could see at the time that the *zaibatsu* had become captives of the military they thought they could control. But the result of the GHQ orders was, ironically, to make Japanese industry strong again. One positive aspect of the purge was to weed out some top-level deadwood from management, although many good people were lost too, and put into control the second- and third-echelon employees who were the actual working engineers and technicians and younger managers with new ideas. This helped to revitalize the companies and made it possible for others to start new companies, such as our own, and Honda Motors, to name only a couple, now that it was obvious that the old giant companies would not be able to dominate everything. But even in the big old companies, the purge put younger and more active, more technically trained executives in charge.

The concept of lifetime employment arose when Japanese managers and employees both realized that they had much in common and that they had to make some long-range plans. The laws made it difficult legally, and expensive, to fire anybody, but that didn't seem like such a bad idea, since workers were badly in need of work, and struggling businesses needed employees who would remain loyal. Without class disputes, despite the Communist and Socialist party propaganda, the Japanese, who are a homogeneous people, were able to cooperate to provide for their common welfare. I have often said that the Japanese company has become very much a social security organization.

In the postwar era, the tax laws make it useless for a company to pay an executive a lot of money, because the graduated tax rises sharply very quickly, and you are very soon in the highest bracket. Company-paid amenities such as worker dormitories and allowances for commuting, for example, help workers make up for the tax system. Tax shelters and tax avoidance are virtually unknown in Japan. Today, the salary for a top management official is rarely more than seven or eight times that of an entry-level junior executive trainee. This means Japan has no multimillion-dollar brass, and companies give no huge executive bonuses, no stock options, no deferred income, no golden parachutes, and therefore the psychological, as well as the real, gap between employees is narrower than in other countries. There may be some exceptions to the general rule, but I am sure they are few.

The national tax agency every year releases a list of the top income earners, and it is always printed in the national newspapers for everybody to see. In 1982 the agency reported that only twenty-nine thousand Japanese citizens had earnings of over eighty-five thousand dollars. And yet a typical Japanese male manufacturing sector worker with a two-child family and the wife not working, according to the Organization of Economic Cooperation and Development, had annual gross earnings about two-thirds of that of his American counterpart in 1983. But the ratio of his disposable income is higher, for at that level he pays lower taxes than the American. The Japanese worker works longer hours to get his money, because he still is somewhat below the U.S. wage, but we in Japan do not think it is wrong to work hard for our pay. In fact a government survey in 1985 showed that most Japanese workers do not take all the vacation time to which they are entitled.

What we in industry learned in dealing with people is that people do not work just for money and that if you are trying to motivate, money is not the most effective tool. To motivate people, you must bring them into the family and treat them like respected members of it. Granted, in our one-race nation this might be easier to do than elsewhere, but it is still possible if you have an educated population.

The interest in education goes back to the Tokugawa era, when the nation was closed to the outside world for nearly three hundred years beginning just after the turn of the seventeenth century. During that period, the society was completely isolated except for a small part of Nagasaki where foreigners could trade. During that time—despite what many people saw some years ago in a popular American television series called "Shogun"—Japan may have been the only country in the world where complete peace reigned for such a long time. I was amazed to read the other day that the forty-year period since the end of World War II is the longest time in the recorded history of Europe that there has been no war there. It is very interesting in this context, then, I think, to realize that in Japan from 1603, when Ieyasu the first Shogun took over, until just before the Imperial Restoration, which ended the Tokugawa era in 1868, a period of more than two hundred and fifty years, there was no war. We call it the Great Peace. Even though samurai carried swords, many of them didn't even know how to use them.

There were very rigid class lines and everybody was locked into a class, with the samurai at the top—there even were many classes of samurai in the system—and the merchants at the bottom. There was one way to break out of your class, though, and that was to become an artist or a scholar. In those days, the arts were encouraged, such as literature, painting, pottery, the Noh theater, Kabuki, tea ceremony, and calligraphy. Scholars in Japanese and Chinese classical literature were very much in demand, and if you were a scholar, no matter where you were born, or what your class, you could move up. So if you were a farmer or merchant, your interest in education would be keen, because that was the only way to be admired by others, and the only route to moving up in your class. All parents wanted to send their children to school, and many private schools were opened.

When the enlightened reign of Emperor Meiji began in 1868, the population of the nation was about thirty million and the number of schools already functioning was about ten thousand. The enrollment at each school was small, of course, in total numbers, so we cannot compare it to today. Now, a junior high school education is compulsory, and 94 percent go on to high school, while 37 percent of the high school graduates go on to college. Today we have a population of one hundred and twenty-one million, but the number of primary and secondary schools is forty-five thousand, which is about the same density of schools as during Tokugawa and Meiji times. Even uneducated parents in the Tokugawa era knew the value of education to their children. If school was available and the child was clever, they would send him to study.

So with this broad interest in education, when Meiji opened the ports and the government decided to introduce Western culture, the interest among the general public to learn about the world was very strong. When the compulsory education system started, literacy developed very fast. The high level of education explains why a worker or even the head of the local union will sometimes rise to become president of a corporation in Japan. For example, Kenichi Yamamoto, the president of Mazda Motor Corporation, joined the company as a graduate engineer and rose from his early job as a shop floor foreman to became the head of the company, then called Toyo Kogyo Company. In 1985, when his company decided to establish a plant to manufacture cars in the United States, he sat down personally with officials of the United Auto Workers Union to talk about a labor agreement. He could do it because he knew all sides of his business; he had even been president of the Mazda employee union many years ago, and he could talk the UAW language.

In our labor relations, we have a kind of equality that does not exist elsewhere. We see very little distinction at Sony between blue- and white-collar workers. And if a man or woman becomes successful as a union leader, we are very interested, because these are the kind of people we are looking for in our management ranks, people who can be persuasive, can make people want to cooperate with them. Management is not dictatorship. Top management of a company has to have the ability to manage people by leading them. We are constantly looking for capable persons with these qualities, and to rule people out because they lack certain school credentials or because of the job they happen to find themselves in is simply shortsighted. There is very little of the adversarial spirit in our companies, and making a living out of opposition to something is not possible.

I do not want to give the impression that relations between company and management in Japan are always sweet, because that is not always the case. Toyota Motor Company suffered a serious strike in 1950 that led to the resignation of top management, and there have been major, if short-lived, strikes in one sector or another since the end of the war. There are strikes almost every day in Japan, very brief ones, to be sure, but the demonstrations make their point with management. However, the days lost in labor disputes have been decreasing since reaching a new high in 1974 after the oil embargo. In that year, Japan lost 9,663,000 man-days of labor to labor-management disputes; the United States lost 47,991,000 and the United Kingdom lost 14,750,000 in the same period. We have improved, and the gap is much wider. In 1984 Japanese industry lost only 354,000 man-days to labor disputes, and the U.S. lost 8,348,000, while in the U.K. the number soared to 26,564,000. Of course, the United States is a much bigger and more diversified place, but the comparison of working days lost between the free world's first and second largest economies is interesting, and Britain's figures seem staggering.

My only experience with a real strike goes back to 1961, on the fifteenth anniversary of our company, and I was put to the test to figure out how to handle it. Our original union was strongly influenced by leftists, and the left picked Sony as a target that year, challenging us, demanding a closed shop. I picked up the union's challenge, saying that I thought the closed shop was unfair. I told them, "A closed shop is a violation of individual rights. If people want to form another union, they have the right to do it. That is freedom and that is democracy." It was quite a challenge, but I sensed the union leaders were getting strong and wanted to dramatize the issue. So did I.

The union leaders knew that we were going to have our anniversary celebration on May 7, and they threatened to strike us that day. They thought that this threat alone would make us give in because they knew how much the anniversary meant to us. I saw it in another light. I knew our employees, most of them personally. I knew we had many who had good common sense, who would approve an open shop, and who would get out of this politically influenced union and join a union that had a more responsible attitude. I had confidence in our good relations with our employees, and I did not want these people who had a feeling of unity with the company to be guided by a few extremists.

I acted very tough. Their leader thought I was bluffing, that I would become agreeable at the last minute because I wanted to have a successful celebration. We had planned to hold the ceremony at our headquarters building, and we had invited quite a few dignitaries, including Prime Minister Hayato Ikeda. We had many bargaining sessions with the union as the anniversary drew closer, and each day they seemed to get cockier, as though they didn't want a settlement. They were thinking we would have to give in, that the company would lose face if it tried to have an anniversary celebration and a party while the streets were full of picketers. I didn't give them a clue as to what I had in mind, but I held my bargaining ground up to the last minute. We came down to the night before the anniversary and nothing was settled. The union leaders stormed out.

The morning of our anniversary the strikers surrounded our building in Shinagawa. The streets were blocked with strikers from our union and others who had been brought in to swell the crowd. Some carried placards denouncing Ikeda as well as Sony. At the same time, some of our engineers had decided to form their own union, and so many of them showed up with their own banners, supporting us, and hundreds of loyal Sony employees were also out in the street, behind the strikers and the engineers. I had appeared in the window in my morning coat, prepared for the anniversary. We had banners strung up announcing the celebration. But Ikeda and the other guests did not come to the Sony building for the celebration, and the strikers thought they had managed to force us to cancel it for a while, but they soon realized they were wrong.

Late the previous night, many of us executives who were staying in the headquarters building day and night during the bargaining called every one of the three hundred invited guests and changed the site of the celebration to the Prince Hotel about a mile away. The prime minister arrived at our celebration unmolested and the party was a great success. Ibuka did the speaking for Sony. When the strikers realized they had been outwitted, the humiliation was theirs. I had slipped out the back way and managed to get to the party at the hotel before it was over. They gave me a round of applause when I walked into the room, and the prime minister said Sony's attitude in confronting extremists should be appreciated by others. The union gave up the strike, and a second union was also formed. Today in the Sony parent company we have two unions, including the original one that is sometimes very difficult to deal with, and we of course also have many nonunion people. In fact, the majority of our employees are not unionized, but our relations with all of our employees are very good.

The reason we can maintain good relations with our employees is that they know how we feel about them. In the Japanese case, the business does not start out with the entrepreneur organizing his company using the worker as a tool. He starts a company and he hires personnel to realize his idea, but once he hires employees he must regard them as colleagues or helpers, not as tools for making profits. Management must consider a good return for the investor, but he also has to consider his employees, or his colleagues, who must help him to keep the company alive and he must reward their work. The investor and the employee are in the same position, but sometimes the employee is more important, because he will be there a long time whereas an investor will often get in and out on a whim in order to make a profit. The worker's mission is to contribute to the company's welfare, and his own, every day all of his working life. He is really needed.

Companies have different approaches to this even in Japan, but basically, there has to be mutual respect and a sense that the company is the property of the employees and not of a few top people. But those people at the top of the company have a responsibility to lead that family faithfully and be concerned about the members.

We have a policy that wherever we are in the world we deal with our employees as members of the Sony family, as valued colleagues, and that is why even before we opened our U.K. factory, we brought management people, including engineers, to Tokyo and let them work with us and trained them and treated them just like members of our family, all of whom wear the same jackets and eat in our one-class cafeteria. This way they got to understand that people should not be treated differently; we didn't give a private office to any executive, even to the head of the factory. We urged the management staff to sit down with their office people and share the facilities. On the shop floor every foreman has a short meeting with his colleagues every morning before work and tells them what they have to do today. He gives them a report on yesterday's work, and while he is doing this he looks carefully at the faces of his team members. If someone doesn't look good, the foreman makes it a point to find out if the person is ill, or has some kind of a problem or worry. I think this is important, because if an employee is ill, unhappy, or worried, he cannot function properly.

Sometimes a person's job or work situation does not suit that person. In Japan changing jobs is becoming more common, but job changing is still rare compared to the U.S. Since we do not have in our system the mobility that the American worker has, where it is easy to quit one job and get another, I figured that we had to do something in our company to handle such a situation. We want to keep the company healthy and its employees happy, and we want to keep them on the job and productive.

All of our engineers are first assigned to work on the production line for a long enough period for them to understand how production technology fits in with what they are doing. Some of the foreign engineers do not like to do this, but the Japanese engineers seem to welcome the opportunity to get firsthand experience. In the United States a foreman can remain a foreman all his life, and that is all right if it pleases him and the company. But I think it is better to move people than to leave them on one job too long where their minds might get dulled.

In order to foster our working relationship as colleagues and to keep in touch, I used to have dinner with many young lower management employees almost every night and talk until late. One night I could tell one of these young men had something bothering him. He was not enjoying himself, and I encouraged him to say what was on his mind. After a few drinks he loosened up. "Before I joined this company," he said earnestly, "I thought it was a fantastic company. It is the only place I wanted to work. But I work for this section chief, Mr. So-and-So, and in my lowly capacity I work for this man, not Sony. He represents the company. But he is stupid, and everything I do or suggest must go through this guy. I am very disappointed that this stupid section chief is Sony as far as my career is concerned."

This was a sobering thought for me. I realized there might be many employees in our company with problems like this and we should be aware of their dilemmas. And so I started a weekly company newspaper where we could advertise job openings. This made it possible for employees to try for other jobs confidentially. We try to move our employees into related or new work about every two years, but energetic employees on the move must be allowed to have this opportunity for earlier internal mobility, for finding their own work level.

We get a double benefit from this: the person can usually find a more satisfying job, and at the same time the personnel department can identify potential problems with managers whose subordinates are trying to get away from them. We have had cases where we discovered a manager was inadequate because so many people working under him asked to be transferred. Our solution is to transfer the person to a position where he or she doesn't have as many subordinates, and that has usually solved the problem. We learn a lot by listening to our employees, because, after all, wisdom is not the exclusive possession of management.

Another important aspect of the internal mobility system is this: occasionally the man we recruited as a guard or some other low-level job answers an ad for a job as an advertising copywriter or a similar type of job, and after examination we find that he is qualified and turns out to be very good in the new job. We often run an ad for a typist or a driver or a guard and people apply without thinking about their true ability, because they just need a job. In the beginning, the personnel department assigns new employees to a job, but personnel departments or managers are not all-knowing, and management is not always capable of putting the right man in the right place every time. Rather, the employee should want to find the right job, so that is why I said to a young worker who was complaining about his foreman, "If you are not satisfied with your job, you should have the right to find a more agreeable one. Why don't you?" If the person selects what he wants to do, he will be encouraged because he got the job he wanted and he will likely apply himself to the new job very diligently. At least that is our experience. We have many jobs and many employees, and there is no reason why we cannot match the jobs with the help of the people who are actually going to do the work.

This is not typical of Japanese companies, unfortunately, but I long ago decided that I wanted a different system, a system where the door to change and improvement was always open. Anything that tended to shut that door, in my opinion, was wrong, and that is why I established the rule that once we hire an employee, his school records are a matter of the past and are no longer used to evaluate his work or decide on his promotion. The book I wrote on the subject struck a responsive chord; two hundred and fifty thousand copies were sold in Japan, an indication of the public's attitude to the system that exists in most other companies even today. For a little while after the book came out, we had difficulty hiring graduates from the "name" universities, because they thought we were prejudiced against them. We were able to explain, however, that that is not the case, but that we were seeking ability, not just people with school pride. Now we get recruits from all the top schools, including the "name" ones.

When our company had just begun, we were novices at management, so we had no choice but to do things in our own unorthodox way. In the beginning, we were small enough so that we could discuss each problem with the entire company and try different approaches until we were satisfied or we solved the problem. I believe one of the reasons we went through such a remarkable growth period was that we had this atmosphere of free discussion. We have never tried to stifle it.

Ibuka is a person with great leadership qualities—he attracts people to him and they invariably want to work with him. In fact, the history of our company is the story of a group of people trying to help Ibuka make his dreams come true. He never believed in one-man management. It was not only Ibuka's genius and originality in technological fields or his ability to look into the future and accurately forecast for us that struck everyone so forcefully, but also his ability to take this group of young and cocky engineers and mold them into a management team that could cooperate in an atmosphere where everybody was encouraged to speak out.

When most Japanese companies talk about cooperation or consensus, it usually means the elimination of individuality. At our company we are challenged to bring our ideas out into the open. If they clash with others, so much the better, because out of it may come something good at a higher level. Many Japanese companies like to use the words *cooperation* and *consensus* because they dislike individualistic employees. When I am asked, and sometimes when I am not, I say that a manager who talks too much about cooperation is one who is saying he doesn't have the ability to utilize excellent individuals and their ideas and put their ideas in harmony. If my company is successful, it is largely because our managers *do* have that ability.

I have had to argue the point loud and long even within

my company. Some years ago, when I was deputy president and Michiji Tajima was chairman of the board, we had a clash that illustrates my point. Tajima was a very fine man, a distinguished gentleman of the old school who had been director general of the Imperial Household Agency, which handles the affairs and details of the royal family. I had some views that angered him and I persisted in trying to push through my viewpoint, although I could see Tajima was opposed—I can't even remember what it was about after so many years. But as I went on, it was obvious that he was getting increasingly irritated and finally he could stand it no longer and said, "Morita, you and I have different ideas. I don't want to stay in a company like yours where you don't have the same ideas that I have and we are sometimes in conflict."

I was very bold in my response because I felt as strongly then as I do now about this issue. I said, "Sir, if you and I had exactly the same ideas on all subjects, it would not be necessary for both of us to be in this company and receive a salary. Either you or I should resign in that case. It is precisely because you and I have different ideas that this company will run a smaller risk of making mistakes.

"Please think of my views without getting angry with me. If you are going to resign because I have a different idea, you are not showing loyalty to our company."

This was new thinking in a Japanese company, and Tajima was taken aback at first, but of course he stayed on. Actually, my argument was not really new in the company. In the very beginning, we had, as I said before, no company song (nobody could imagine the thoughtful, introspective Ibuka singing), but we did have a statement called the "Sony Spirit," a statement in which we believed. We first said Sony is a pioneer and that it never intends to follow others. "Through progress, Sony wants to serve the whole world," we said and went on to say that in doing so the company would be "always a seeker of the unknown."

We also said this: "The road of a pioneer is full of difficulties, but in spite of the many hardships, people of Sony always unite harmoniously and closely because of their joy of participating in creative work and their pride in contributing their own unique talents to this aim. Sony has a principle of respecting and encouraging one's ability—the right man in the right post—and always tries to bring out the best in a person and believes in him and constantly allows him to develop his ability. This is the vital force of Sony."

Our idea was that people were at the heart of what we were trying to do. As we looked around at Japanese corporations we saw that very few companies were doing what we were, because the personnel departments acted like gods, assigning people and moving them around and molding people to jobs.

I have always made it a point to know our employees, to visit every facility of our company, and to try to meet and know every single employee. This became more and more difficult as we grew, and it is impossible to really know the more than forty thousand people who work for us today, but I try. I encourage all of our managers to know everybody and not to sit behind a desk in the office all day. I enjoy showing up at a factory or a branch office and chatting with people when I can. Not long ago I found myself in downtown Tokyo with a few extra minutes in my schedule, and I noticed a small office of Sony Travel Service. I had never been there, and so I just walked in and introduced myself. "I came here to show my face," I said. "I am sure you know me by seeing me on TV or in the newspaper, so I thought you might be interested in seeing Morita in the flesh." Everybody laughed, and I went around the office chatting with the staff, and in those few minutes we all felt good about our sense of shared effort. On a visit to a small Sony lab near Palo Alto one day, our manager, an American, asked me if I would pose for some pictures and I said I would be happy to. Before the hour was over, I had posed with all thirty or forty employees and I said to the manager, "I appreciate your attitude. You understand the Sony family policy."

On the twenty-fifth anniversary of Sony America, Yoshiko and I flew to the U.S. where we had a picnic or a meal with all the employees. We arranged it so that we could have a picnic with our New York staff and could sit down to a meal with the three shifts at our Dothan, Alabama, tape plant and also at our San Diego factory. We dined and danced with employees in Chicago and Los Angeles. It was a very satisfying thing for me, and I think they were pleased to see me and my wife. It was not just part of my job; I like those people. They are family.

II

A company will get nowhere if all of the thinking is left to management. Everybody in the company must contribute, and for the lower-level employees their contribution must be more than just manual labor. We insist that all of our employees contribute their minds. Today we get an average of eight suggestions a year from each of our employees, and most of the suggestions have to do with making their own jobs easier or their work more reliable or a process more efficient. Some people in the West scoff at the suggestion process, saying that it forces people to repeat the obvious, or that it indicates a lack of leadership by management. This attitude shows a lack of understanding. We don't force suggestions, and we take them seriously and implement the best ones. And since the majority of them are directly concerned with a person's work, we find them relevant and useful. After all, who could tell us better how to structure the work than the people who are doing it?

I am reminded of my argument with Chairman Tajima on differences of opinion and conflicting ideas. There is no possibility of the world progressing if we do exactly the same things as our superiors have done. I always tell employees that they should not worry too much about what their superiors tell them. I say, "Go ahead without waiting for instructions." To the managers I say this is an important element in bringing out the ability and creativity of those below them. Young people have flexible and creative minds, so a manager should not try to cram preconceived ideas into them, because it may smother their originality before it gets a chance to bloom.

In Japan, workers who spend a lot of time together develop an atmosphere of self-motivation, and it is the young employees who give the real impetus to this. Management officers, knowing that the company's ordinary business is being done by energetic and enthusiastic younger employees, can devote their time and effort to planning the future of the company. With this in mind, we think it is unwise and unnecessary to define individual responsibility too clearly, because everyone is taught to act like a family member ready to do what is necessary. If something goes wrong it is considered bad taste for management to inquire who made the mistake. That may seem dangerous, if not silly, but it makes sense to us. The important

(OPPOSITE TOP) *Reunited after the war in September 1945, the family is at home in Kosugaya, the three brothers in uniform for the last time. First row, left to right: Yuki (Kyuzaemon's sister), Kyuzaemon, and Shuko. Back row, left to right: Kazuaki, Akio, Kikuko, and Masaaki.*

(OPPOSITE) *In 1947, Tokyo Tsushin Kogyo moved from a bombed department store to a barrack in Gotenyama, the same site Sony headquarters now occupies. From left to right: Akira Higuchi, Kazuo Iwama, Masaru Ibuka, Akio Morita.*

(ABOVE) *A Sony family photograph, 1951, with the company's 483 employees. Ibuka and Morita stand front row center, and Iwama is directly behind Morita.*

The first factory and headquarters built by Sony.
The "T" stands for Tokyo Tsushin Kogyo.

(LEFT) An electric rice cooker—
a product that never worked properly.

(ABOVE) The first magnetic recording
tape and tape recorder marketed
in Japan, 1950.

On September 17, 1970, Sony became the first Japanese firm to be listed on the New York Stock Exchange. From left to right: Robert Haack, president of NYSE, Akio Morita, and Albert Fried, NYSE specialist for Sony.

(ABOVE LEFT) Sony's first transistor radio, 1955.

(ABOVE) The world's first videocassette system.

The Morita family at home on New Year's Day, 1974.
Left to right: Naoko, Hideo, Yoshiko, Akio, and Masao.

Longtime friend Leonard Bernstein relaxes at
the Morita residence in Tokyo.

Masao Morita graduates from Georgetown University in June 1979.

With Deng Xiaoping in China, September 1979.

The Princess of Wales at the opening of the expanded Sony Bridgend plant in Wales.

Meeting with President Reagan at the White House during the Keidanren mission to the United States in June 1984.

edge and experience. And if he is new to your company, I said, well, a child's mistake does not have to be dealt with by disowning him. It is more important to try to get to the cause so that you can avoid the problem in the future. And if it is made clear that the cause is being pursued not to cause damage to an individual's future but to help all employees learn, the result will be a valuable lesson rather than a loss. In all my years in business I can recall very few people I have wanted to fire for making mistakes.

Right after we formed our American company, we needed a lot of people in a hurry to establish our sales organization because business got very good very fast. Some of our new employees were good and some, we realized later, we shouldn't have hired. We had trouble with one man and I was exasperated and constantly worried about him. Finally, I discussed his case with my American colleagues. "What can we do with this guy?" I asked one day. They all looked at me as though I was slow-witted. "Why, fire him, of course," they said. I was stunned by the idea. I had never fired anybody, and even in this case it had never crossed my mind. But to solve a problem by firing the man was the American system. It seemed so clear and straightforward and logical. I began to think America is a manager's paradise; you can do anything you want to do. Then a few months later I saw the other side of the coin.

We had a district sales manager who looked very promising, so promising, in fact, that I sent him to Tokyo on an extended trip to meet everybody at the home office and get acquainted with the philosophy and spirit of our organization. He did beautifully, impressing everybody in Tokyo. He came back to the States and went to work and continued to please us until one day, without any warning, he came into my office and said, "Mr. Morita, thanks for everything but I'm quitting." I couldn't believe my ears. But it was no joke. A competitor had offered to double or triple his salary, and he thought he couldn't refuse it. This is the American way, I realized. I was very embarrassed and embittered by this episode, and, frankly, I didn't really know how to handle it. Months later, I went to an electronics show and there at the booth of one of our competitors was this traitor. I thought we should avoid each other, but instead of hiding from me, he rushed over to me full of greetings and conversation, as though there was nothing to be ashamed about. He introduced me around enthusiastically and demonstrated his new product, just as if there had been no breach of faith between us. Then I realized that for him, and in the American system, there had been nothing wrong with his departure with all of our marketing information and our corporate secrets. Apparently, this sort of thing happened every day, and that is a far cry from managerial paradise. I vowed that my company would do its best to avoid adopting this aspect of American managerial technique.

I also discovered soon that in Western countries, management lays off workers when a recession sets in. That was also a shock because in Japan we just do not do that unless we have been brought to the direst point. In the wake of the oil embargo, Japan suffered heavily because of our total dependence on foreign sources for oil. We experienced a one-year inflation rate of over 25 percent in 1973–74, and some companies simply couldn't keep their shops running, so they had to send people home. But it was impossible for those people to sit around at home when their company was in trouble, so there were cases where employees started drifting back to the company, cleaning up, mowing lawns, offering to do any odd jobs. One electrical appliance company sent employees to local electrical shops to help the retailers, who were also suffering, by becoming unpaid salesmen. This was not something that came from the management side. It came from the workers themselves, who see their jobs in the context of a shared fate with the company. I have heard of a case where a laid-off worker in Osaka who came back to his plant confided to a reporter that he was shamed by his wife, who said, "How can you sit here at home all day doing nothing while your company is in such trouble?"

It was not always like this, of course. In Meiji times, when the *zaibatsu* were the economic rulers of the country, any attempt at labor-organizing was branded radical, or worse, Communist, which was outlawed. There was no real democracy before the war. Coal miners, mill workers, and factory laborers were exploited. Lifetime employment was a one-way street in those days. That is, workers were required to stay loyal with a spirit of "serve but one master." But the employer could fire anybody at any time. People could be fired on the spot. The apprentice system was also notorious, something very few of our youngsters realize today. When an apprentice took service with an employer, he was forced to work a few years without any payment at all. This was called "courtesy service." They worked ten or twelve hours a day, and the average apprentice was given only one or two days off a month. Right after the war, when the new, liberal labor laws were enacted, many businessmen feared the laws would lead to the collapse of Japanese industry. So, even though this system of being unable to fire anybody might have seemed dangerous, the Japanese businessmen went through a rough period of trying to turn the situation to their advantage. They did it by promoting the familial concept, and in making the best of what they thought was a bad thing, they created something new and durable. Management transformed itself at the same time. Now that the *zaibatsu* were gone and family fortunes were virtually wiped out, everybody became a worker.

We were fortunate, despite everything, to have the new labor concepts forced on us after the war, concepts that the Western countries had learned not all that many years earlier after decades of labor exploitation and strife.

Not all businessmen were exploiters during the bad old days, but there is a difference between old-fashioned paternalism and the shared-fate and egalitarian system that exists today. I cannot understand why there is anything good in laying off people. If management takes the risk and responsibility of hiring personnel, then it is management's ongoing responsibility to keep them employed. The employee does not have the prime responsibility in this decision, so when a recession comes, why should the employee have to suffer for the management decision to hire him? Therefore, in times of boom we are very careful about increasing our personnel. Once we have hired people, we try to make them understand our concept of a fate-sharing body and how if a recession comes the company is willing to sacrifice profit to keep them in the company. Their wage increases or bonuses might also have to be sacrificed, because we all must share this difficulty. They know that management does not lavish bonuses on itself—only workers get bonuses under our system—and, as I have mentioned before, there are no "golden parachutes" for managers except a simple lifetime parachute of guaranteed employment and a life of constructive work. And when a company is in trouble, it is the top managers who take salary cuts before the lower-level employees.

I do not like to have my managers think they are a special breed of people elected by God to lead stupid people to do miraculous things. The world of business has some peculiarities. For instance, in the world of the arts, nobody will recognize a person as an artist unless he is outstanding, excellent, a virtuoso. Nobody would pay to hear Horowitz and Kempff and Serkin play the piano unless those men were outstanding performers. It is no exaggeration to say that a circus tightrope walker or an aerialist is the same. They all have excellence of technique, which they perfected only after long and hard training. And most important, they know that any little mistake they make will be obvious to the audience immediately. It could destroy their whole career, and for the circus performer it could be fatal.

But the remarkable thing about management is that a manager can go on for years making mistakes that nobody is aware of, which means that management can be a kind of con-job. This is because management, despite the work of the Harvard Business School and others, and the increasing number of holders of advanced degrees in business administration, is an elusive thing that cannot always be judged by next quarter's bottom line. Managers can look good on the bottom line but at the same time may be destroying the company by failing to invest in the future. To my mind, the performance of a manager is measured by how well that manager can organize a large number of people and how effectively he or she can get the highest performance from each of the individuals and blend them into a coordinated performance. That is what management is. It does not start at the bottom line of the balance sheet, which can be black one day and red the next, no matter what you do. I told my managers recently, "What you are showing to your employees is not that you are an artist who performs by himself on the high wire, but you are showing them how you are attempting to attract a large number of people to follow you willingly and with enthusiasm to contribute to the success of the company." If you can do that, the bottom line will take care of itself.

There are many styles of management, and some work fine in their own context but not in others. For example, Sony America was under the direction of Harvey Schein from 1972 to 1978, and our U.S. business really flourished with him at the controls. His approach was not Japanese, but based on pure, hard, straight, and clear logic. I guess that is what I found attractive about him during my negotiations with him for the CBS-Sony joint venture. The problem with the logic game, however, is that it leaves little room for the human factor.

Our old-style familial company was unusual or rare in the United States, although Tom Watson, Sr., built IBM into an industrial giant by using some of the same people-oriented policies we use. There were a few others among the smaller concerns in the U.S. But Schein did not believe that this kind of management would help the expansion of Sony America. We talked a lot about this, and he got my authority to streamline the company. I thought it was an interesting and reasonable experiment. He Americanized the company totally and did a very fine job of it. He recruited a new group of top executives and fired some of the previous group, and he installed a budgeting system that kept tight financial control of everything. He even flew economy class himself when he traveled on domestic flights. He considered cost in everything, and as far as making a profit was concerned, there was no match for him.

In 1975, when we were ready to introduce Betamax, which was to become our future "cash cow," I envisioned a huge domestic advertising and promotion campaign that would be carried out regardless of budgetary considerations. My feeling was that this first home-use video cassette recorder needed to be introduced to the people with a massive campaign, because it was the first of its kind and people had to be shown how they could use the product in their daily lives and how it could become an asset and something more than a toy. But my Sony America (Sonam) president was reluctant to spend the money. He said if we spent a lot on this promotion and if he could not bring in enough sales, we would lose money. I told him over and over, "You must also consider the return that comes in five or ten years, Harvey, not just the immediate return." He had his own plans for introduction and was satisfied with them. I wasn't.

As the introduction date drew near, I began to worry about what the campaign would look like and what its impact would be. The more I knew of it, the more worried I got. I didn't think it was impressive enough to match the innovative nature of this brand-new product. That summer I was with my family at our cottage in Karuizawa, and I couldn't get my mind off the problem of the Betamax introduction. I wanted it to be a stunning introduction that would grab the imagination of Americans and show them how this machine could change their lives, as I knew it would. That night I went to bed troubled. I couldn't sleep, tossing and turning until I could stand it no longer.

In the middle of the night, I grabbed the phone and called Harvey. He was in a meeting in New York. I got him out and yelled at him, "If you're not going to spend a million or two million dollars on the Betamax campaign in the next two months, I will fire you." I had never said anything like it, and he had never heard me sounding like that. It made an impression, and I felt better.

He spent the money, and Betamax was well and properly introduced. But I discovered later that what they did at Sonam was shift the money from other parts of the business, so our total advertising expenditure remained the same. It meant a cut in the promotion budget for audio equipment and TV, which were then very active. Their sales might have been even more active if the ad and promotion budgets hadn't been cut back by the Betamax promotion. But I'll never know.

The trouble with American management of the Sonam operation in the early days under Schein was that profit was the main goal. In my view, profit doesn't have to be so high, because in Japanese companies our shareholders do not clamor for immediate returns; rather they prefer long-term growth and appreciation. Our bank loans are solid at favorable rates of interest. Of course we have to make a profit, but we have to make a profit over the long haul, not just the short term, and that means we must keep investing in research and development—it has run consistently about 6 percent of sales at Sony—and in service.

Too often the idea was sounded that service was a nuisance, and when that philosophy took hold, service quality dropped dramatically. Stocking of parts means an increase in inventory, hence more interest loss, so using good Harvard Business School logic, the thing to do, I was told, was to decrease the service components stock. When we planned to open an extensive service center in Kansas City to establish a complete servicing network, I had a very difficult time convincing Sonam management that this was a necessary and good idea. My argument again and again with Harvey Schein and others was that by saving money instead of investing it in the business you might gain profit on a short-term basis, but in actual fact you would be cashing in the assets that had been built up in the past. To gain profit is important, but you must invest to build up assets that you can cash in in the future.

In the electronics industry today, everything is changing rapidly; in fact the only thing we can be certain of is that the business will never stand still. The competition between companies in Japan is fierce. We have gone from tape recorders to video tape recorders to compact discs, from vacuum tubes to transistors, semiconductors, integrated circuits, very large-scale integrated circuits, and we have biochips to look forward to in the future. This onward rush of technology will one day enable people to have facilities at their command in their homes that are not even hinted at yet. It will be an exciting future.

It may sound curious, but I learned that an enemy of this innovation could be your own sales organization, if it has too much power, because very often these organizations discourage innovation. When you make innovative new products, you must re-educate the sales force about them so the salesmen can educate and sell the public. This is expensive; it means investing sufficient money in R&D and new facilities and advertising and promotion. And it also means making some popular and profitable items obsolete, often the items you can make the most profit on because your development costs are paid for and these products have become easy for your salesmen to sell.

But if you are nothing but profit-conscious, you cannot see the opportunities ahead. And where compensation is tied to profits, as it is in most American companies, very often a manager will say, "Why should I sacrifice my own profits today for the guy who is going to follow me in this job a few years from now?" Too often in the U.S. and Europe, managers will abandon work on a promising product because development costs seem too high. That can be very shortsighted and can lead to the inability of a company to compete.

Sometimes salesmen can get out in front of the public without actually leading them. When we first marketed our portable black and white video tape recorder, the U-Matic, we got an order almost immediately for five thousand units from an American distributor. I told him the order seemed too large for the market at the time. Not many people were psychologically prepared to buy such a device. I said that with an innovation like the U-Matic, a lot of educating has to be done: one must prepare the groundwork among the customers before you can expect success in the marketplace. It is a time-honored Japanese gardening technique to prepare a tree for transplanting by slowly and carefully binding the roots over a period of time, bit by bit, to prepare the tree for the shock of the change it is about to experience. This process, called *nemawashi*, takes time and patience, but it rewards you, if it is done properly, with a healthy transplanted tree. Advertising and promotion for a brand-new, innovative product is just as important. In the case of the early U-Matic, little had been done to prepare the American public for this new device, and it was no surprise to me that the distributor and the retailers could not sell them. Then, in reaction to the disappointment of the failure, the distributor did the worst possible thing from our point of view: he discounted them heavily to get rid of them, cheapening our image.

I have sometimes been accused of moving too fast, of being impatient (my New York office staff once gave me a red fireman's helmet as a present because they said I was always in such a hurry). But I am also a person who can apply a kind of sixth sense to people and products that might defy logic. Something told me that the market was not yet ripe for a large sale of video portables, and I was right. Advertising and promotion alone will not sustain a bad product or a product that is not right for the times. Home video was the right product and proved to be a durable success, but its time was a bit later.

What I can sometimes sense in a product, I have also been able to sense in personnel, I believe. I think I have hired many more creative employees than mediocre ones. They haven't always agreed with me, which is fine, of course. One of the best examples of this is Norio Ohga, the young music student who asked so many audacious questions of our salesmen in 1947 that they finally brought him around to the company to talk to the engineers.

Ohga advised us on the musical side of things for many

years before he joined Sony. He made one of our first tape recordings of the full orchestra of the Tokyo University of Arts, with himself as baritone soloist in Brahms's German Requiem. I tried very hard to get him onto the Sony staff, but he was extremely reluctant. When he first came to visit Sony, while he was still a student, he started arguing with me, not knowing exactly who I was or what my position was. The staff was amused by his brashness, and when I left the room he asked them about me. They said, "That's Morita, Mr. Tokyo Tsushin Kogyo." He says he was embarrassed, but I doubt it. It certainly didn't change his style. He went off to Germany to study, and we asked him to write us about developments in electronics there. I sent him one of our first transistor radios to show off, and we kept in touch while he studied and sang his favorite roles, Wolfram in *Tännhauser*, the title role in *Don Giovanni*, and Count Almaviva in *The Marriage of Figaro*. He finally returned to Japan, got married, and gave concerts with his wife, the pianist Midori Matsubara. In 1959 I asked him to come with me to Europe on a trip to find new agents for transistor radios. We had a fine trip and I didn't broach the main subject I had in mind until we were aboard the SS *United States*, where I had him trapped for the four days and ten hours of the Southampton–to–New York crossing.

On that trip, we walked a lot, ate a lot, exercised a lot, and talked a lot, of course. Ohga, a strapping, barrel-chested fellow, with a resonant voice, criticized Sony in beautiful tones, and I was most interested in what he had to say. He didn't pull any punches. "Your company is full of engineers," he said, and from his tone of voice I could tell he didn't mean it as a compliment. "Since these engineers started the company," he continued, "from their point of view they think it is right that they should continue to run it. But from an outsider's point of view, the company is old-fashioned and poorly run." It was a fresh point of view, and startling, because we still thought of ourselves as quite daring and original managers. We couldn't see what he saw from outside, that perhaps we had been resting on our oars, that we were getting out of date after over a decade in control. He elaborated at some length, and finally I said, "All right, you join us and you will be one of the management team." He had fallen into my trap, I thought. But he still held out, saying that he wanted the freedom to be an artist, not a salaryman tied to a desk. I said he could still give concerts and also work for us full-time, that we would work it out between us.

After we got back to Japan, my wife and I went to his wife, Midori, and appealed to her to help us get him on board. Midori was a high school classmate of Yoshiko. I do not know who was eventually most persuasive, but Ohga finally joined the company as general manager of professional products and in a year and a half was in charge of all consumer tape recorder operations. In 1964, after only five years in the company, and when he was only thirty-four, he became a member of the board, something unheard of in traditional Japanese companies, but Sony still thought it was anything but traditional, despite Ohga's criticism. In his first year he did many nontraditional things, including hiring almost forty people away from other companies.

When Sony was new and small, we could steal people from other companies and get away with it, but now that we are so large it is not considered the right thing to do, although we still keep on scouting for talent. Besides, it tends to undermine the loyalty of your own company's staff by slighting the people who are trying to earn promotions. When I was starting Sony, I found many people from among my classmates at school, which is one of the traditional sources. I even called on people with whom I had gone to elementary school because I knew them and their families. But I long ago ran out of these personal friends and acquaintances and had to recruit in other ways. Ohga, in his early days with us, would go through the booklets of new graduates put out by each school and mark the promising ones for us to recruit.

III

Once you have a staff of prepared, intelligent, and energetic people, the next step is to motivate them to be creative. For a long time, the Japanese have been branded as imitators rather than creators. But I think it would be downright foolish to say that what Japanese industry has accomplished in the past forty years has been anything but creative. The work being done in biotechnology, new materials such as ceramics and fibers, opto-electronics, and other fields all speak for themselves. And certainly our contributions in production technology and quality control have been creative.

We all learn by imitating, as children, as students, as novices in the world of business. And then we grow up and learn to blend our innate abilities with the rules or principles we have learned. Dr. Makoto Kikuchi, our research center director, likes to point out that imitation is the first step in a child's learning process and that the original meaning of the Japanese word *manabu* (to learn) is *manebu* (to imitate).

When Japan joined the world after more than two centuries in isolation, the Japanese were ignorant of so much that had been learned and developed abroad during those centuries. Led by the government and the enlightened leadership of the Emperor Meiji, Japan reached out all around the world for these "new" ideas and technologies. In a way this was done in self-defense, because when the Western countries demanded that Japan open its doors, they also imposed unequal treaties on Japan, pacts that did not allow Japan to protect her economy and infant industries. A strong industrial base together with a strong military seemed the only way to survive as a member of a rather greedy and predatory international society.

Some people think that the Japanese ability to create the country's present industrial establishment is something that was learned in the four decades since World War II, but they just do not know their history. From the depths of agrarian isolation, Japan started on its industrial journey in the last third of the nineteenth century, and by 1905—only about one generation—the industrial and economic might of the nation had been raised to such a height that tiny Japan, with a population of about thirty million, was able to defeat both China (1894–95) and Imperial Russia (1904–1905) in war. At the beginning of World War I in Europe, Japan was the major military and industrial power in Asia. This is history, and I am citing it only to point out that the economic miracle of Japan since 1945 should be seen in perspective. Early in the development process the Meiji government realized it could devise economic plans and set industrial goals to fulfill the plans, but government leaders soon realized they could not run the factories and produce the goods. And so government and industry devised a system of cooperation and support, for the benefit of the nation. Some aspects of the system are being dismantled only today.

Comparing the two periods—the Meiji era and the post–Pacific War era—would be useless, but one striking fact must be noted, and that is that all Japanese have shared in the struggle to rebuild the nation and its peaceful industrial plant since the end of the war. And they have shared the fruits of their success for the first time in history, as the Japanese standard of living reached top world levels. Of course, Japan reached out again in these last four decades for technology, to attempt to catch up with developments it had missed, and we bought technologies for direct use and to improve upon.

Japanese steel makers bought technology for the basic oxygen conversion system from the originating companies in Austria, but within less than a decade Japanese companies were selling improved steel-making technology back to those same companies. As another example, we at Sony took the basic transistor and redesigned and rebuilt it for a purpose of our own that the originators hadn't envisioned. We made a completely new kind of transistor, and in our development work, our researcher, Leo Esaki, demonstrated the electron tunneling effect, which led to the development of the tunnel diode for which he was awarded a Nobel Prize seventeen years later, after he had joined IBM.

I was on the board of IBM World Trade when the award was announced and was actually attending an IBM board meeting in Paris at the time. An assistant brought news to IBM chairman Frank Carey at our meeting, and Carey proudly told his board members that this was the first time an IBM scientist had won a Nobel. He was beaming, naturally, and there was applause all around. Then Dr. Emanuel Piori, the head of IBM research, went to him and quietly explained the background. When Carey called on me, I only said, "We are very pleased." Actually it was an understatement. Esaki's Nobel was the first Nobel Prize for any Japanese scientist working in industry; all the other laureates have been professors. And Sony was, relatively speaking, a very young company on the Japanese industrial scene.

Dr. Kikuchi, our research center director, says that regardless of whatever arguments one might make about what he calls the "adaptive creativity" that Japanese scientists and technicians used during the catch-up phase in Japan's development and the so-called "independent creativity" practiced today, there is no doubt that Japan is now a full-fledged member of the world's technological community. Japan, the United States and Western Europe now treat each other on equal terms. When technical meetings are held in Japan, such as the meeting on so-called fifth generation computer technology held in Tokyo in 1984, top researchers from around the world gather to learn of Japan's technical progress. At that 1984 conference, speaker after speaker from abroad pointed out how the Japan project, lightly funded by the government and participated in by many Japanese companies, had stimulated their governments to invest in artificial intelligence projects that had been neglected until there was news of Japan's project.

As Dr. Kikuchi has pointed out, there are different kinds of creativity. I told a gathering of Europeans and Americans at the Atlantic Institute in Paris in December 1985 that the key factor in industry is creativity. I said there are three creativities: creativity in technology, in product planning, and in marketing. To have any one of these without the others is self-defeating in business.

To clear up a few myths that still linger about the subject of Japanese creativity, I must emphasize that a unique feature of Japanese technological development is its independence from defense technology. It is well known that much of American and European technology is spun off of defense work funded by government. This has been beneficial, of course; but in Japan, where we have no defense industry to speak of, we have made perpetual changes in the consumer marketplace, bringing technological innovation into the home with commercial use technology. And interestingly, in the reverse of the flow in the United States and Europe, now Japanese nondefense know-how is being sought by the defense establishments of both the U.S. and Europe. In fact, an agreement has been signed on the exchange of technology between Japan and the U.S. concerning imaging technology using Japanese-designed charge-coupled devices, which convert analog information into digital information that can produce finer and more useful and adaptable images.

Also, I think it is worth pointing out that in Japan most advanced engineering and scientific research has been carried out by national universities, not private ones. These national universities tend to avoid influences from outside and jealously guard their independence, especially from the private business community. That is why cooperation between industries and universities is more difficult here than elsewhere. In the United States, exchanges of human and research resources are common between universities and the private sector.

The major burden of research is borne by private industry in Japan, which contradicts the notion that Japanese business and government cooperation is the key to Japanese commercial success. In fact, in 1984, 77.7 percent of the R&D in Japan was paid for by business enterprises, and only 22 percent by government. Some of us in business feel the government isn't really helping, but is creating impediments to innovative change and developments with excessive intervention and obsolete regulations.

The highly educated work force of Japan continues to prove its value in the field of creative endeavor. In the recovery from the war, the low cost of this educated labor was an advantage for Japan's growing low-technology industry. Now that the industrial demand is for high technology, Japan is fortunate to have a highly educated work force suited to the new challenge. And even though labor costs are high, the intelligence of the labor force is one factor that will continue to be an advantage for Japan's industry.

There is growing discontent in Japan today with the current educational system, which forces students to spend much of their time learning how to pass examinations in order to get into good schools. This system does not leave them enough time for experimentation and original thinking. The system has served us well up to now, but ways are being explored to make the system more efficient and relevant to the new times we are living in. We have always demanded original thinking from our employees, and we have received a lot of it. From a management standpoint, it is very important to know how to unleash people's inborn creativity. My concept is that anybody has creative ability, but very few people know how to use it.

My solution to the problem of unleashing creativity is always to set up a target. The best example of this was the Apollo project in the United States. When the Soviet Union launched the world's first artificial satellite, Sputnik, and then sent the first human being into outer space, it was a shock to the United

States. Many nations that had always looked to the U.S. as the great innovator and creator of so many good things could hardly believe that any other country could have the ability to be first in space. America began a program to catch up, but when President Kennedy set a very clear target—going to the moon within ten years—everything changed. The target was a clear challenge. It meant an enormous leap forward would be needed. Nobody knew how to do it, all was theory. The studies had to start immediately. How much power would be necessary? What kind of navigation system would be needed? What kind of computer would have to be developed? And then there was need for new materials. Carbon fiber was invented; even such simple but useful things as Velcro came from that program. The inertial navigation system, a whole new concept, was invented and is in use in our airliners today.

In order to reach one target, many people became creative. Managers had to determine goals and go for them, encouraging workers to excel. In fact, the Zero Defects programs of NASA were a great influence on Japan's quality control programs. We had had one bout with American high-quality standards during the Korean War (1950–53), when U.N. military procurement in Japan gave an enormous boost to Japanese industry and introduced military standards that required higher quality than was common for ordinary civilian products. We Japanese took the military standards and the Zero Defects programs to heart.

The "patron saint" of Japanese quality control, ironically, is an American named W. Edwards Deming, who was virtually unknown in his own country until his ideas of quality control began to make such a big impact on Japanese companies. Americans awoke to the message of this prophet but did not take it as seriously as the Japanese did. In fact, to win a Deming Award for quality is one of the highest distinctions a Japanese company can attain. We at Sony have always been fanatics about quality. Simply, the better the original quality of a product the fewer service problems that have to be faced. We were pleased and proud—and taken by surprise—to hear that a Sony cassette recorder was taken to the moon aboard the Apollo 11 spacecraft and used to play music back to the earth. Although NASA spent large amounts of money to develop zero gravity reliability assurance into every item used in the program, down to such things as mechanical pencils, the recorder the astronauts used was an off-the-shelf model, which had been tested and found to be acceptable without any need to refer back to us. We didn't know about it in advance, and I jokingly chided our engineers after I heard about it, saying they had obviously overdesigned the tape recorder. "It doesn't have to work in zero gravity," I said. "It just has to work anywhere on earth." When an engineer or a scientist is given a clear target, he will struggle to reach it. But without having a target—if your company or organization just gives him a lot of money and says, "Invent something"—you cannot expect success.

That is the trouble with Japanese government research institutes. Government believes that if you have a big laboratory with all the latest equipment and good funding it will automatically lead to creativity. It doesn't work that way. When I was a student, one of Japan's top electrical companies built a new laboratory in a lovely wooded campus in central Japan. It was beautifully designed and outfitted with the latest equipment, and the scientists had gorgeous workstations that were the envy of their peers. The company thought that if they threw money at these scientists they might get some results. Very little came from the lab, except that many of the researchers used their time to do research for their advanced academic degrees at company expense. The company made a lot of Ph.D.'s, but no products to speak of. The government has also followed the same path with about the same results. In industry, we must have the theoretical background, and we must have the pure research that precedes development of new things, but I have learned that only if we have a clear goal can we concentrate our efforts.

I do not mean to deny the value of pure or basic research. In fact, we are heavily engaged in it right now, and I believe that in the future Japanese industry must put more effort into this field, because this kind of research is essential for the creation of new technology. Japan's spending for basic research is now increasing at a faster rate than spending for general research and development. But Japan should not be complacent. A report from Japan's Science and Technology Agency in 1985 said that Japan's involvement in fundamental research "cannot be said to be adequate." And it pointed out that even though Japan's R&D investment is higher than that of the three major European countries, the ratio of spending for basic research is lower and seems to be gradually decreasing in universities and government institutions, which means the load is increasingly falling on industry.

When we started our company and even before we took stock of our abilities, the number of people we had, and what their talents and expertise were, Ibuka said, "Let's make a tape recorder." This was even before we knew what the tape was made of or how it was coated—or even what it looked like. We set out to make special, innovative products, not to indulge in pure science. But as we grew we had to move more and more into this realm to make our products and their components, to devise our own proprietary items like transistors, semiconductors, integrated circuits, and charge-coupled devices. Gradually, the lines between different kinds of research tend to overlap. At no time did we look to the government for help. Our perhaps peculiarly Japanese reaction when we learn of some new development or come across a phenomenon, is invariably "How can I use this? What can I make with it? How can it be used to produce a useful product?"

When video recording was being used in the United States by the major broadcasting stations, we thought people should have the same capability in their homes. The big TV machines that the stations used were cumbersome and very expensive. We started working toward our target to bring this machine into the home. As we devised each new model, it seemed more and more incredible to us that we could make it so small and so well. Yet it was not small enough for Ibuka. But nobody knew exactly where we were headed until he tossed that paperback book onto the conference table and said that was the target, a videocassette the size of the book that could hold at least one hour of color program. That focused all the development. It wasn't just a matter of making a small cassette—a whole new concept of recording and reading the tape had to be devised.

Our brilliant researcher, Nobutoshi Kihara, came up with the system that did away with the blank spaces between the bands of recorded material on regular videotape. These empty bands (called guard bands) were placed there to avoid interference, or spillover, as each band of program material is recorded and played back. But this meant that half the tape was going unused except for providing separation between the bands of program. Kihara thought, why not record onto the empty spaces, greatly increasing capacity and avoiding interference by using two recording-reading heads and angling the heads about ninety degrees from each other so that each head could not read or interfere with the recorded track next to it. A new revolving head drum had to be designed and a different mechanism developed, but after many months of testing, his group produced a system that worked beautifully, and we had built a brand-new video system for home use, with the best picture yet attainable.

We were justifiably proud of Betamax. In Japanese the word pronounced "beta" refers to a brushstroke in painting or calligraphy that is rich and full, without skips or white spots. Kihara used it to refer to the use of all the tape without leaving space for the guard bands. The sound, *beta*, so resembled the Greek letter beta and its scientific overtones, that we coined the brand name, Betamax, from it.

Management of an industrial company must be giving targets to the engineers constantly; that may be the most important job management has in dealing with its engineers. If the target is wrong, R&D expenses are wasted, so there is a premium on management being right. And to my mind this means that people who are running a business ought to know their business very well. If the accountant had been in charge of our little company in 1946, our company would be a small operation making parts for the giants. Likewise, someone who is only a scientist is not always the best person to have at the helm.

The late Peter Goldmark was a remarkably creative man, a brilliant engineer. He invented the long-playing record and he eventually became the head of CBS Laboratories. He got the idea for a type of video recording that used black and white photographic film and electron-beam printing. He demonstrated his idea to the CBS board, and they were enthusiastic about it. Of course nobody else on the board, including Chairman Bill Paley, had a technical background. They were all novices at engineering technology, and so they had no way to judge the invention. Goldmark had a good record on inventions and was also a very capable salesman of his ideas, and perhaps nobody asked the right questions. In any case, the board decided to invest a lot of money in this system. Goldmark came to me to try to sell the idea, hoping to enlist us in using the same system, but we were already deeply involved in video recording using the much simpler magnetic system.

"Peter, we are experts on video recording," I told him. "We have been working on magnetic video recording for a long time, and it works beautifully. We don't think this is the way to go." He was disappointed, but I told him I thought a photochemical method was just too complicated; too many things could go wrong with it. CBS went ahead with the system (they called it EVR) and spent a lot of money on it before they finally abandoned it. Although it was creative, it was not feasible as a business venture.

As another example, RCA went into the video disc business with a mechanical capacitance system, but in the end had to write off many millions because the system was a flop. Whether the design, the technology, the merchandising, or the promotion was bad, the failure was a failure of management. Managers who do not have the capability to judge from a technical standpoint whether a product is feasible or not are at a tremendous disadvantage. I have always felt that the idea that professional managers can move from one industry to another is dangerous. Even being in the business and being knowledgeable about it is no guarantee that all the possible opportunities will be exploited and that mistakes will not be made, but at least the odds are on your side.

Texas Instruments showed good foresight in making a radio frequency transistor at the same time we were also struggling with it. (They had also licensed the technology from Western Electric.) TI became a principal supplier of transistors to IBM and to other industrial companies as well as to many involved in U.S. defense contracting. They later invented the integrated circuit, a great achievement in the area of semiconductor technology. Texas Instruments also supported the Regency company, which put the first transistorized radio on the market a few months before ours. Yet TI did not make moves to develop and take advantage of the huge market they might have had in the consumer field. The Regency radio, as I mentioned earlier, was on the market for only a short time. We would have given them a good run for their money if they had stayed in, but there was never a fight because TI apparently saw no future in small radios. But we did.

It is possible to have a good idea, a fine invention, but still miss the boat, so product planning, which means deciding how to use technology in a given product, demands creativity. And once you have a good product it is important to use creativity in marketing it. Only with these three kinds of creativity—technology, product planning, and marketing—can the public receive the benefit of a new technology. And without an organization that can work together, sometimes over a very long period, it is difficult to see new projects to fruition.

It has been said that the creativity of the entrepreneur does not exist in Japan anymore because the nation has so many giant companies. But venture capital is available now as never before, and so we will see the results from new small, innovative companies. We promote entrepreneurship right within our own large company by the way we manage. We have a group system in which each group, such as TV, video, magnetic, audio, has its own management with total responsibility for what it does. Within each section, each chief has responsibility in his field. So when he or his staff comes up with an idea or a new invention, or a new technological means or process, he has the authority to present it to top management. If management, which has the ability to understand technology, sees the possibilities favorably, we give the authority to proceed. If we do not, there are sometimes options beyond just dropping the project.

One young Sony researcher recently came up with a system of plasma display that might one day be adaptable for computers and even flat TV monitors. But the idea seemed very far in the future to us, too far to invest a lot of time and money in at the moment. We supplied him with some capital, and he acquired some more and has set himself up in business. We were reluctant to let go of such a talented employee, but we felt that since his desire to become independent was so strong, he could apply his talents better in his own environment.

As an idea progresses through the Sony system, the original presenter continues to have the responsibility of selling his idea to technical, design, production, and marketing staffs and seeing it to its logical conclusion, whether it is an inside process or a new product that goes all the way to market. That way the family spirit continues to prevail and the group or those within the group can feel they are not only a part of the team but entrepreneurs as well, contributing profitably and creatively to the welfare of all of us in the family.

AMERICAN AND

JAPANESE STYLES

The Difference

I

I once complained to an American friend that it was becoming difficult to find anything actually made in the United States these days, and he said, "Why don't you take some of our lawyers, a genuine Made-in-America product!" We both laughed over the joke, but it isn't really funny.

The lawyer has become in my mind a major symbol both of the difference between American and Japanese business and management styles and of a weakness in the American system. I have spoken out quite frankly on the subject of lawyers in speeches in many places in the U.S., including the John F. Kennedy School of Government at Harvard University.

Americans know that legal problems are constantly involved in almost all of the relations between individual companies and between companies and the government and its agencies, such as the Securities and Exchange Commission and

171

the Fair Trade Commission. Americans seem to take it in stride, but I can't. These legal problems have a severe impact on how business is conducted and, worse, on how businessmen see their role in America. American businessmen seem to think it is natural always to be looking over their shoulders to see who is coming up behind them with a lawsuit. They must always be protecting themselves from attacks from behind instead of moving ahead and looking far into the future. The intrusion of lawyers and the legal mentality into so many facets of American business is in contrast to Japanese management style and philosophy, but as Japanese business has become more internationalized, we Japanese have had to become more aware of the legal profession. I hope we do not go the way of the Americans in this regard. I prefer the Japanese system, although I have learned a lot from the American system. I don't believe all that we do in Japan is good, because it is not, but I believe a better understanding of the differences may clear up some misconceptions.

I met Dean Graham Allison of Harvard's Kennedy School of Government at the Shimoda Conference, a periodic gathering in Japan of American and Japanese intellectuals, businessmen, and others, named for the town that became the site of America's first consulate in Japan. The conferences are a great opportunity for communication, for analysis from both sides, for expressing opinions in an attempt to increase understanding, and for just getting to know people. In my discussions with Dean Allison, I must have been pretty animated on the subject of lawyers, because he invited me to come speak at the school, and in his letter of invitation he assigned me a provocative title: "The Role of Lawyers in Handicapping Entrepreneurial Efforts in the United States."

When I began researching my subject, I discovered that other businessmen have been worried about the problems that lawyers create for business and for American society generally. My friend John Opel of IBM wrote an article a few years ago titled "Our Litigious Society," so I knew I was not alone in my view that lawyers and litigation have become severe handicaps to business, and sometimes worse. I was once told by an American friend that in some cases lawyers step in when there is a traffic accident and sometimes take 65 percent of the insurance money or the court award, leaving the victim only 35 percent. It is an astounding situation from our point of view.

There are over five hundred thousand lawyers in the United States, and I understand that every year more than thirty-nine thousand people pass the bar examinations, so the number of lawyers continues to grow. Many people take law degrees in the U.S. even though they do not intend to practice law. In Japan we have approximately seventeen thousand lawyers, and the number grows only by about three hundred persons a year. The bar examination is so difficult that less than 3 percent of those who take it pass it. Those who pass it go to the National Legal Training Institute, where they choose to pursue one of three branches of the law: public service as a prosecutor or as a judge, or private practice.

The three hundred annual graduates of the institute are usually divided almost equally among prosecutors, judges, and private-practice lawyers. Of course, there are thousands of young people who study law and get degrees and then move into private companies where they do corporate legal staff work very much like American lawyers, but they do not practice before the court. Others who are trained in law sometimes sit as arbitrators. In Japan, we have no huge law firms as in the United States, where dozens of lawyers' names cover the front door—sometimes the front wall. Also, when someone files a lawsuit in civil court, he is required to pay a nonrefundable filing fee based on the amount being sued for. If he loses the case, he must also pay the court costs. This is one reason why in our early days we were hesitant to go to court in Tokyo against Balcom Trading over the tape recorder patent infringement case; we couldn't afford to lose if the case dragged on for a long time, building up the court costs.

Even though we are not busy in Japan creating lawyers, our courts are still jammed with cases that take years to settle, which is partly a function of the small number of lawyers. This state of affairs also tends to discourage casual litigation, because people know when they go into court that it may take a very long time to reach a settlement. Therefore, most ordinary disputes between people and even many between companies are settled by arbitration. But as crowded as Japan's court calendar is, it is nothing like the American situation where, according to Opel's calculations, in the year 2010 there will be nearly a million cases on appeal.

While the United States has been busy creating lawyers, we have been busier creating engineers. We have twice as many engineering graduates, which means, taking the relative size of our countries into account (the U.S. has about twice the population of Japan), four times the ratio of engineers. In the electronics field alone, each year we graduate about twenty-four thousand engineers, to about seventeen thousand in the U.S.

With this situation in mind, I flew to Boston for my speech on a June day in 1982 and drove to the Harvard campus where Dean Allison met me. As I looked out over my audience in Faneuil Hall, I thought to myself, there are probably a lot of lawyers here, and this is America, so I had better start out with a disclaimer. I said, "First I wish to make it very clear that what I am about to say is my personal observation and not an opinion having any legal meaning. I don't need any legal problems."

The audience was anything but hostile, and they chuckled at my opening observation. But I couldn't help saying what was in my heart and mind. I told about my first experience with American legal procedures in setting up our company and about how much I learned. Although I had known quite a bit, for a Japanese, about the law in the early days of our business, it was pretty much centered around patents and things directly relating to our products. We knew nothing of contracts, of consolidated accounting, or other complicated matters like dealing with American government agencies, which you cannot do yourself but must have a lawyer do for you.

I said we have many lawyers in our company today and are involved with many law firms in America and elsewhere, and they give us valuable advice. "But if we listen to lawyers too much," I said, "we cannot do any business. The lawyer's role is very important for the businessman, but I also think that it poses a danger. Even if the lawyers think of all the possible risks, an unpredictable thing may happen." I told of my American friend who was so afraid of falling and hurting himself in the bathtub that he had the tub covered in rubber—and then one night he fell down in his bedroom and broke his leg.

When I had warmed up to the subject, I made the point that "if you have so many lawyers, they have to find business, which sometimes they have to create. I know there are many lawyers sitting here. But I think that is a fact. Sometimes nonsensical lawsuits are generated by lawyers. In this country everybody sues everybody." Contingency cases, which are frowned upon in Japan, are common in the United States, and I know of cases now in the U.S. courts involving large sums of money that I believe were thought up by an outside lawyer and sold on a contingency basis to an American company.

Worse, in my opinion, is that nobody seems to trust anybody in the legalistic climate that has been created in the U.S. I often say to my assistants, "Never trust anybody," but what I mean is that you should never trust someone else to do a job exactly the way you would want it done; so therefore, do not put the burden on someone else to fulfill your wishes. In Japan we customarily trust each other, which is why government and industry have managed to get along so well since the war, even though they often squabble.

In the United States businessmen often do not trust their colleagues. If you trust your colleague today, he may be your competitor tomorrow, because people frequently move from one company to another. It is almost inevitable in this situation that mutual trust and confidence are lost all across the board. Management doesn't trust its employees, and employees don't trust management. The government doesn't trust business organizations or industry, and industry doesn't trust government. Sometimes at home the husband doesn't trust his wife, and the wife doesn't trust her husband—although that isn't strictly an American characteristic. About the only person you can trust in America, it seems, is your lawyer. The conversation and correspondence between the lawyer and client are protected, legally. All other things can be disclosed in court, so how can you trust anybody else?

I have had my difficulties with the American legal system, and so I feel qualified to talk about it. We established our company in the United States as Sony America, an American company, and we have been good business citizens of America. We had to learn about American government and legal procedures right away and I was lucky to have a lawyer like Edward Rosiny to make the introductions. It was not easy for me to grasp why some things were necessary, but I learned to comply with the endless legal requirements. However, I think in America there is such a thing as legal harassment, and here is a good example:

In 1968 the Electronics Industries Association filed a complaint with the Treasury Department claiming that Japanese TV makers were selling their sets in the United States at lower prices than in Japan, in short, dumping them and causing injury to domestic makers. Sony was investigated and found not to be dumping, but because all Japanese companies were suspected, Sony continued to be subjected to an incredibly tedious, inefficient, time-consuming, and costly investigation for many years to come. Finally, in 1975 we were excluded from this television dumping ruling, which we had no reason to be included in in the first place. But for technical reasons, it took another eight years to clear the case.

While this investigation was going on, in 1970 Japanese TV makers including Sony were named defendants in a private antitrust lawsuit filed by an American TV maker, National Union Electric Company (NUE), which used the brand name Emerson. That suit also charged dumping. It took ten years of hard work by some of my best legal staff people and outside lawyers before the Federal District Court in Philadelphia delivered a judgment in our favor, saying in particular that Sony's well-known position as the highest priced seller in the U.S. market makes it "an illogical candidate" for membership in a low-price conspiracy. Yet it took another two and a half years to have the judgment confirmed by the Court of Appeals.

I thought that might be the end of it, but I was wrong. A coalition of American color TV makers and their unions filed a petition with the International Trade Commission claiming injury from increased Japanese color TV exports. President Jimmy Carter didn't go along with the recommended duty increase of 20 percent, but he negotiated an orderly marketing agreement with the Japanese government restricting shipments for three years. My company was covered by the agreement, even though our sales in the U.S. showed no sign of the kind of increase that could cause injury to domestic makers.

Well, if that wasn't enough to wear us out, along came two duty petitions seeking to place higher duties on our products. And even when the Treasury Department concluded in these cases that Japanese-made electronics were not subsidized by the government, Zenith sued the U.S. government over the ruling! They challenged the ruling and said that the refund of the Japanese commodity tax on exported goods was a subsidy. Three years later, the U.S. Supreme Court dismissed the Zenith case. I must say that all of this—and there is more I will not mention—indicates the use of the law by American companies to harass and actually block Japanese imports. These companies spent millions of dollars in the legal battles, but they failed to make themselves more competitive against the Japanese makers. The result was a great deal of bitterness and a lost battle. The only ones who profited from it were the lawyers, not the consumers, the American companies, or the Japanese firms. And so if I used the phrase "handicapping entrepreneurial efforts" in my speech, as Dean Allison suggested, I think it was apt.

One of the things that bothers me the most about the problems that can be created by lawyers is illustrated by the National Union Electric case I mentioned earlier. While this case was dragging on, it struck me that it was costing everybody a lot of money, and I thought it would be wise to come to some kind of agreement to end these costs. The parent company of NUE was Electrolux, and I went to see the chairman, Hans Werthen, and suggested we talk about settling the case. But he said he had no control over the case and would have to get his lawyer's OK. I see nothing wrong with asking and taking a lawyer's advice, but why give them so much control? In this case, Werthen was even worried that if he settled with Sony he might be sued by his own lawyer!

Werthen made a deposition to our counsel in 1978 and recounted our meeting, saying, "I had to tell [Morita], however, much as I sympathized with him, this lawsuit is absolutely out of my hands. I told him that I have a deal—we have a deal with our legal people here that they handle the lawsuit against a sort of compensation that depends on the outcome. . . . That means that I cannot start to give orders to my lawyers to say dismiss this one or bring this one. They must handle it. I told Morita that I would hardly be in a position to give orders in this case. . . ."

There is no proof that his lawyer controlled this case in order to get a large attorney's fee in the end, but I have to strongly suspect that this was the case, because Werthen said to me that his lawyer represented his company on a contingent fee basis, and the amount of possible recovery in this case—under the old law that allowed for treble damages if proved—was three hundred and sixty million dollars. Whatever the truth was in this particular incident, a combination of the system of treble damages and private lawsuits, which are allowed under the 1916 Revenue Act in suspected unfair competition cases, plus contingent fees, seems to give incentive to clients and their lawyers to bring private antitrust actions in order to share the recovery of damage awards between them. The idea must have come from lawyers, and that is why I say it is the lawyers who create problems.

I believe there may be some justification for contingency cases. Sometimes it enables people who could not afford to hire a lawyer to make a legitimate claim, and I know it is legal in the United States, and not actually illegal in Japan. But I do not think that contingency cases should be applicable to large industrial companies.

Many Americans seem proud of the adversarial relationship between government and business, as though their aims are naturally antagonistic. In Japan we do not see it that way. To put it bluntly, whether we like it or not, the government is a partner in our business without owning a single share of Sony stock or running any risk. And the American government is a partner of American business, too, in the same way. The Japanese government takes away more than 50 percent of our profits, and that in a sense makes it a majority partner. So from our government's viewpoint, it wants its partner to work hard and make a profit. By doing so, business is able to keep people employed, enabling the company and its employees to pay taxes rather than to go on the public dole. This is done with a long-range viewpoint. So while we often have our disagreements with the government and its bureaucracy, which actually runs the government, and while I often criticize specific government programs or policies, I know the relationship is basically supportive.

The American system of management, in my opinion, also relies too much on outsiders to help make business decisions, and this is because of the insecurity that American decision makers feel in their jobs, as compared with most top Japanese corporate executives. The legal requirement for disclosure puts the manager's performance on show every quarter and the main evaluation of an executive too often is done in this shortsighted way. Obviously, after the Great Crash of 1929 the reasons for regulation and/or constant public reporting were evident to everyone, and the objective of protecting the shareholders was a worthy one. But the SEC and the FTC became like policemen. And maybe that is justified in the United States, where there have been so many cases of executives being arrested for economic crimes.

In Japan a person who holds an executive position of trust and who violates it is really disgraced, and because of our closed-circle society, it would be impossible for him to continue to do damage to company after company, as some have done in the U.S. and even in Europe. Often if some major failure or illegality takes place somewhere within the company, or if there is a breach of trust with the consumers, it is the president who resigns to accept responsibility for the failure of the company to do what was correct. Rarely is such an executive personally held responsible for the failure.

For example, in 1985 the president of Japan Air Lines resigned after a JAL 747 crashed, killing five hundred and twenty people in the worst single-airplane disaster in history. Several years before, he personally visited the survivors and the families of the dead in an accident that was less disastrous. The head of a famous Tokyo department store, who was known for his autocratic and flamboyant ways, created a sensation when the business reputation of his fine old company was damaged by the scandal of having misrepresented and sold some bogus Persian antiques as real. When he refused to resign to take responsibility for it, his board defied long-standing tradition and actually voted him out. Since Japanese management of a company is long-range and collective, the departure of any one top official is not likely to change the long-range goals of the company or the way it deals with its employees and suppliers. In this case, the scandal was so humiliating to this firm that the board felt it was necessary to repudiate not only the president but also the changes of style he had brought to the job of running the company. It is very rare, though, for a Japanese board to have to fire a top executive.

But the differences between U.S. and Japanese companies go beyond the cultural. If you ask a Japanese executive, "What is your most important responsibility?" he will invariably say that continued employment and improving the livelihood of the workers is at or near the top of the list. In order to do that, the company must make a profit. Making a profit will never be at the top of the list. Most of the American business executives I know put the highest priority on return to the investors or this year's profit. They have the responsibility because the investors gave it to them, and to stay in their jobs they have to continue to keep the investors happy. The board of directors represents the investors, and if top management fails to give the return the investors feel they need, he will be fired. For that reason he is entitled to use the factory and the machinery of the company, and also the workers, as tools to accomplish his aim. This can be detrimental.

Visiting an American television plant in the Midwest a few years ago, I commented to the manager that I thought he really needed to buy some more modern equipment in order to improve the company's productivity. He shocked me when he told me that his compensation was based on the company's financial performance and that he was not going to do anything, like making long-range investments, that might cut his compensation for the sake of the next manager who would be along in a year or so. I have also noted in our joint venture dealings that we in Japan like to take our depreciation quickly, on a constant percentage, and get on with the business, whereas our American partners always seem to want to take their depreciation over a long period, on constant value.

After the war, both the labor law reforms and the destruction of the family-controlled holding companies were major contributors to Japan's reconstruction. We also devised a union system in which the company family became the labor unit rather than the impersonal industry-wide kind of unions that finally developed in the United States. Of course the Japanese company unions belong to associations of unions that set goals and generally attempt to coordinate the concerns and demands of the member unions. But we have labor peace in Japan mainly because management does not use labor as a tool and tries to be aware of the concerns of labor. Some companies are, of course, better at this than others.

In Paris not too long ago, someone said rather innocently to me that Japan is a capitalistic country. I said that it would appear so, but that actually, it would be more accurate to say Japan has a socialistic and egalitarian free economic system. When the laws were changed after the war, it appeared to many Americans as well as Japanese that the swing to the left could be dangerous. The labor laws that made it virtually impossible to fire people seemed a terrible intrusion into the traditional discretionary powers of management, especially to the older managers. But they were forced to accept these laws and they turned them to everyone's advantage. Japanese managers thought that if everybody could have a familial attitude—and after all, Japanese tend to feel that way almost instinctively about their "Japanese-ness"—perhaps it would be easier to pull Japan out of the hole in which it found itself. That was the spirit that created what an American first called "Japan Inc."

Generally, in the United States, management's attitude toward the labor force and even the lower-level executives is very hierarchical, much more so than in Japan, an Oriental country where Westerners always expect to see such hierarchies. When I visited the Illinois television assembly plant of Motorola, one of the first things I noticed was that the offices were air-conditioned, but out on the shop floor it was stifling, people were dripping with sweat, and big noisy fans were blowing the hot air around. The workers were plainly uncomfortable, and I thought, "How can you get quality work from people laboring under such conditions? And what kind of loyalty can they be expected to show to the big bosses in their cool offices!" In Japan people often used to say that the shop floor where the goods were made was always more comfortable than the workers' homes. That has changed as the Japanese workers have become more affluent, and air-conditioning has become more common at home. By the middle of 1984, more than half of Japan's homes and apartments had it. But back in the late fifties, we air-conditioned our factories before the offices.

Amenities are not of great concern to management in Japan. The struggle for an office with a carpet, a water carafe, and an original oil painting on the wall is not common. Just recently a U.S. company, the maker of highly complex computerized graphics equipment, formed a joint venture with a Japanese company and the Japanese partner said to his foreign associate: "We would like you to design the showroom, but please allow us to design the office space upstairs." It seemed reasonable enough. The showroom was beautifully appointed, with soft lighting and comfortable chairs for visitors and clients. The equipment was highlighted using modern display techniques, and there were video demonstrations and elegant four-color brochures on the company and its equipment. Upstairs, the entire office staff was housed in one big open room without partitions, just a grid of desks with telephones, filing cabinets and other necessary furniture in a simple, very Spartan arrangement. The U.S. partner raised his eyebrows, and his Japanese colleague explained, "If Japanese clients come into the office of a new and struggling company and see plush carpet and private offices and too much comfort, they become suspicious that this company is not serious, that it is devoting too much thought and company resources to management's comfort, and perhaps not enough to the product or to potential customers. If we are successful after one year, we might put up low partitions. After two or three years, we might give the top executive a closed office. But for now we have to all be reminded that we are struggling together to make this company a success."

Exactly my sentiments. We want everybody to have the best facilities in which to work, but we do not believe in posh and impressive private offices. Or perhaps I should say we do not give such things priority. At Sony we have comfortable offices everywhere and some new and impressive buildings, but our headquarters in Tokyo is nothing more than a converted factory building. We have made it comfortable and functional, but it still bothers me a bit that visitors have to climb two short flights of stairs to get to the reception desk. Generally, in Japanese industry, the investment goes into those things that relate directly to the product. And often the building that houses a factory site will look very much like a warehouse. But inside it will have all the essentials. Too often I have found in dealing with foreign companies that such superfluous things as the physical structure and office decor take up a lot more time and attention and money than they are worth. Obviously, in some businesses it is important to put on a show for the clients, but people in the hardware business rarely need to do this. We like to give thought to the atmosphere within our plants, to provide a comfortable, simple, and pleasant work environment, which we believe has a direct effect on product quality.

When we started the company, clothing was scarce and expensive on the black market. People came to work in an odd assortment of gear; returning soldiers wore bits of their uniform or old-fashioned suits that had been saved for many years. If a person was fortunate enough to have a good suit, he didn't want to wear it to the office where he might risk burning a hole in it with acid or soiling it. Some of our employees just didn't have the money to invest in a work jacket. So with company money we bought a jacket for everyone to wear in the office. Pretty soon these jackets became a symbol of our company family. As the company prospered, we could have done away with the jackets—we used to have a summer jacket and a winter one—because we were all being better paid and could afford our own, but everybody seemed to like the idea, and so we just decided to continue to provide them. In the beginning, we executives had a different colored name tag from the others, but we eventually adopted the same kind worn by everyone else. Today these jackets and tags are being used everywhere, even where class distinctions made people hesitant to wear them at first. Many of us liked our blue jackets, and I still wear mine occasionally.

But in the early seventies, when diplomatic relations were restored with the People's Republic of China and contacts increased and news coverage picked up, the papers often had pictures of large groups of Chinese in their Mao jackets all looking alike, and some people around Sony began to joke that when a group of us gathered for a meeting we looked like the people in the pictures from China.

I wanted a change. And so on Sony's thirty-fifth anniversary I asked the design departments of several Tokyo department stores to compete for the contract to design and supply the entire company with new jackets. They came up with some very good designs, I thought, and some of our people wore the jackets to see how they worked out on the job. There was no clear favorite. Finally, I took the problem to my friend, the fashion designer Issey Miyake. He came to the company and watched how the people worked. He went into the plants, the labs, and the offices to observe the kinds of movements they must make, and about a year later he came up with a simple and ingeniously designed gray jacket with red piping that has sleeves that can be removed, turning the jacket into a kind of vest that can be worn all year around. That ended the complaints; I figured correctly that even if people were not too pleased with the jackets, they couldn't very well complain when they were wearing something created by one of the world's top fashion designers. So nobody could doubt it, I made it a point to insist that Miyake put his label in every garment. Today one of those jackets on a Sony employee is as good as a credit card in business establishments near our facilities. The wearing of that jacket makes a person feel that he is part of our team effort, and merchants in the neighborhood will often give credit to someone who asks for it just on the strength of the jacket and the person's name card.

II

Japanese attitudes toward work seem to be critically different from American attitudes. Japanese people tend to be much better adjusted to the notion of work, any kind of work, as honorable. Nobody would look down on a man who retires at age fifty-five or sixty and then to keep earning money takes a more menial job than the one he left. I should mention that top-level executives usually have no mandatory retirement age, and many stay on into their seventies and even their eighties.

At Sony we have mandatory retirement from the presidency at sixty-five, but to utilize their experience and knowledge we keep former executives who have retired as consultants. We provide them with office space and staff, so that they can work apart from the day-to-day affairs of the company, at Ibuka Hall, a building located five minutes away from the headquarters building. From time to time, we ask them for advice and they attend conferences and other events as representatives of Sony. Many of those people who retire from managerial jobs find executive positions in smaller companies or subsidiary companies of Sony where their managerial experience and skill are needed and valued.

Workers generally are willing to learn new skills. Japan has never devised a system like the American, in which a person is trained to do one thing and then refuses to take a job doing anything else—and is even supported by government funds while he looks for a job that suits his specific tastes. Because of Japan's special situation, our people do not have that luxury. And our unemployment rate lately has not reached 3 percent.

One old style of management that is still being practiced by many companies in the United States and by some in Japan is based on the idea that the company that is successful is the one that can produce the conventional product most efficiently at cheaper cost. Efficiency, in this system, becomes a god. Ultimately, it means that machinery is everything, and the ideal factory is a perfectly automated one, perhaps one that is unmanned. This machinelike management is a management of dehumanization.

But technology has accelerated at an unparalleled pace in the past few decades and it has entailed digesting new knowledge, new information, and different technologies. Today, management must be able to establish new business ahead of its competitors, rather than pursue higher efficiency in manufacturing conventional products. In the U.S. and Europe today, old-fashioned low-level jobs are being protected while the new technologies are being neglected.

More important, an employee today is no longer a slave to machinery who is expected to repeat simple mechanical operations like Charlie Chaplin in the film *Modern Times*. He is no longer a beast of burden who works under the carrot-and-stick rule and sells his labor. After all, manual labor can be taken over by machine or computer. Modern industry has to be brain-intensive and so does the employee. Neither machinery nor animals can carry out brain-intensive tasks. In the late sixties, when integrated circuits had to be assembled by hand, the deft fingers of Asian women were greatly in demand by U.S. companies. As the design of these devices became more and more complicated, along came more sophisticated machinery, such as laser trimmers, which required not deft fingers but agile minds and intelligence. And so this upgrading of the workers is something that every country will have to be concerned about, and the idea of preserving old-fashioned jobs in the modern era does not make sense. This means educating new employees and reeducating older employees for new challenges.

That is not all. At Sony we at times have scientists participate in sales for a while because we don't want our scientists to live in ivory towers. I have always felt they should know that we are in a very competitive business and should have some experience in the front lines of the business. Part of the training program for graduates who enter Sony as recruits fresh out of university includes a program where nontechnical persons undergo a month of training at a factory and technical persons work as salespeople in a Sony shop or department store, selling our products.

Japanese labor practices are often called old-fashioned in today's world, and some say the old work ethic is eroding in Japan as it has elsewhere, but I do not think this is inevitable. As I see it, the desire to work and to perform well is not something unnatural that has to be imposed on people. I think all people get a sense of satisfaction from accomplishing work that is challenging, when their work and role in the company are being recognized. Managers abroad seem to overlook this. People in America, for example, have been conditioned to a system in which a person sells his labor for a price. In a way, that's good because people cannot coast; they know they have to work to earn their money or be fired. (I also think the way Americans make their children do work to earn their allowance is a fine idea; in Japan we often just give the money without requiring anything of our children.) In Japan we do take the risk of promising people job security, and then we have to keep motivating them. Yet I believe it is a big mistake to think that money is the only way to compensate a person for his work.

People need money, but they also want to be happy in their work and proud of it. So if we give a lot of responsibility to a younger man, even if he doesn't have a title, he will believe he has a good future and will be happy to work hard. In the United States, title and job and monetary incentives are all tied together. That is why, if a young person has a big job, management thinks he has to have a big salary. But in Japan we customarily give raises each year as employees get older and more experienced in the company. If we give an unusually high salary to one person, we cannot continue to give him annual increases indefinitely. At some point, his salary will have to level off, and at that point, he is likely to get discouraged. So we like to give the same sort of raise to all. I think this keeps our people well motivated. This may be a Japanese trait, but I do not think so.

I believe people work for satisfaction. I know that advertisements and commercials in the U.S. seem to hold up leisure as the most satisfying goal in life, but it is not that way in Japan yet. I really believe there is such a thing as company patriotism and job satisfaction—and that it is as important as money. It goes without saying that you must pay good wages. But that also means, of course, that the company must not throw money away on huge bonuses for executives or other frivolities but must share its fate with the workers. Japanese workers seem to feel better about themselves if they get raises as they age, on an expectable curve. We have tried other ways.

When we started our research laboratory, we had to go out and find researchers, and because these people had more education and were, naturally, older than our normal new employees we decided they should have higher wages, equivalent to U.S. salary levels. One suggested plan was to put them under short-term contract, say three years, after which we would decide whether to renew or not. But before we decided on this new pay scheme, I asked the new employees whether they would prefer the more common system of lower pay to start, but with yearly increases, or the three-year contract at a much higher wage.

Not one of them asked for the American-level salary. Everyone opted for long-range security. That is why I tell the Americans I meet that people don't work only for money. But often when I say it, they respond, "Yes, I see, but how much do you pay the ones who really work hard?" Now this is an important point. When a worker knows he will be getting a raise each year, he can feel so secure that he thinks there is no need to work hard. Workers must be motivated to want to do a good job. We Japanese are, after all, human beings, with much in common with people everywhere. Our evaluation system is complex and is designed to find really capable persons, give them challenging jobs, and let them excel. It isn't the pay we give that makes the difference—it is the challenge and the recognition they get on the job.

My eldest son, Hideo, may not be the best example of the typical Japanese worker, but he has an interesting and, I think, typical view of work in Japan. He has studied in Britain and the United States, and all his life he wanted to work for Sony. He went to work as an Artists and Repertory man at the CBS-Sony record company on the urging of Norio Ohga. He and I felt that for him to come directly into Sony headquarters would be wrong, because of the family connection and the overtones of nepotism. So he was proving himself at CBS-Sony. He worked with foreign and local artists and became famous and successful in the record industry in Japan. He worked very hard, from about noon until three or four o'clock in the morning, doing his regular office business during the day and then dealing with musicians after they finished their work. Hideo doesn't drink, and so it was hard for him to sit around the Tokyo discos and bars with these rock stars, drinking Coca-Cola while they relaxed with whiskey in the wee small hours of the morning. But it was important for him to do this, and although he could have gone on a long time resting on his laurels, he took stock of himself on his thirtieth birthday and made a decision.

As he put it, "In the record business, there are many people in their late thirties and early forties wearing jogging shoes and white socks and jeans and T-shirts to the office. I looked at those guys and said, I don't want to be like that when I am forty or forty-five. This business is fine and I have been successful, and I have no reason to leave it. If I keep this job, I thought, I might end up being a top officer of CBS-Sony, but I didn't want to see myself at fifty coming into the office at one o'clock in the afternoon in jogging shoes and white socks saying 'Good morning.' I felt I had to prove to myself after seven years in the record business that I could work from nine to five, like ordinary people."

He was assigned to the Sony accounting division—quite a change, you might think, from the artistic side of the record business—and some might have wondered whether he could make it or not, but I believed he could. His attitude is very Japanese, despite his international upbringing:

"All jobs are basically the same. You have to apply yourself, whether you are a record A&R man, a salesman on the street, or an accounting clerk. You get paid and you work one hundred percent to do the job at hand. As an A&R man, I was interested and excited and happy, but naturally as long as you are satisfied with your work and are using your energy, you will be happy. I was also very excited about the accounting division. I found out something new every day, struggling with a whole bunch of invoices and the payment sheets, the balance sheet, the profit and loss statement, and working with all those numbers. I began to get a broad picture of the company, its financial position and what is happening day to day and which way the company is heading. I discovered that that excitement and making music at the studio are the same thing."

▲

In the late sixties a European Commission internal memo on Japan was leaked, and a great stir was created because it referred to the Japanese as "workaholics" who live in "rabbit hutches." There is no doubt that inadequate housing is a major problem in Japan, and nobody could deny that the Japanese are probably the hardest working people in the world. We have many holidays in Japan, but only about the same number as the United States. We do not give long summer vacations, even to our schoolchildren.

At Sony we were one of the first Japanese companies to close down our factory for one week in the summer, so that everybody could take off at the same time. And we long ago instituted the five-day, forty-hour week. The Japan Labor Standards Act still provides for a maximum forty-eight-hour workweek, though it is soon to be revised downward, and the average workweek in manufacturing is now forty-three hours. But even with up to twenty days of paid vacation a year, Japanese workers managed to take fewer days off and spend more days on the job than workers in the United States and Europe.

It was only in 1983 that banks and financial institutions began to experiment with the five-day week, closing one Saturday a month, and eventually the whole nation will move closer to the five-day week. Still, International Labor Organization data show that Japanese work longer weeks and have fewer labor disputes than workers in the U.S., the U.K., France, or West Germany. What I think this shows is that the Japanese worker appears to be satisfied with a system that is not designed only to reward people with high pay and leisure.

At Sony we learned that the problem with an employee who is accustomed to work only for the sake of money is that he often forgets that he is expected to work for the group entity, and this self-centered attitude of working for himself and his family to the exclusion of the goals of his coworkers and the company is not healthy. It is management's responsibility to keep challenging each employee to do important work that he will find satisfying and to work within the family. To do this, we often reorganize the work at Sony to suit the talents and abilities of the workers.

I have sometimes referred to American companies as being structures like brick walls while Japanese companies are more like stone walls. By that I mean that in an American company, the company's plans are all made up in advance, and the framework for each job is decided upon. Then, as a glance at the classified section of any American newspaper will show, the company sets out to find a person to fit each job. When an applicant is examined, if he is found to be oversized or undersized for the framework, he will usually be rejected. So this structure is like a wall built of bricks: the shape of each employee must fit in perfectly, or not at all.

In Japan recruits are hired, and then we have to learn how to make use of them. They are a highly educated but irregular lot. The manager takes a good long look at these rough stones, and he has to build a wall by combining them in the best possible way, just as a master mason builds a stone wall. The stones are sometimes round, sometimes square, long, large, or small, but somehow the management must figure out how to put them together. People also mature, and Japanese managers must also think of the shapes of these stones as changing from time to time. As the business changes, it becomes necessary to refit the stones into different places. I do not want to carry this analogy too far, but it is a fact that adaptability of workers and managements has become a hallmark of Japanese enterprise.

When Japanese companies in declining or sunset industries change their line of business or add to it, workers are offered retraining and, for the most part, they accept it eagerly. This sometimes requires a family move to the new job, and Japanese families are, again, generally disposed to do this.

III

Who owns a company anyway? Is it the managers, the shareholders, or the workers? The question is not as simple as it sounds. In Japan we feel that the company must be as much concerned with the workers as with the shareholders. I understand very well the importance of stockholders. We have many of them, and more than 40 percent are non-Japanese. The duty of management is to use their funds effectively and to give them a return on their investment greater than they could have realized if they had used it themselves in some other way. But this does not always mean dividends. It could also mean growth in the value of the stock they hold, which is considered more important than dividends in Japan, since the tax rates on growth of the value of the stock are lower than rates on dividends. A company that reinvests in itself instead of paying out dividends will in the long run be returning more to the shareholders, and certainly more than many companies in the United States and Europe that pay dividends out of fictitious profits.

Sometimes fights between companies, expecially in take-over attempts, can lead to some strange battles that drain the vitality from companies. The unfriendly takeover hasn't yet happened in Japan, though one major case was pending at the beginning of 1986 but failed by midyear, and many business-men think this tactic, common in America, may one day take hold here.

My argument with the American system in this regard can be illustrated by the case of a joint venture company founded with only four million dollars more than fifteen years ago in Japan. The company became phenomenally profitable very quickly and began paying handsome dividends, yet retained plenty of earnings. In fact, by 1985 the company had built two new plants completely out of retained earnings, without re-sorting to any loans, and there was still over one hundred mil-lion dollars in retained earnings in the bank. Then the American partner's parent company came under attack by a corporate raider, and to fend off the raider the company had to buy its own stock at a very high price. To do this they needed cash, and their eyes fell on the joint venture company in Japan and its earnings. They told their partner in Japan that they wanted an immediate dividend declared, taking more than three-fourths of the retained earnings, so they could fight the takeover. The Japanese partner didn't want to sacrifice the earnings, but the pressure was so intense he could not resist.

In Japan we believe one of the most important things in a company is the workers' morale; if the workers lose their enthusiasm for the company the company may not survive. The employees view loss of retained earnings as a threat to their job security. We feel a company that sells its assets has no future. It seems to be difficult for some Westerners to un-derstand this idea we have in Japan that the company belongs not only to the shareholders and the managers. The sharehold-ers can take their money out any time they wish. In America the managers can leave when their contracts expire, and the workers can drift in and out. But I believe in most cases workers want job security, even in the United States and Europe. The workers are the people least able to defend themselves and yet they are indispensable to both management and shareholders.

In the sixties and seventies, when Japan was becoming more liberal and international in outlook, there was a defensive spirit in the country. Some old-line businessmen were against letting foreign companies in at all and wanted more and more barriers erected. I was going the other way, and I tried to encourage liberalization and the entry of foreign goods into the country. I established Sony Trading Company and began importing foreign goods, all sorts of things, from refrigerators to Falcon jets and sundries, and I hoped to see more foreign companies on Japanese soil.

I first established in Sony America a division called "U.S. Sell to Japan Division," and we did a lot of advertising for companies that wanted to sell products to Japan. At first I thought there was no real enthusiasm on the U.S. side, but the inquiries began pouring in and eventually we had eleven thousand of them, some from top U.S. companies such as Whirlpool Corporation and the Hoover vacuum cleaner company. We began bringing many products into Japan, but we had some problems with our suppliers. Whirlpool, for example, made a fine large refrigerator, but its motor ran on the American voltage system of one hundred and ten volts. In Japan our standard voltage is one hundred volts. We told Whirlpool that they should change the motors in the units they ship to Japan, and until they did we had to install a voltage converter in each unit they shipped to us. It took five long years for Whirlpool to start replacing the standard U.S. motor with one that was usable in Japan. In the beginning the Whirlpool machine was bigger than any refrigerator available in Japan, and although it was noisy and vibrated, it sold well. But Japanese makers began building bigger refrigerators, too, and their designers were more sensitive to the need for quiet running mechanisms for use in our small Japanese houses, where kitchens are not normally very far from the bedrooms. Unfortunately, the American refrigerator was not able to maintain a competitive edge in the market.

At present, we are devoting much of our energy to importing helicopters made by L'Aerospatiale of France. For the 1986 Tokyo summit of industrialized nations, we were able to sell three large Aerospatiale Super Puma helicopters to the government for VIP use. In fact, of the four hundred and thirty-nine helicopters in Japan in October 1985, one hundred and thirty-six were Aerospatiale machines. We also became agents for Falcon jet aircraft, but unfortunately there are few airports in Japan and the transportation ministry regulations are strict, so we have had few sales. The reason, I believe, is that the distances in Japan are not great and commercial carriers have a very effective system. Sony is the only company in Japan that owns a corporate jet, aside from the newspaper companies.

My activities abroad for Sony and as a member of the Morgan Guaranty Trust International Council, the Pam American board, and the IBM World Trade board put me in contact with many fine businessmen from all around the world, many of whom have become good friends of long standing. I suppose it was natural, then, that I was called on to help Texas Instruments come into Japan. I had known Pat Hagerty of TI since 1955, when we discussed a possible joint venture. Even though it never worked out, Hagerty and I became close friends. When TI developed integrated circuits (IC), everybody in the electronics business in Japan was interested in the technology. At that time (1968), TI's chairman was Mark Sheppard, and he was adamant about how TI would make its entry into Japan: he would not sell any IC licenses to a Japanese company unless TI had its own wholly-owned company in Japan. TI wanted to come in to manufacture ICs and sell them in the Japanese market, too.

But under the existing Japanese regulations, the only way TI could come in was through a joint venture with a Japanese firm. TI's technology was well respected, and having TI in Japan, many realized, would be a good thing for our industry and for the nation. Besides, lots of companies wanted that IC technology. And so I was approached to try to work out a compromise. I offered TI a joint venture with Sony—we were also a maker of semiconductors—and the Ministry of International Trade and Industry seemed agreeable to the arrangement by which we would sell our 50 percent in three years. We hit a snag when the TI side said they needed a guarantee in writing from the government saying that the sale of our 50 percent of the company would be approved three years hence. Getting a government agency to approve something in advance is a challenge in any country. "You must trust us," I told one of the TI ne-gotiators, but he insisted it had to be on paper. We finally created a satisfactory written document that just barely man-aged to satisfy the American lawyers. TI ran the joint venture as though it were wholly owned and did a very fine job of it, which was what we intended, and as we had assured the TI lawyers, our share was sold to TI three years later.

Some years after the Texas Instruments joint venture went through, I helped General Motors chairman James Roche in his negotiations to buy 35 percent of Isuzu Motors. It was the first major automotive deal of its kind and had to be handled very discreetly in those days. The mood in Japan in April 1971, when James Roche arrived, was very defensive. Newspaper headlines speculated on the motives of this giant company, and the terms they used had military overtones. They talked of "invasion" and "bridgehead" and speculated that Roche was coming to take over Isuzu Motors.

What had stirred things up was a visit by Henry Ford II just before the Roche visit in which, at a Tokyo press confer-ence, Ford criticized Japan severely on the slow pace of its trade liberalization. In fact, Ford was quite blunt and his bluntness irritated many people. I knew James Roche as a fellow member of the Morgan Guaranty Trust International Council, and while the trip was being prepared, I was asked by the Morgan rep-resentative in Tokyo to advise Roche, brief him when he ar-rived, and help arrange some appointments for him. I thought it was a good idea, because the Ford visit could have been counterproductive for those of us who were trying to promote liberalization and less parochialism in the country. Another antagonistic performance might set back the cause of liberal-ization and internationalization for years.

I wanted Roche's first impression on the Japanese to be a positive one. The day Roche arrived, I rented a room at the Tokyu Hotel at Haneda Airport. Reporters waiting at the air-port were told that Mr. Roche was tired and that he would want to wash up and rest for a half hour at the hotel before meeting them. I went to the room early so that I was not seen by the press and was waiting in the room when Roche arrived. I spent the half hour briefing him. I had arranged his appoint-ments with Kiichi Miyazawa, the minister of international trade and industry, and with the chairman of the Chamber of Commerce and Industry, which became headline news events. I had prepared the shape of his first press release, his press announcements, and a kind of script of the questions I thought he would be asked at the press conference. His aides had many questions, and we discussed everything in great detail. I suggested that he explain GM's interest in Japan and his current mission with a soft touch, because at that time Japan was in a rather tense mood, as though suffering from an allergy.

The press saw the story of GM's interest in Japan as one of the most important stories of the postwar era, and the papers were fighting each other for exclusive pictures and information on what GM was planning to do. I advised Roche to say flatly that GM was not interested in taking over Isuzu Motors, which it was not, and he did so. As it turned out, all the questions I had anticipated were asked, and Roche took my suggestions on how to answer them. At that time a foreign company needed government approval to buy more than one-third of a Japanese company, and I helped smooth the way with industry and the government figures who were concerned with the GM-Isuzu plan. The plan worked smoothly and with little adverse publicity.

Many years afterward, I was delighted to learn that GM continued to be grateful for my advice. Several years ago I was invited to lunch by the head of GM Japan, who told me he had been reading the company files before he came to Japan and said, "I know very well how much GM owes you." It gave me a great deal of pleasure and encouragement for the future to know that some giant companies such as GM can show those human qualities we think Japanese companies excel in rather exclusively. After Roger Smith became chairman of GM, he visited Japan and asked to come chat with me. He thanked me for what I had done for GM more than ten years before.

IV

The primary function of management is decision-making and that means professional knowledge of technology and the ability to foresee the future direction or trends of technology. I believe a manager must have a wide range of general knowledge covering his own business field. It also helps to have a special sense, generated by knowledge and experience—a feel for the business that goes beyond the facts and figures—and this intuitiveness is a gift only human beings can have.

I was having lunch in New York one day with Professor Peter Drucker, the management expert, and Bill Bernbach, the advertising man whose agency created many fine campaigns for us, including the popular and successful "Tummy TV" series. The subject of management came up, and Drucker said, "When I speak with Japanese managers they don't seem to me to be rational in their thinking. The strange thing, though, is that they end up coming to the correct conclusions. How is that possible?"

Bernbach pondered it for a while. "My profession is advertising and I don't know much about business administration," he confessed. "But in order to make rational decisions, you have to know all of the facts and the environment that surrounds the facts. But it is probably impossible for a human being to know everything. American managers may believe that they are rational, but they are only rational on the basis of the facts that they have come to know. There are bound to be lots of facts and environmental factors that they don't know. If these are missing, it is natural that no matter how rational a conclusion might seem, it's going to be off base.

"Compared with this," he went on, "Japanese managers seem to have a kind of Oriental 'sixth sense.' Probably instead of putting one fact together with another, they grasp a general idea as a whole and then use this information, together with that 'sixth sense,' in making decisions. This way they have a better grasp of the general idea than one can get only through careful reasoning."

I use Bill Bernbach's comment to illustrate the point that it is essential that the people who run the business know the business and the environment and are prepared to take risks based on their knowledge and indeed even on this so-called sixth sense. I hope the reader will not consider it too much of a boast if I refer to my hunch that the portable stereo player, the Walkman, would be a successful and popular product despite a lot of skepticism within my own company. I was so certain of this that I said, "If we don't sell one hundred thousand pieces by the end of this year, I will resign my chairmanship of this company." Of course I had no intention of doing that; I just knew this product would be successful.

In the United States today, because managements are so highly mobile—I am told that the average white-collar employee works at three different companies in his lifetime—it is common that the man running a company knows little or nothing about the technical side of the products his company makes. If that is the case, he will naturally lack this intuition about his products and their impact on the market, especially if he is, say, an accountant running a consumer products company. There are remarkable exceptions to this, of course, but I believe they are few. It is my observation that such an executive, lacking knowledge and unsure of himself, will hesitate to take risks, will feel the need to justify his every move, and will often turn to the consulting firms.

Next to lawyers, I think these people are the most overused and misused businessmen on the scene in the United States and Japan. I use consultants selectively and have found the best ones can do valuable information gathering and market analysis. But their use can be brought to ridiculous extremes, and it has been. Often when the market research proves to be wrong, the excuse is heard that market conditions changed after the study was done. So what is the use of it? Mainly, I am afraid, to avoid risking jobs. I know of a case where the American home office of a joint venture company didn't think that the plans of the Japanese partner were right, so they had their American representative in the joint venture employ a prestigious management consulting firm based in Tokyo to do a study.

It happened that the American representative, who is a vice president of the joint venture, agreed with the Japanese partners about their plan and had told his home office so in a recommendation to them. But his boss in the States didn't trust his own man in Tokyo or the Japanese partner. When the American in Tokyo discussed the project with the consulting firm, he told them the whole story and the results he "expected" they would find. It may be coincidence that they found just what he was looking for. The Japanese firm was right all along, as was proved later, but it cost the company a large sum of money for the consultant's fee; a great deal of time was lost while the executives were interviewed; it subtly undermined the trust between the partners; it made their representative feel and look foolish and ineffectual; and nothing new was learned. But an executive in the United States in charge of the international operations of his company had covered himself in case the project failed.

If I have written a lot about top management and workers so far, I have not meant to exclude middle management, which is so important and in Japan differs from the Western model. Many Japanese companies operate on the "proposal" system, in which middle management is expected to come up with ideas and concepts to be proposed to top management for judgment. This of course differs from the concept of one-man or small-team management that is so common in the West, and especially in America, where it may be a legacy of the frontier or pioneer spirit. (In Japan we have been exposed to American movies since before the war, and we have come to assess the American spirit in those terms, which is probably not altogether a good or accurate thing. But we like the idea of "fighting spirit," and sometimes in sports and even business we admire the player with the best spirit, even if he loses.) It may sound like a contradiction to say that Japanese companies, as opposed to Western companies, are run by consensus in light of what I have already written about the individuality we prize at Sony and other Japanese companies such as Honda, Matsushita, and some others, where a strong central figure traditionally makes bold decisions, seemingly all by himself. But it is not a contradiction.

The concept of consensus is natural to the Japanese, but it does not necessarily mean that every decision comes out of a spontaneous group impulse. Gaining consensus in a Japanese company often means spending time preparing the groundwork for it, and very often the consensus is formed from the top down, not from the bottom up, as some observers of Japan have written. While an idea may arise from middle management, for example, top management may accept it whole or revise it and seek approval and cooperation all down the line. When I pulled my bluff on the Walkman, threatening to resign, my colleagues knew that I was ahead of them, that I was using all of my experience and knowledge of marketing and consumer psychology in making my decision. And because of it they committed themselves 100 percent to helping make the project a success. If we had failed with the Walkman, I could not have pointed to any market research as the cause of the fiasco.

Once a decision is reached, whether it originally came up from the shop floor or down from the front office, it is the Japanese way for everyone to devote every effort to implementing it without the sniping and backbiting and obstructionism that is sometimes seen in some Western companies. It is a fine situation to be in, because everybody is doing his share of the work, but getting there can be difficult.

My second son, Masao, worked for Morgan Guaranty Trust in New York and London for two and a half years after he graduated from Georgetown University, and he finds the Japanese way of reaching consensus and planning tedious. His viewpoint is very interesting to me, and very Western. "In a Japanese company they like to have meetings," he complains. "They spend hours and hours at it, and I am always frustrated because I want to know exactly why we are meeting and what we are going to decide. I have trouble keeping my eyes open after the first five minutes. At Morgan I worked in foreign exchange trading, and time was so precious that we didn't waste it in meetings. If we had to make a presentation, we would always give the conclusion first, and if anybody wanted to know how I arrived at the conclusion they would ask. In Japan they like to explain first and they don't tell what they have decided until the very end. But sometimes it is difficult to understand all the explanation without knowing where it is headed."

This is a problem that seems to bother foreigners who are exposed to the system. A journalist who came to Japan to do a lot of interviews of Japanese businessmen visited me near the end of his trip. I asked him what his impression was and he was very frank. He said that after several weeks he had finally figured out how to understand the Japanese: "I don't have to listen to the first part of what they say. I only have to begin to pay attention when they say 'however . . .' because up to then they are expressing everybody else's ideas. After that they expressing their own ideas." You have to be very patient in dealing with the Japanese. It takes most Japanese a long time to tell people what is really on their minds.

The group management system of Japan, where decisions often are made based on proposals from younger management, can be an advantage for a company. Young managers can be expected to remain with the same company for twenty or thirty years, and in ten years or so they will move into top manage- ment jobs. Because of this the young managers are always look- ing ahead to what they want the company to be when they take it over. If top management looks down at middle and lower management and is always pressing them to show profits this year or next, as is common in the West, and fires these managers for not producing profits, it is killing the company. If a middle manager says his plan or program may not break even now, but will make big profits ten years from now, nobody will listen to him, and he may even be fired.

Our encouragement of long-range plans from up-and- coming employees is a big advantage for our system, despite all the meetings and the time spent in discussing and formu- lating plans. It enables us to create and maintain something that is rare in business in the West: a company philosophy. Since our employees stay with us a long time, they can main- tain a consistent outlook. Company ideals do not change. When I leave the company, the Sony philosophy will continue to exist. In the United States it is rare for any company to have its own philosophy, because whenever top management changes, the new person imposes his own very strong views. In fact very often boards of directors will go far out of the field of business of their company to bring in a new top officer to "clean house" and change everything in the company.

Recently, one of these outsiders came into an American company, closed down several factories, laid off thousands of employees—and was hailed by other executives in articles in *The Wall Street Journal* as a great manager. In Japan such a performance would be considered a disgrace. Closing factories and firing employees and changing corporate direction in a business slump may be the expedient and convenient thing to do and may make the balance sheet look better at the end of the next quarter, but it destroys the company spirit. And when the business rebounds, where will the company go to get ex- perienced workers who will produce quality goods and work hard and loyally for the company?

I think one of the main advantages of the Japanese system of management over the American or the Western system in general is this sense of corporate philosophy. Even if a new executive takes over he cannot change that. In Japan the long-range planning system and the junior management proposal system guarantee that the relationship between top management and junior management remains very close and that over the years they can formulate a specific program of action that will maintain the philosophy of the company. It also may explain why in the initial stages progress is very slow in a Japanese company. But once the company communicates its philosophy to all employees, the company has great strength and flexibility.

When crises hit various industries, such as after the oil shocks of 1973 and 1979, Japanese companies showed this flexibility. Shipbuilding companies began to manufacture antipollution equipment, computer software, even dishwashers. A mining company began to make bowling machines. A textile company, Kanebo, started making cosmetics and is now a major factor in the local market. When movie attendance declined, a Japanese studio started a leisure industry using its movie theater properties.

More recently, with the fall in world demand for steel, steel makers, already the most efficient in the world, have begun to sell their byproduct gases, such as carbon monoxide and hydrogen, to chemical companies as feedstock, which also lessened the chemical companies' reliance on petroleum. Now there is lively competition among Japanese steel makers in marketing these gases.

In another recent example, a Japanese steel company joined with an American semiconductor maker to produce silicon wafers for making masterslices for semiconductor gate arrays and very large-scale integrations for telecommunications circuits. This was the first case of a steel maker entering the market for semicustom logic chips. The steel company's experience as an efficient producer of small-batch customized steel products, using computerized production control and quality assurance systems, seems to make a fine fit with the American manufacturer. Both companies will learn from this experience, and especially the employees of the Japanese firm, who will be looking into the future having had the experience of working in a shrinking industry.

Such corporate moves make more sense to me, as a Japanese manager, than some I have seen in the United States. Americans pride themselves on being rational in their business judgments: the total logic of the American business schools seems to be cold, deemphasizing the human element. We in Japan see the bases for success in business and industry differently. We believe that if you want high efficiency and productivity, a close cordial relationship with your employees, which leads to high morale, is necessary. Sometimes it is more important to generate a sense of affinity than anything else, and sometimes you must make decisions that are, technically, irrational. You can be totally rational with a machine. But if you work with people, sometimes logic often has to take a backseat to understanding.

COMPETITION

The Fuel of

Japanese Enterprise

I

"If Japanese business management is so good," asked an American friend, "why do eighteen thousand Japanese businesses go belly up each year?" The answer is this: for the same reason they fail elsewhere. As I pointed out in an earlier chapter, there is no magic or secret that will make a Japanese company successful unless a lot of the right things are done, and they must be done by the managers of the business; they can't be done by bankers or bureaucrats.

The glory and the nemesis of Japanese business, the life's blood of our industrial engine, is good old-fashioned competition. It is a severe kind of competition, and sometimes it is so severe that I am worried about its export to other countries. We Japanese are competitive not only in business, but even in life. During the war, the militarists used the emperor's name as a way of getting obedience, by issuing orders in his name rather than their own. And Japanese would compete with each other to show how devoted and loyal they were to him. In the Tokugawa era, great arrogant swordsmen would come into a village and issue a challenge to all comers, just like the gunfighters in the Old West of the United States. Seeing who was best was a pastime for many of these people.

But there was then and there exists now a fine line between competition and destructiveness. In China they say you should not break a person's rice bowl. In Japan it is understood that you must not destroy a worthy competitor—you must leave him his honor, his face. Still, Japanese competitors are often cutthroat, and it is this keen competition at home that makes our companies so competitive abroad. In business competition, as fierce as it is, the unwritten understanding of competition for a share of the market is not for a single company to greedily take everything. However, if a company simply cannot compete, its competitor will not keep it afloat.

In the retail business, from the great department stores to the hundreds of thousands of Mom and Pop shops from Hokkaido to southernmost Okinawa, competition is understood to be the normal way of doing business. If we cannot compete in price, we will compete in service. We Japanese also tend to be fad-oriented and somewhat fickle in our tastes for the new, and so one day it's a Baskin-Robbins ice cream store and a year or so later it's Haagen-Dazs and maybe tomorrow Famous Amos.

The competition in our domestic market makes the consumer a king. In Japan today there are more makers of civilian industrial products than in any other country on earth, including the United States. And these companies—nine automobile makers and two heavy truck makers, more than one hundred machine tool makers, and over six hundred electronics companies, for example—are the survivors of the competitive struggle. At one time, there were forty makers of television sets; today there are only six major ones.

I think I have to point out, though, that what I have been talking about mainly are Japan's really strong industries, all of which export their goods, as well as sell them on the local market. It is in the competition for the local market share that these companies develop the ability to compete abroad. These are companies engaged in electronics, automobiles, cameras, home appliances, semiconductors of some types, precision machine tools, and the like. These are industries that impact directly on the rest of the world and are, I think, of the most interest to the readers of this book. There are many other industries in Japan—chemicals, aluminum, pulp and paper, to name only a few—that are in dire straits and are even being phased down. There are more than seven thousand textile companies competing for a piece of a shrunken market. They have found they cannot compete with cheap textiles from China, Hong Kong, Taiwan, Southeast Asia, and elsewhere, and so they have upgraded the quality of the goods they supply, but eventually they found competition even in high-grade textiles tough. Some companies have been literally junking and breaking up machinery as they scale down. They had to break up the discarded machinery to prevent some ambitious novice from buying it and setting up a business.

As I said earlier, the smartest and best-financed and -managed companies in declining industries have managed to diversify into other fields and some continue to do so. Some so-called "sunset" industries get government support, and companies get low-cost bank loans to help them phase out of one field and retrain employees for another. There are five major steel-making companies in Japan; all are readjusting to a new era when steel orders are shrinking because of competition with imported steel. They are attempting to lessen their dependence on steel orders and are competing with each other on another battleground: selling byproduct gases, as I have said before, contracting out engineering capability, and making ceramics.

The copper industry, too, which sees optical fiber replacing copper wire for transmitting information in telephone communications, homes, and even automobile electrical systems, is moving into optical fiber. In fact, these companies got off the mark so fast that they were able to grab nearly 70 percent of the world market by the beginning of the eighties.

Several Japanese sewing machine makers who fell on hard times because of decreasing demand worldwide have upgraded their old electromechanical technology with the addition of microprocessors and have gone heavily and successfully into electronic typewriters, printers, word processors, and office automation equipment.

We have a free economic system in which anybody can start any kind of legitimate company, so if something turns out to be a good product, people leap in in big numbers, and they compete with each other tooth and nail for the business. A few years ago Yamaha decided the time was right to challenge Honda for a bigger share of the Japanese market in motorcycles and motorscooters. Honda had a clear lead then, but was investing heavily in a new automobile assembly plant in the United States, and so Yamaha put out a line of new models and began a lively advertising campaign. The Honda management responded instantly, despite its heavy financial burden. It struck back with a new model introduction every single week for over a year! Yamaha could not keep up, and in the end there were top-level resignations at Yamaha.

Share of market is more important to Japanese companies than immediate profitability. If the purchase of an expensive new piece of machinery will depress short-term profits but can be expected eventually to increase the company's share of the market, the decision will almost always be to make the investment in the long-range future of the business.

This interest in building for the future in order to stay competitive became a source of trade friction in 1985. Japan's semiconductor makers continued to invest in new plants and equipment at a time when the world market was in decline and American companies were laying off workers and closing down capacity.

Outwitting an opponent in some clever deal is not what the Japanese are interested in. A legendary samurai intellectual martial arts expert named Miyamoto Musashi once wrote a book on the strategy of combat, and when it was reprinted in an English-language translation as *A Book of Five Rings* a few years ago, it became a cult book among some foreign businessmen who were told that a study of this thin volume would reveal the key elements—the secret—of how to win the business battle with Japan. One New Jersey bookseller's catalog even described the book as "Japan's answer to the Harvard MBA."

But the answer to the Harvard MBA is not a book by an ancient swordfighter. It lies on the shelves and the showroom floors of stores all around the world: good quality products that people want and in such variety that any consumer whim can be satisfied. This is how Japanese goods managed to take so much of the U.S. market. And I would say that the best way to compete with the Japanese would be to examine the successful Japanese products for design and construction and innovative concepts. We did not "invade" the American market as it is sometimes charged; we just sent our very best products to America, products that were recognized for their quality and price. These products were the survivors of the competition in the Japanese marketplace.

Since we began making the world's first featherweight headphones to go along with our Walkman stereo player, we have made more than fifty million sets and the number of models grows. In Tokyo today, you can see and try out more than two hundred different models of headphones by a dozen makers at a single store. The variety of models of televisions, video cassette recorders, laser disk players, CD players, video cameras, still cameras, cars, vans, motorcycles, scooters, computers, printers, leisure goods, household appliances, clothing, and communications equipment—the list is almost endless—is the greatest in the world. And because Japan's consumers are fussy, we cannot sell anything that is not of high quality. After-sales service is crucial; we still make house calls, and the company that lets up on any aspect of production or delivery or service will lose customers. An American in the cosmetics business was shocked to hear that it is not unusual for a wholesaler in Japan to send a single lipstick by messenger all the way across the city to a retailer with a waiting customer. If he didn't, it was explained, he might lose the retail shop's business.

Nearly 70 percent of today's Japanese consumers live in the urban corridor from Tokyo, on the main island of Honshu, to Fukuoka, on the southern island of Kyushu. Reaching these consumers, who all see the same network television programs and read the same national newspapers, is easy. Satisfying them is hard. And the high rate of competition among Japanese companies for their disposable income is where we have honed our competitiveness for international trade battles. Japan's one hundred and twenty-one million people are more and more urbanized—only 12 percent are employed in primary work such as farming, and about 80 percent of those farmers earn part of their income in nonagricultural jobs. When we established the Sony Corporation, half of all Japanese were employed in the primary industries. We could see the increasing sophistication of the consumers as our business developed; it became easier to sell higher technology as more and more people came into the city from the farm.

From the beginning, Ibuka and I knew that we were after quality above all. When we came to the American market, we made sure that we had service personnel trained to handle the problems that might come up, and we charged high enough prices to support that effort. Today we have secured markets in the United States and Europe, and I keep telling my managers that we must not be complacent about what we have achieved, because everything is changing very rapidly, not only in the field of technology but also in people's perceptions, thinking, fashions, tastes, and interests. Any company that is slow in grasping the meaning of these changes will not survive in the business world, especially in the high-technology electronics field. Complicating things is the fact that it is hard to predict change, not that it has ever been easy.

When Ibuka and I introduced Betamax to the market in 1975, we established our marketing policy to promote the new concept of time-shift. It was my idea that we had to create a market for the video cassette recorder by educating people and giving them new ideas. I gave speeches telling people Betamax was really something new. "Now you can grab a TV program in your hand," I said. "With the VCR, television is like a magazine—you can control your own schedule." This is the concept I wanted to sell. I knew the competition would soon be upon us, and I wanted to beat it and move people into VCR as fast as possible. I was thrilled with the idea myself. After all, we had been working toward this for twenty-five years.

People were so impressed with television from the earliest days and were so aware of its impact that they didn't think much about TV's major drawback, which is that no matter how good or entertaining the programs are, the information is flowing away as fast as it is being received. If I miss reading my *Time* magazine or *The New York Times* or *Asahi Shimbun* today, I can pick it up tonight and get exactly the same messages with the same initial impact. But even though TV carries a strong impact, if you are not there to see it, you lose everything, and in that case TV has failed in its mission to inform and entertain people.

In the fifties and sixties, popular programs in the United States and later in Japan caused people to change their sched-

ـules. People would hate to miss their favorite shows. I noticed how the TV networks had total control over people's lives, and I felt that people should have the option of seeing a program when they chose. The television broadcasters should not be upset because the programs would be seen with commercials, only at a different time. Of course, to them it meant that people would not be watching the current show and its commercials while they were catching up with the news or the entertainment program they had missed earlier. But it was that control of people's lives that I felt was unfair.

In any case, when we introduced the concept of time-shift with our Betamax, we were hit immediately with a lawsuit by Universal City Studios, Inc., and Walt Disney Productions, because they said that taping from the air violated their copyrights. Of course we fought that. Some motion picture executives, equally shortsighted, were against us, too, saying people would build up libraries of films that would hurt the movie companies' interests.

We won the lawsuit, although it took eight years and we had to carry it all the way to the U.S. Supreme Court. And I was delighted to have the Supreme Court use my phrase, "time-shift," in its ruling that taping off the air does not automatically infringe copyright laws. The concept of time-shift has now become common, and although the phrase sounds like something new, any tape recording of a speech, or musical performance, or news event, or any film, including your home movies, represents time-shift. I have been dealing with time-shift all my life, from the time my mother and I listened to those old classical records, to when Norio Ohga said he needed a vocal mirror. Introducing the concept to video had to await the right equipment. Our video cassette recorder was the first vehicle available to the general public to bring the concept of time-shift to video. Our Japanese competitors were right behind us. We had no American competitors.

II

The continued vigorous competition we have in Japan has also changed the way we look at how we work. In the past, it was important to produce a large stock of a product at the lowest possible cost, but now the life cycle of our products is getting shorter and the cost higher, and if we build up huge inventories, we may find ourselves with a stock of outdated goods. The premium is now on how quickly and efficiently we can get a new product onto the assembly line. In the past we could run a particular model for a year and a half or two years; now we must change models in just half a year, and often sooner. Sometimes it seems like a great waste to put so much investment, so much sophisticated technology, and so many highly complex procedures into such a short cycle, but if we try to lengthen the product cycle and market a model longer by sticking to an old design, our competitors will be in the marketplace with a new model trying (and perhaps succeeding) to take the business away from us. So in design work and in the application of new technology, we have to be ingenious, and on the production lines we have to do a lot more educating of our employees so that they can quickly learn to work on new models without confusion with the old.

I reminded my managers at a worldwide meeting in 1985 that our major competitor came onto the market in Japan with a small compact disc player only seven months after we introduced this new technology in 1984 with our small CD-5 player. In fact, the competing machine was even a bit smaller than ours. Initially, we had not produced enough stock of the new tiny CD player—it was an instant hit—before other small players began to appear on the market, so we were short just at the time we needed to have big stocks on hand. Fortunately, our customers who couldn't get the tiny model CD-5 bought out all of our more expensive models instead, so the story had a happy commercial ending for us. Then we announced a new player, which is even thinner than our competitor's model, and a lot of accessories, including one that will play CDs through a car radio from a tiny FM signal transmitter. It is frequently said in Japan, quite rightly, that the thrust of Japanese industry in the seventies and eighties has been toward things that are light, thin, short, and small. We expect that this will hold for the future as well.

I keep urging my staff to try to figure out ways to cope with the speed of change and turn it to our competitive advantage, because it is obvious that change is a constant and you cannot turn it around, slow it down, or frustrate it. The problem this makes for the production side of an enterprise is obvious: you must keep educating the production people. And the pressures are also very heavy on the marketing people, who are being called on to market products that didn't exist before or models that have new and unfamiliar features.

In the competitive struggle for the biggest share of the market, all sorts of unscrupulous things can take place, including industrial espionage. In this age there are some businesses, even in Japan, dedicated to information access for industrial espionage. The more we become an information-oriented society, the more accessible all kinds of information become. For example, there is no sure method of protecting software now. Once software is created and put into use, it can easily be stolen. We used to think that patents could be used to protect software. The Japanese government had a dispute with the United States over this and reluctantly agreed that software should be regarded as intellectual property and not as industrial property and that therefore copyright law, not patent law, should apply. But in reality how can you tell if something has been stolen when that something is virtually invisible? I believe software is unique and requires some new form of protection; neither patent nor copyright laws seem right to me. This is a difficult area, but I think new concepts are needed.

In California's Silicon Valley, the trade in information is very lively—consultants by the hundreds, newsletters, and magazines all offer information. During the early development of computers, inventors were notorious for some of the things they did, such as bribing nightwatchmen to allow them into the labs and workstations where they could examine the circuitry of a rival machine.

California is crawling with people attempting to sell technical information. Consultants spend a lot of time digesting government contract awards, research grants, literature from technical meetings, and other sources in order to be able to give or sell advice to manufacturers. Some of the shady ones are always attempting to buy data from employees of progressive companies, and big money is said to be available for an employee who will pass out company secrets. Several Japanese companies have been involved in buying such secrets, and some were caught in an FBI sting operation back in 1982, when representatives of two Japanese computer makers and more than a dozen Americans were involved in the sale of data on a new IBM computer design. I have laid down strict rules against this kind of practice.

The absurd aspect to me is that every year in the United States hundreds, or maybe thousands, of technicians, researchers, and executives of American high-technology firms are given layoff notices, are fired, or just quit. When they go to a new company, they take on a new allegiance and they bring with them all the previous company's secrets, or all the ones they were allowed to know. Without the loyalty that comes with long-term employment, it seems to me impossible to ever stop the kinds of leaks and thefts that American business suffers every day through disloyalty and dishonesty.

We are so careful with our secrets that we are constantly reminding our people not to talk about their work in public. This is a problem in Japan where it is a custom for section chiefs, foremen, and others to relax after work over drinks and dinner with their coworkers. Tongues oiled by beer, sake, and whiskey do tend to wag, and the friendships that develop from these sessions, I believe, are valuable. But obviously the information that might slip out to be heard by an eavesdropper could be quite damaging.

At Sony we are protected from this, to a great extent, by our own company-run, nonprofit bar called the Sony Club, although it was not established to prevent information leaks. I started it when I realized managers were spending too much money to entertain their subordinates. (We encourage this kind of entertainment because it fosters the family spirit.) The Sony Club is in an unmarked building near our headquarters, and only Sony people are allowed in, so that at any time everybody in the place, every bartender, cook, waitress, and service person, is a Sony employee. Nobody else, no matter how important, is ever admitted. Executives from section chief up get a credit card for the club, and their bar bills can be automatically deducted from their paychecks. Besides all of its obvious advantages for economy and reinforcement of our feeling of solidarity in the company, we also have a barrier to the leakage of company secrets.

I learned very early in the United States never to listen to ideas from outsiders. Some companies, eager for a competitive edge, might grasp at an outside idea, but I always felt it was a mistake that could create severe legal problems. If you listen to some idea peddler and then say, "I know that. I've been doing it that way for a long time," you still might be in difficulty if you do anything remotely like his suggestion. Edward Rosiny, my first legal teacher in the U.S., made me promise never to listen to outside ideas. The only way to do this, he insisted, was to look at ideas from patents. If a patent had been granted, we could ask to see the data describing it in detail, since it would be a protected matter on public record. Then we could evaluate the idea and decide whether we would like to license it.

Rosiny told me of one New York company that was hit by a lawsuit when a man told the president of the company he had a surefire way for the company to double its business. He was dismissed as a crank, but some months later the company decided to raise its prices all across the product line drastically. The crank filed suit. This was his idea, he said. His surefire plan was to double the business by doubling prices. He lost the suit, of course, but it took time and money to deal with it. I did not want to be involved in such nuisance suits.

III

It worries me that the idea of business competition seems to have been lost in many places in the non-Communist world. In Europe, and especially in France, there are people in power who believe that one company making a product under state ownership is sufficient to supply them with what they need. The European system still generally emphasizes decreasing competition to increase profits. They like to have a monopoly with a small number in control. It does not work to the advantage of the consumer or the employee.

In the United States they cheer people who take risks— venture capital is available in America as nowhere else on earth. Venture capital is still not freely available in Japan, probably because our big companies are horizontal in structure and have the resources to fund their own new projects. This puts the small entrepreneur at a disadvantage, but he, just as we at

Tokyo Tsushin Kogyo did back in the forties, must find a market niche and go after it with new ideas. Some are doing this today, though now it is more difficult in a highly technical business like ours than it was forty years ago because the amount of investment needed is very large. Banks are still reluctant to lend money to unknowns, although venture capital is becoming more available. We were fortunate that we could start with so little money, and we were lucky to have had such a distinguished group of advisers to give us credibility with potential investors. Our true capital was our knowledge and our ingenuity and our passion, and I think those qualities are still salable today.

It is a pleasant surprise that China has begun to understand the free market system in agriculture and some services and is allowing some free market competition. The Soviet Union, too, has flirted, off and on, with the idea of introducing some capitalist incentives into their system, but the Chinese under Deng Xiaoping are very serious about it.

In 1979 I flew to Beijing in our Falcon jet to make a call on Chinese government leaders. My friend Henry Kissinger helped to arrange for me to meet with Deng. My trip was originally one of those "paying respects" visits, and the planned meeting with Deng was not made public. China has been a customer of our products for quite a while and for several years the giant billboard at the corner of Wangfujing Street and Chang An Boulevard in downtown Beijing, adjacent to the Beijing Hotel, was devoted to advertising our products. Besides visiting with officials, I was also going to take a look at the state of Chinese modernization, and particularly at their electronics industry. I went to Shanghai, where I had a chance to visit some factories and talk to a lot of people, and then did the same in Beijing. My hosts were surprised to get the news that the top man wanted to see me.

I spent an hour with Deng Xiaoping, sitting in big overstuffed armchairs in a huge room with high ceilings and Chinese murals in the Great Hall of the People. He was full of questions about how my company had grown so fast in such a short time, and he wanted to hear some of my opinions and suggestions on China's modernization, which was just getting under way then. The Chinese were beginning to look to Japan for technological help. I told him frankly that there was a lot of inefficiency in the then-new modernization projects. "You are wasting a lot of valuable time and money," I told him, "which I know you can't afford." For an hour, with two interpreters, we discussed the situation, although he made me do most of the talking. He didn't show very much emotion, but during our discussion he ordered his top officials in the electronics division to meet with me later to get more details.

At the end of the seventies, the Chinese push to modernize was done with a great amount of enthusiasm. Their bureaucrats and experts traveled to Japan, the United States, and Europe and began buying up factories and technologies that could only be utilized by people with skills that were in very short supply in China. They signed contracts for construction of facilities they could not even supply with enough electric power. Worse, everywhere they went they insisted upon seeing the most modern, automated equipment, ignoring the fact that their own first need was to give employment to their growing population and that therefore they should be concerned about building labor-intensive industries. Visiting Chinese always wanted to see Japan's most automated factories, its latest computerized systems. They tried to buy many things that were wisely denied them because they could not have handled them in that stage of their development. Soon some of the companies that had supplied equipment and plants to the Chinese were being criticized for "overselling." It was not their fault; the Chinese insisted that they knew what they wanted. Sometimes two competing ministries or divisions bought duplicate equipment, not realizing what they were doing.

I was frank with Deng. I told him I had visited a factory in Shanghai and found a very early model automated soldering machine not being used because the quality of the solder was so poor that the parts it soldered were not usable. I found people sitting around smoking and talking at assembly lines, unable to work because the right parts were not being delivered to them in time. In their rush to modernize, the engineers and managers indulged their personal interests, so they would buy a machine, or even a whole plant, without attempting to coordinate the activities of the whole industry toward any kind of goal.

In one Shanghai plant, I was surprised to see a brand-new automated machine removing the insulation from the ends of wires to be soldered into electrical circuits. Wire-stripping like this is a simple operation that can easily, and economically, be done by hand. The machine was so fast that if it ran for only one shift it could yield enough wire to last the factory for a whole month, hardly the kind of machine that will help solve the unemployment problems of China. There was no engineering management. In their rush to "modernize," they were buying ready-to-operate plants outright from Japan to make color television tubes, integrated circuits, and other parts. But there was no overall plan for how all these plants and their equipment would coordinate. And in designing products they weren't concerned enough with local conditions and what the people needed, and could use, all crucial design criteria.

And then the government announced a new law, permitting joint ventures between foreign companies and Chinese government-owned companies. Under the joint venture law they said they were ready to admit private ownership, remittance of a "reasonable" amount of profit abroad, some freedom of foreign ownership, and foreign top management. But a basic problem even today is that the Chinese are not comfortable with the way business in general works in free nations. For example, on wages, they unilaterally decided that a person who worked in a joint venture company would be paid more than a Chinese who works in an ordinary state-run plant. The reason, I was told, was because a worker in a joint venture factory would be required to work much harder than the workers in ordinary Chinese government-run enterprises, which are well known for their inefficiency. I told them this pay differential idea was a mistake, that joint ventures should begin with wage levels that are equal to those of the government-run businesses, and any increase should be granted only after there was some definite improvement in efficiency and productivity.

They also hoped to earn foreign currency by exporting the products made for the home market in the new plants. It seemed such an elementary mistake from our point of view that it would not need commenting on, except that they seemed to be thinking about it seriously. I pointed out that if they wanted to make consumer goods for the Chinese public, such as televisions and radios and home appliances, those goods must be simple, utilitarian, and economical. They would have to be adjusted to suit local conditions, like power supply, and would have to be very sturdy to withstand the heat and humidity of some regions of their enormous country and the dryness and cold of others. The goods would also have to be easy to repair, I said, because if they could distribute goods widely, they would still have a tough time building a service network over such an enormous portion of the earth. This means that the goods would have to be designed for durability and would have to leave the factory perfectly produced and tested for reliability. Quality control would be essential, if they really cared about serving their people. But reliability and durability have always been a problem in China, where the stories of breakdown are topics of general conversation.

They should understand, I told them, winding up, that such sturdy, simple goods would never be competitive in sophisticated free-world markets, where consumers looked for other features. "If you want to earn foreign currency in the electronics industry," I told them, "there is only one way to do this. You have to do assembly work for foreign companies on a complete knockdown basis, merely adding your inexpensive labor at first. It would be impossible to make goods for the domestic market and goods for export at the same plant."

I admire Chinese courage and determination. They have learned a lot about modern industry in a short time, but they have a long way to go. Japanese and European products are now competing on the local markets in China, in limited areas. But the contrast in quality and design between anything produced locally and the foreign goods is still striking, although Chinese goods have improved and I am confident that the improvement will continue. The joint ventures at work now making foreign-designed products seem to be progressing. Many Japanese and European companies are happy with the work they are having done there in the textile trade, such as Hanae Mori, Yves St. Laurent, and Pierre Cardin. By 1985 Chinese textile exports had reached four billion dollars.

But the factor that has energized Japan to produce ever-new and better products, as it energizes large segments of the American industrial and commercial establishment, competition in the local marketplace, is still missing. And without that spur, progress is hard to achieve. In the eighties the liberalization in the service trades—it became legal to open a bicycle repair shop or a tearoom, for example—began to give some sense of competitive improvement to the people. Control of many government enterprises was taken from the iron hand of the Communist party leader and put back into the hands of professional managers who, at least, knew something about the business in which they were engaged. And a return to competitiveness may be on the way. In some places, ironically, competition has arisen with the aid of the Japanese. A munitions factory in Chongqing is assembling Yamaha motorcycles and motorscooters, and a competitor is producing Honda products, carrying the long-standing domestic battle to yet another country.

Since 1979, the Chinese government has achieved remarkable success in increasing productivity in the agricultural area with the introduction of a market mechanism, socialist style. The rural development policy also resulted in a reasonably smooth shift of the labor force into labor-intensive light industries. In the modernization process of big state-owned industries, however, the outcome has been different and this sector still lags.

My China experience wasn't my first look at a Communist industrial establishment. My wife and I had been invited to the Soviet Union five years earlier. Yoshiko and I were advised before we left for Moscow to take bottled water and towels and toilet paper because conditions were said to be primitive in the Soviet Union. But it was a needless precaution. We received nothing but the red carpet treatment from the minute we arrived. At the airport, a big black Chaika limousine drove right up to the plane to get us. We didn't even have to bother with the usual immigration and customs formalities. There was a female interpreter for Yoshiko and a male interpreter for me, in addition to our guide and hosts. They tried to be very accommodating and were with us every minute, it seemed.

At one point Yoshiko said, "I would like to eat some piroshki." The interpreters looked at each other, puzzled. "Piroshki," said her interpreter, patiently, "is what the laborers eat—it is not something that you should eat." But Yoshiko insisted and after much discussion between the interpreters and many phone calls, we were finally taken to a place where laborers were standing around eating piroshki. We joined them and enjoyed those delicious little pastries filled with meat and vegetables.

Our host was Jerman Gvishiani, who was then deputy chairman of the Council of Ministers for Science and Technology, and is now deputy chairman of the State Planning Committee. He is a friendly, sophisticated man who speaks perfect English. I had met him in San Francisco at a party given by Steve Bechtel, Sr., right after a meeting sponsored by the Conference Board and Stanford Research Institute. I was amazed to see this Russian playing marvelous jazz piano and circulating with such ease and suavity in a capitalist environment.

In the U.S.S.R. he was just as expansive. He insisted we try dishes from his home country, hearty peasant food. He took us to see factories in the suburbs of Moscow and Leningrad, and I watched them making radios and television picture tubes and assembling television sets. I saw everything there was to see, but I was not impressed. The Soviets were then eight to ten years behind Japan and the West in their consumer electronics technology. They worked with crude tools and awkward and inefficient production technology. It was obvious to me that the lack of quality and reliability was directly attributable to the indifferent, plodding attitude of the workers and a management that had not figured out how to motivate the engineers and the production workers. Even the Soviet citizens make ironic jokes about how badly designed and poorly made things are, but I believe quality has improved since my visit.

At the end of the trip, my host brought me to his office, where he was joined by an official from the Ministry of Communications and a group of bureaucrats. Gvishiani smiled and said to me, "Now, Mr. Morita, you have seen our factories and you understand our ability. We don't have inflation or wage increases in our country. We have a very stable labor force. We offer to share this with your country in the form of subcontracts."

He seemed very proud of what he had shown me, and perhaps for someone who had watched the Soviet people struggle along through the years, the progress seemed phenomenal. But I was not encouraged by what I had seen.

I looked around the room at the faces waiting for me to say something. I asked Gvishiani if I could really say what was on my mind. He said that I should, by all means. And so I did.

"I am going to tell you the truth," I said. "In Japan we used our top talent and our best brains and spent years seeking

ways to increase the efficiency and the productivity of even
such a simple thing as a screwdriver. We have racked our brains
and made detailed studies and experiments to decide just what
is the exact and precise temperature for a soldering iron in
each particular application. You do not make any such effort
here; there appears to be no need to do it, because nobody
seems to care.

"Frankly, Mr. Gvishiani, I am very sorry to criticize anything after you have been such a fine host and shown me all
around, but I must tell you that I could not bear to see Sony
products being produced under such conditions as you have
here. I cannot offer you our product technology yet."

He took it quite calmly and motioned to one of his assistants who proudly handed him a small, crude, boxy Soviet-
made black and white transistorized television receiver.

"Mr. Morita," he said, "this is a television set we are now
planning to sell in Europe. What do you think of it, please?"
Again I had to ask him, "May I really say what I think?" He
nodded.

I took a deep breath. "Mr. Gvishiani, there is wonderful
artistic talent in the Soviet Union," I began. "Your musicians,
your dancers, your artistic heritage are grand and your performers are world-renowned. You are fortunate that you have
both technology and art in your country.

"But why don't I see both exhibited in this television set?
Since you have art and technology in the Soviet Union, why
do you not combine them to come up with wonderful things?
Frankly, gentlemen, knowing what we know of the market and
consumer preferences, we would not consider such an ugly
television to be merchandisable."

There was a moment of stunned silence and then Gvishiani
turned to the communications ministry official: "Will you please
respond to Mr. Morita's comments?"

With all seriousness, the official said, "We understand what
you are saying, Mr. Morita. But art is not under our jurisdiction!"

It was an incredible answer. I started to feel bad and I
said, "Oh, I understand that. I have said all that I wanted to
say. If you give me one of these televisions, I will bring it back
to Tokyo with me and let my engineers give you our recommendations as to how it could be improved." I did, and our

engineers wrote a long report back suggesting some redesign of circuitry and other ways to improve the set. But no Sony technology.

Although the idea of true competition for the consumer's benefit has not made much headway in the Soviet Union, the experiment in China may stimulate it. But right now the Russians and the Americans have another kind of competition, and this military competition is a major drain on both economies, despite the spinoff effect of defense technology. In the Soviet Union technology seems centered on such things as the space program and the defense program, certainly not on consumer goods. Design and even technological quality lags where the public is concerned.

We do a lot of business with the Soviet Union in broadcasting station equipment. Sony is the largest maker of this kind of equipment in the world. Of course, we sell only with the approval of the Coordinating Committee for Exports to Communist Areas. Similarly, we also do a great deal of business with China in broadcast equipment. We are often asked for technology through licensing agreements by both countries, particularly for Trinitron television tube technology. But we still do not produce anything or allow anything to be produced in the Soviet Union or China under our name. A long time ago Fiat sold a factory and car-making technology to the Soviet Union, and as a result many cars turned up all over Europe that looked just like Fiats but were really only the inferior Soviet version. Fiat's reputation suffered because of this, and we don't want the same thing to happen to us.

I spoke to Gvishiani in Salzburg a couple of years later during the music festival. "You must come visit us again," he said to me. But I have not had another opportunity.

IV

Having said so much about how competition has worked to make our industry great, I must admit there is another side of the picture, which is that excessive competition is at work in our society today. It exists in education and in social life, and it has actually destroyed many young lives. The competition for a place in school is intense. And because entrance to the "best" schools is based completely on merit, the only way to get in is through competitive examination. This has led to the making of Japan's famous "education mothers," who force their children into a very difficult and cheerless life of drill and study. Some years ago, when we moved into a new house in the Aoyama district of Tokyo, I discovered there was a prep school for kindergarten in the neighborhood.

The University of Tokyo is perhaps the most famous institution of higher learning in Japan, and it can be proud of its many thousands of brilliant graduates, who have been prime ministers and top bureaucrats and diplomats and leading businessmen. But a former president of the university said to me one day, "The freshmen arrive here after a lifetime of cramming and they are completely exhausted." It is a sad joke in Japan that for many students, almost no learning takes place at university. Once the students have entered the university they have worked so hard to attain, they assume they have achieved their goal in life. They are so tired out that they have no will left or feel no need to study further. Almost no one ever fails once he has made the grade into a university. In Japan university is very difficult to get into and easy to pass out of as a graduate; in the United States and Britain it is the opposite: easier to get into but more difficult to graduate from.

The spirit of competition in Japan even pervades the government ministries. To outsiders it may appear that the Japanese government is one smooth-functioning organization. It is composed of many very well-trained, intelligent graduates of all the elite universities, and Japan may have the most highly trained and competent bureaucracy in the world today. Those bureaucratic experts are often jealous of their territorial authority, and often there are battles between bureaus or sections within the ministries and between the ministries.

Our newspaper competition and our television competition have caused severe problems. The quality of television programming has deteriorated to low levels because of the competition to air the most popular shows. In the newspaper field, cool heads have solved one problem but caused others. Because we have almost total literacy and because our country is all in one time zone, we are able to have national newspapers, and so the competition for news is very keen. The major newspapers have airplanes and helicopters, and some even have photographic darkrooms aboard so that the photographers can process their film while the plane is on the way back to Tokyo from a faraway assignment. Tokyo's *Asahi Shimbun* used our filmless Mavica camera at the 1984 Los Angeles Olympics and transmitted the pictures from each event over a phone line from a Sony cellular telephone installed in a car the *Asahi* team used to visit all the major venues. *Asahi* beat every other paper with these instant, digitalized pictures. This was an experiment that worked much to our satisfaction. I didn't go to the Olympics, but I enjoyed the pictures.

The eagerness for news and the largenumbers of reporters assigned to cover any event, however, cause big problems for everybody. Reporters and TV cameramen often camp overnight outside the homes of persons in the news and sometimes harass people who come and go. Sometimes the sheer numbers are staggering. At all the government ministries and major agencies, reporters who normally cover the activities and the persons in those ministries have established clubs that set the rules of coverage and conduct. This tends to stifle "enterprising" reporting, but if hundreds of reporters all zero in on one cabinet minister or one set of bureaucrats to get a story, nobody would ever get a night's sleep.

Despite some of its darker aspects, competition, in my opinion, is the key to the development of industry and its technology, and I think that is true in the United States as well as in Japan. Any interference with free and open competition should be minimum. In that respect, the Reagan administration's new approach to the antitrust laws has been most welcome in bringing back a reasonable approach to the problems that is more in line with the realities of the economy. We in Japan must also contribute our effort to lift some unnecessary restrictions and limitations on the free functioning of the marketplace. Obsolete and meaningless business customs and practices must be done away with. I have always challenged conventionalism and I will continue to do so.

But I would like to give one word of caution to my American friends. American diplomacy was once described by George Kennan as "legalistic and moralistic." I think it is still true today. Each country has a different historical and cultural background, just as individuals do, and to assume that one can apply American ideas and American legal doctrine everywhere in the world, as some Americans seem to think, would be wrong.

What I am getting at is that often the competition we face for markets leads to misunderstanding. That is why I have always advocated the idea of more personal contacts among top business executives from around the world. Lawyers often advise us not to get together, fearing that the possibility of such a meeting might be used to incriminate us in an antitrust case. I do appreciate their advice, but there is nothing in antitrust law that says business executives cannot and should not get together and know each other a bit better. With appropriate safeguards provided, sponsorship by governments, and public availability of the minutes, such meetings would create the basis of better understanding and should be encouraged. An outstanding example is the ongoing series of meetings between British and Japanese electronics industry associations, now in its nineteenth year. Certainly in the meetings of the so-called Wiseman's Group, and later the Japan–U.S. Businessmen's Conference, and in the meetings of the U.S.–Japan Advisory Commission in 1984, important steps were made toward developing mutual understanding.

But more effort is needed to find broader understanding. I was interested to see the outraged American reaction when the fourth year of so-called "voluntary" automobile restraints was announced in 1985. After Japanese makers for three years held down shipments of cars to the U.S., officials of the administration in Washington, including the U.S. trade representative, said that a fourth year of restraints would not be necessary, because the American industry had got its "breathing space." It had retooled and its cars were now competitive.

The sizes of the bonuses to American auto executives for 1984 were so big that there were editorials in the papers calling them nothing short of scandalous. But General Motors and Ford were asking for huge increases in the number of Japanese cars they could sell under their brand names in the United States. The smaller Japanese companies that had very low quotas under the old restraints were eager to see the restraints end so they could begin to ship more cars to their customers in the U.S. Wise people in MITI saw that if there were no restraints at all, everybody would begin shipping as many cars as possible, and the result could be chaos and anger in the United States if the exports became torrential. So the Japanese government decided to have another year of quota restraint, and raised the numbers by about 24 percent, a considerable increase, but knowing the competitive nature of our own people, probably lower than the number they would have shipped if they were not under any restraint at all. This increase gave bigger quotas to small companies whose cars were being sold by American companies as what are called "captive imports" (the Mitsubishi cars made for Chrysler, the Mazdas made for Ford, the Isuzus made for GM).

The announcement caused a great commotion and outrage in Detroit and the industrial Midwest. Some U.S. newspapers ran editorials saying the Japanese should continue to abide by the old restraint quotas, even if there were no formal curbs in effect. Congressmen were screaming. They didn't understand the Japanese competitive mentality. And then to our surprise, some American automobile makers began to complain—not because Japan was shipping too many cars, but because they were not getting enough of an increase in the number of the cars they import! The shipments under the increased restraint quotas for Japanese cars gave Chrysler a 70-percent increase in the number of Mitsubishi-built cars they could import over the previous year's quota, and GM got a 211.8-percent increase in Suzuki cars and a 140-percent increase in Isuzu vehicles. Both these two companies and Ford increased their capacity to supply Japanese cars to their American customers. It became Japan's turn to wonder what was going on. Why are congressmen and others complaining about Japanese competition when American automobile companies themselves are increasing their purchases and even complaining that they cannot get enough cars?

Competing in a market we understand, such as our own, Japanese companies sometimes misbehave with their cutthroat tactics. Companies will go after an increase in share of market by cutting prices to the bone, sometimes to the point where there is no chance of anybody making a profit on the product. The winner for market share becomes the one who can afford to lose money in the market the longest. Such practices have caused misunderstanding and hard feelings in business circles in some countries, particularly in Southeast Asia, where Japanese companies have brought their competitive tactics with them in disregard of the system of their host country. But in the case of automobiles, American companies are participating in Japanese practices, and if they do not know the market and the consumers best, I don't know who does.

TECHNOLOGY
Survival Exercise

I

We Japanese are obsessed with survival. Every day, literally, the earth beneath our feet trembles. We live our daily lives on these volcanic islands with the constant threat not only of a major earthquake, but also of typhoons, tidal waves, savage snowstorms, spring deluges. Our islands provide us with almost no raw materials except water, and less than a quarter of our land is livable or arable. Therefore, what we have is precious to us. And that is why we learned to respect nature, to conserve, to miniaturize, and to look toward technology as a means of helping us survive. We Japanese do not think of ourselves as deeply religious people, although we are; we tend to believe that God resides in everything. We are Buddhists, Confucianists, Shintoists, and Christians, but we are also very pragmatic. We often joke that most Japanese are born Shinto, live a Confucian life, get married Christian-style, and have a

Buddhist funeral. We have our rites and customs and festivals steeped in centuries of religious tradition, but we are not bound by taboos and feel free to try everything and seek the best and most practical ways of doing things.

One of the most significant value concepts that we have cherished from ancient times is a term that does not bear simple literal translation, *mottainai*, which can be pronounced "moat-tie-nigh." It is a key concept, one that may help explain a great deal about Japan, the Japanese people, and our industry. It is an expression that suggests that everything in the world is a gift from the Creator, and that we should be grateful for it and never waste anything. Literally, *mottainai* means "irreverent," "impious," but more deeply it carries the connotation of a sacrilege against heaven. We Japanese feel that all things are provided as a sacred trust and actually are only loaned to us to make the best use of. To waste something is considered a kind of sin. We even use the expression *mottainai* to refer to the profligate waste of something simple, even water or paper. It is no wonder that we have developed this concept that goes beyond mere frugality or conservation; it is a religious concept. I know that the concept appears to a degree in the West and elsewhere in the East, but in Japan it carries special meaning. Struggling for survival under the constant threat of harsh times and natural calamity, attempting to produce goods with a minimum of raw materials, both became a way of life for the Japanese, and so the wasting of anything was considered shameful, virtually a crime.

In the old days when Japan was completely isolated, we had to handle any calamity by means of our own resources. We had food shortages and earthquakes, and fires burned the wooden houses of our cities many times, forcing people to start rebuilding their lives from scratch. We became skilled at crisis management. Some people who were in Japan just after the war marveled at how the Japanese went about rebuilding the cities that in 1945 were reduced to huge fields of rubble by the bombings. More than one person has written that we seemed to go about it as though another natural disaster had struck, as it had on September 1, 1923, when the great Kanto earthquake jolted Tokyo ferociously, toppled its tall buildings, and set fire to hundreds of thousands of homes. The incendiary and high-explosive bombings of World War II did similar damage.

I remember walking from our temporary factory in the Shirokiya department store to Tokyo Station every evening after work in 1946, a walk of about a mile, and no buildings were standing, nothing but a few chimneys and many steel safes of the shops and factories that once filled the area. For a mile in any direction, you could see only waste. Thousands of B-29 Superfortresses had dropped incendiaries on the major cities, going after the concentration of industry there—a planning mistake of the Japanese. Almost half of our aircraft engines were produced in one city. All of the airplanes were assembled in two cities, and 90 percent of the electron tubes in three cities.

But in both eras, after natural and manmade disaster, the city was rebuilt with a speed that amazed even some Japanese. Accustomed to dealing with privation and natural calamity, some families after the war managed to move into the bomb shelters of their burned-out homes, while others built shacks using corrugated iron, cardboard, and wood scraps for shelter. They accepted their misfortune as something that had to be endured but no longer than was absolutely necessary, and they immediately went to work rebuilding, ingeniously fashioning cooking stoves from rubble and odd bits of shattered metal, patching together remnants of usable material from among the charred ruins. In rebuilding the city, new ways were sought and new technologies employed in an attempt to learn how better to survive the next calamity, whatever and whenever that might be.

The Imperial Hotel, designed by the great American architect Frank Lloyd Wright, withstood the shock of the 1923 earthquake (in fact, it was formally opened only hours before the quake), and his techniques were studied and emulated. Advanced construction technology was the result, and that technology is being improved constantly in earthquake laboratories at Tsukuba University and elsewhere in Japan today. In these labs earthquakes are simulated and are used in tests of building foundations and construction methods. With the aid of computers, simulations are possible that were never available before and, as a result, Japanese building technology is probably the best in the world. It has to be, because it is so much a matter of survival.

We are also great savers, and not just savers of money, although we are pretty good at that, too. When I first went to the United States I was astonished to see Americans throwing away their newspapers. I could hardly believe that after a quick glance at the headlines over breakfast they would just throw the paper aside or into the garbage. Some people saved them until the bundle got big and then carried the bundle to the trash heap. They would save the day's TV program schedule page and throw out the rest. I was also astounded at the sheer size of the newspapers; in Japan the newspapers are much thinner. I had never seen anything like the Sunday edition of *The New York Times*, which sometimes weighs several pounds. After a while in America it seemed almost natural to throw papers away.

While I was in New York, I met a Japanese who had been in the States for quite a while and he confided to me that he was embarrassed about a problem that he could not solve and with which he thought I could help him. Of course I said I would be glad to help him. "What is your problem?" I asked. But he wouldn't tell me.

"You must come to my room," he said. So I went to his room and discovered the problem immediately. The tiny place was almost completely filled with newspapers—stacked up against the walls, under the bed, filling the closets. He couldn't bring himself to throw them away and he didn't know what to do with them. I arranged to have them hauled away, to his great relief, and I explained that *mottainai* was not a concept ingrained as widely in American society as in Japan.

The literacy rate being what it is, Japanese magazines, books, and newspapers proliferate. Our use of paper extends from religious objects, art, and books to coverings for lamps and windows, to wrapping and packaging and decoration of many kinds, and all of this makes Japan the second biggest producer of paper in the world, after the United States, turning out over one hundred and ninety million tons a year. Yet Japan has the highest recycling rate in the world—in 1984 we collected 50 percent for recycling. (In the U.S. the figure is 27 percent; in France, 34 percent; in West Germany, 38 percent; in Holland, 46 percent; and in the U.K., 28 percent.) One old-fashioned but effective method we use is to have the paper dealer go through the neighborhoods periodically with a loudspeaker on his truck or cart collecting old newspapers and magazines and giving toilet paper in exchange. That might look a little odd on the streets of New York, but it would probably be a wise thing to do. We also recycle large amounts of aluminum, steel, glass, zinc, copper, lead. People in Japan very loyally separate their garbage to help make recycling work.

Because we have always had to practice conservation for survival, we Japanese feel it makes more sense and is more economical to heat a body with a foot-warming brazier or electric heater than to use all the energy it takes to heat an entire room (or house) in order to make one or two persons comfortable. Even the hot Japanese bath serves the whole family (the washing is actually done outside the bath), bringing body temperatures up in the winter to easily survive dinner in a drafty Japanese-style house before getting into warm bedding for the night. In America huge houses are heated in the winter and cooled in the summer for the convenience of a few people, and to the older generation of Japanese like me this seems like a waste, but we are doing it in Japan now, too. Sometimes we must take our coats off in the winter because it is so hot in many offices and we must put them on in the summer because of the air-conditioning. After the second oil embargo, Japanese prime minister Masayoshi Ohira tried to get Japanese businessmen and bureaucrats to wear a kind of modified summer safari jacket to work instead of a shirt and tie and jacket, so that building temperatures would not have to be brought down too far, and he even tried it himself for a while. He even posed for the press in what he called his "energy-saving suit," but the Japanese have too much of a sense of formality to be quite so casual and it never caught on. But office building temperatures were adjusted to save energy, and people just sweated more. At Sony we make it a point never to overheat or overcool any of our buildings, and we have a sign at our main office explaining our policy to visitors.

Up until the first oil embargo, our economic growth seemed to many Japanese to be based on the assumption that oil resources were unlimited, that all we had to do was go out and find them, and that with these resources we could expand our industries indefinitely. We learned once again the meaning of *mottainai* when the oil crisis came. But we also learned how to apply the principles that underlie the expression, and today with a much-expanded economy we use less crude oil, coal, and natural gas than we did in 1973 because we have learned how to be efficient.

The ability of Japanese to work together came to Japan's aid at the time of the oil crises. Japan was then and is now almost 100 percent dependent on others for oil. And so this oil became precious to us and ways to conserve it were foremost in our minds. All Japanese industry was charged with the responsibility of conserving, or of devising ways to use less energy in our factories, and was challenged to make products that would use less energy. Actually this was right down our alley. Ibuka had been a fanatic about low power consumption; it is one of the main things that led him to want to use the transistor.

We looked at all of our factory operations and at our products and made design changes where we could save even small amounts of energy. Within a few months of the embargo, we had modified our Trinitron picture tube design from indirect to direct heating of the cathode element to cut consumption by 12 percent. We also restudied all forms of power consumption at Sony, in our factories and offices as well as in the products. I had made the same kind of energy analysis when my wife and I were building our new home in the Aobadai district of Tokyo, in 1969. I wanted a heated swimming pool in the basement, but there were two problems: first, humidity would rise to the upper floors, and second, the heat loss from the pool would be great and wasteful. Ninety percent of the heat loss would be due to evaporation, I calculated. I solved both problems by devising a plastic foam barrier to cover the entire surface of the pool, sealing in moisture and heat—and I patented the idea in the United States and Japan.

In 1973 every maker of home appliances went to work to cut power consumption, and in fact they competed with each other to see who could produce products using the least power; low power consumption became a major selling point and a new point of competition. At the time, I was disappointed to see how little was done in redesign of products in other countries, but I supposed in countries, that had their own oil, like the U.S. and Britain, such a crisis did not have the heavy impact on every single citizen that it did in Japan. We realized that if we were cut off, we were finished. Some of the most pessimistic people were warning that Japan would have to be prepared to go back to its agrarian roots if worse came to worst. Realistically, we knew that there would be oil, at a price, but we knew that changes had to be made. We could no longer be extravagant, and our dreams of continued economic growth might be cut short. In fact, the first oil embargo dropped our real gross national product growth from 8.8 percent in 1973—the highest of the industrialized countries—to −1 percent in 1974, the biggest growth loss among those countries that year.

Because of the crisis, we became efficient. Using the latest technologies, we designed lighting that consumed less power and more efficient generators. Soon people who visited the Ginza and saw the blazing lights there and other places around the country could hardly believe that we were burning less energy. Factories learned to recycle waste heat and gases and how to make products with less energy. Automobile fuel efficiency was greatly increased by new technology. And soon we began to realize that we could get more efficiency out of a barrel of crude oil than almost anybody else.

One interesting aspect of the oil situation is that because our country is small, we use less oil for transportation than for industrial purposes, whereas in the United States the situation is reversed. There, more than half of every barrel of crude oil is used for transportation. For a time, we envied the British for having their own North Sea oil, but as oil prices plunged and a glut hit the world in the eighties, Britain's expensive North Sea oil became a burden on the country. We are still 99.7 percent dependent on imports for oil, 100 percent dependent for aluminum, iron ore, and nickel, over 95 percent dependent for copper, and over 92 percent dependent for natural gas. We cannot get away from our worry about being cut off, and we attempt to keep at least a 100-day supply of oil in storage tanks and parked supertankers, just in case something should happen. This is prudent, of course, but it is also, I believe, a legacy of our recent agrarian past and sense of vulnerability.

When you are told from childhood on that the metal object you hold in your hands comes from iron ore mined in countries far away, which is transported to Japan at great expense and is produced in furnaces that use gas and coal from other far-away places, such objects seem very valuable. In America it may be practical to make a production run of, say, automobile axles, check them later and discard the ones that do not pass inspection. In Japan simple economics do not allow us to do this. Our general philosophy throughout industry in Japan is that everybody is an inspector and that the goods being made must be made correctly at every single stage of the operation.

This is natural to us. It is a cautious and conservative philosophy, but it has worked well for us. In America a certain number of rejects is expected, but we have always tried to avoid a single reject. You can imagine how concerned we were, back in the 1950s, when we had so few resources, when the number of usable pieces in the total production of our first transistors was only 5 percent. The major mission of everybody involved, day and night, was to get that yield up over 90 percent, which we did in a matter of months. I discovered very early that for Sony the cost of after-service overseas was so expensive that quality assurance at every stage of manufacture was cheaper in the long run.

I also learned that the attitude in America is much more easygoing as far as raw materials are concerned than in Japan. America has so much of everything—oil, coal, copper, gold, uranium, timber—that even today Americans do not seem to take conservation seriously. I am reminded of the American expression, "There's plenty more where that came from." We have no such expression.

Our people also seem naturally more concerned about precision. It may have something to do with the meticulousness with which we must learn to write the complicated characters of our language. But for whatever reason, when we tell one of our Japanese employees that the measurement of a certain part must be within a tolerance of plus or minus five, for example, he will automatically strive to get that part as close to zero tolerance as possible. When we started our plant in the United States, we found that workers would follow instructions perfectly. But if we said make it between plus or minus five, we would get it somewhere near plus or minus five all right, but rarely as close to zero as the Japanese workers did. We discussed what to do about this, and in no time had the answer. For the U.S. specifications, we just set the tolerance at plus or minus two, and in that range the American workers consistently gave us what we needed. If we have the need and demand zero tolerance from the American workers, we can get it if we specify it.

I do not for a moment discredit the foreign worker. Sometimes you have to use a different approach where people are accustomed to different approaches. I am sure American executives who have dealt with Japanese workers in Japan have had equally interesting experiences. When we started assembly of Trinitron sets in San Diego, we were working with employees who were inexperienced, and we were, of course, concerned with quality. We had to impress on these new workers just what we expected of them and also why. We discussed it with our operating executives there, Mike Morimoto, Junichi Kodera, and Ron Dishno, who were going to be responsible for the assembly operation. The answer was simple: show each employee what would happen to the set if his or her operation wasn't done properly. Sets were made with a certain poorly wired joint, for example, and the employees dealing with that part of the assembly could see what was wrong with the picture and trace it back to the source, a poor solder joint or connector, or whatever. Very soon we were getting the same quality in the U.S. that we were getting in Japan. For a time after we opened our plant at Bridgend in Wales, we were shipping the locally made parts back to Japan for inspection and then returning them to the British plant for assembly, until we were certain that all the parts were up to standard.

We Japanese have always been eager to develop our own technology, absorb aspects of technology from abroad, and blend them to make suitable objects or systems. We still use Chinese characters in our language, together with a purely Japanese syllabary, which overlays the rather simple Chinese grammar with our own very complex one. The second of our syllabaries is designed to pronounce foreign words phonetically. Any new foreign word can be brought into the language this way, with our own way of pronouncing it, of course, but without having to create a string of Chinese characters to approximate the sound. Written Japanese is also a simple language to speed-read because to get a quick sense of what a piece of writing is about, all that is needed is a quick scan of the Chinese characters. That is technology, too.

It was an accident that several Portuguese were aboard a Chinese trading ship (or maybe a pirate ship—we are not sure) that stopped in 1543 at the tiny Japanese island of Tanegashima, off the southern coast of Kyushu, for supplies. The Portuguese had two matchlock guns with them and they went hunting on the island while the ship was being provisioned. When Tokitaka, the lord of the lonely island, saw these new weapons, he insisted on learning more about them. The Portuguese apparently agreed to teach him how to shoot, and by the time they were ready to leave, Tokitaka decided he had to have both guns, for which he paid the Portuguese a very high price. He ordered his head swordsmith to make duplicates, and so firearms were introduced into Japan. It is said that within a few years the Japanese version of the Portuguese weapon, now called a Tanegashima in Japan, was better than the original, something for which I cannot vouch.

Japan had a long fascination with guns that ended tragically in 1945, and today Japan is the least-armed of the world's industrialized nations. Lord Tokitaka's island, perched close to our southernmost main island in the Pacific Ocean, turned out to be a geographically logical position for the establishment of the National Space Development Agency's launching site, where its newest rockets launch communications and weather satellites. It is an irony of history that Tanegashima has pioneered leading-edge technology for Japan twice. The technology being explored from the island today puts tools for survival into our hands, such as the ability to communicate with the rest of the world through geostationary satellites, and meteorological satellites that give crucial weather data and solar observations that we share with other countries in the Western Pacific.

In the sixteenth century, Japanese soldiers led by Toyotomi Hideyoshi invaded Korea, and among the people brought back to Japan were Korean potters and other craftsmen who had perfected different kinds of ceramics and metalwork using techniques not then used in Japan, which they taught Japanese craftsmen. The Japanese thirst for technology has, then, always been great. I have already mentioned the period of the Meiji restoration, when we sought everything we could find by way of new technology from the West, and we learned how to make all sorts of new things, from hoopskirts to locomotives.

But my idea of technology and its usefulness for mankind does not start with the latest inventions of whatever age. You can have great technology and not know how to make proper use of it. And you can have simple technology and it can save your life.

On a January day in 1974, a couple of fishermen were walking through the reeds in a lonely spot near the Talofofo River on the island of Guam, on their way to set some shrimp traps, when they noticed some unusual motion nearby. They stopped and waited. In a few moments, the reeds parted, and out darted a short, wiry, bearded man in a kind of burlap uniform. Startled to see the fishermen, he dropped his traps and raised his hands in a prayerful gesture, then lunged at one of the men. The two subdued this strange creature and tied his hands. At the local police station, he drew himself to attention and identified himself as Corporal Yoichi Yokoi of the Imperial Japanese Army Supply Corps. He had gone into hiding when the American forces retook Guam in 1944 and had eluded detection and capture for twenty-eight years. He told an incredible story of survival.

Yokoi had been a tailor before being drafted in 1941. He served in a supply unit in China before being transferred to Guam in March 1944, not long before its fall. After American troops recaptured the island, he was presumed dead by Japanese military authorities and was posthumously promoted to sergeant. A memorial tablet was placed in his family's Buddhist altar, but both of his parents died believing he was still alive. Except for anemia, he was in excellent health. All he wanted to eat when he was taken to the hospital was "something salty." He had gone twenty-eight years without the taste of salt. He bathed in and took his drinking water from a small stream near his cave. He dug the cave eight feet below ground level using a spent artillery shell as a shovel; he shored up the roof with bamboo; and he fashioned drains and a latrine for sanitation.

He had been ordered to burn his army uniform when the island was taken by the Americans, and he and two others had retreated to the deserted end of the island. The other two lived separately, he said, and died years before Yokoi was discovered. For his clothing he stripped the pliable bark from pago trees and made thread of it, which he wove into cloth on a makeshift loom. Then he cut the cloth with the tailoring scissors he had saved and sewed trousers, shirts, and jackets. He made needles by pounding and shaping pieces of brass cartridges. He found a discarded American ammunition box and some spent machine gun shells, which he used as containers. He found bits of discarded junk floating in the river and, on the shore, a piece of cloth, some wire, a Schlitz can. Wire made belt buckles, plastic made buttons. He squeezed oil from coconut pulp, and used the coconut shells for containers.

He also learned to make fire by rubbing sticks together,

and kept fire by weaving a rope of coconut fiber. Once lit the rope would smolder for days and could be used to start a cooking fire by blowing on it. He ate an occasional wild rat he trapped in a handmade snare. He also captured a deer every once in a while and smoked the meat over his hearth in a basketlike contraption he devised to cut down the amount of smoke that could escape through his ventilation shaft. He trapped fresh-water shrimp and fish and managed to grow some vegetables.

Yokoi came home to a hero's welcome. He got his back pay, wrote a book, and now he makes personal appearances, lecturing on living with nature.

Few of us can expect to have to duplicate Sergeant Yokoi's ordeal, fortunately. I recount this story of his survival to make the point I began with, that technology can be directly related to survival at its most elemental level. Technology refers not only to the marvels that make life so comfortable for us today.

II

Perhaps it is because of our need for the means of survival that Japanese science tends to concentrate more on the applied than on the theoretical. We have taken many basic ideas and turned them into practical objects, in many cases products not even thought of by the originators of the basic technology. This is inevitable, of course. A good example in Sony's history is the way we transformed the transistor for radio uses. Today we are developing new materials for uses in machines that are not off the drawing board, but that we know will be needed along the developmental time line.

The biggest difficulty is moving a new technology into people's lives. Once the public recognizes the advantage this technology brings, they come to expect it. What housewife would want to go back to the washboard? For another example, until computers and on-board microprocessors were common, few people realized that they could have automobiles that use so much less fuel, that ride so comfortably, and that are safer because of better engineering made possible by computers. For safety, many models now have sensors that turn on the lights automatically at dusk, and windshield wipers that start up when the first drops of rain fall. Smaller, more economical engines are made possible because very small on-board computers make them so efficient. Ceramic parts are appearing more and more in auto engines, making them more heat-resistant and more durable. New plastics are replacing steel. Optical fiber will soon replace copper and aluminum wire in electrical systems. We have cars that warn us verbally when a system or component is in a dangerous condition, if a door is open, the fuel is low, and so on. And we have automatic direction finders coordinated with a map on a cathode ray tube display on the dashboard. We have a CD ROM (read only memory) disk that holds thousands of maps, which will pinpoint the car's position on the map display, moving in real time as you drive along. With this device, it should be impossible to get lost. I expect there will be crash avoidance systems and a whole lot more, and all because a small microprocessor with great capacity is put on board.

However, considering everything that has been done with automobiles, and allowing for all the added aids and conveniences to come, there is little in the basic nature of the auto that is likely to change. Four wheels, an engine, and a body will remain standard for personal ground transportation, and the automakers are approaching a peak. All of the improvements in some way go to make automobiles safer than ever before, better, and more reliable, but the automobiles soon will not really be very different from each other, as their reliability continues to improve. From the viewpoint of someone interested in merchandising, I believe that people are growing accustomed to these automotive advances—the general public expects them—and styling will become the main difference in consumers' minds. The technological improvement is taken for granted, as it should be, as it progresses and becomes a part of our lives.

When I began driving a car, the act itself was almost a specialized technology, and to pass the examination I had to know all about the mechanics of the engine and the drive train. Today this is not necessary. We rely on specialists to fix our cars if and when they give us trouble. Sometimes I regret that it has become impossible to tinker with a car engine, but then the compensation is that I don't have to park my car on a hill at night so I can get it started the next morning; I have other things to which I can devote my time. People my age and even younger can still remember when having a flat tire was common. Today it is rare.

I remember when people were constantly having to replace the vacuum tubes and other parts in their radios and early television sets, when drugstores and variety stores in the United States had testing machines where people could bring suspect vacuum tubes from their ailing TV sets, check them, and buy replacements if necessary. All this has disappeared with the advent of the transistor, diode, semiconductor, integrated circuit, and better production systems for assembling the sets. Automatic soldering machines and better and finer quality control, in addition to new materials that are more durable and more reliable, have greatly diminished service needs.

But as new-product quality and reliability and advancement become commonplace, we in industry are challenged to create things that will be new and intriguing enough to bring the customers to us. Obviously, we can never expect to survive in business if we do not keep improving what we offer to the public, and that takes new technology.

The reproduced music people now can hear in their homes is the most accurate in history, thanks to the laser technology of the new compact disc players. The compact disc technology, in which a tiny laser reads information embedded on a plastic-coated aluminum record (there is no need of a stylus riding in grooves as on old-fashioned records), was the opening of a new era in which people can hear music exactly as it was played by the musicians. Only the music is heard, without annoying sounds like tape hiss and record surface noise from scratches or debris in the grooves and with the dynamic range that went into the music as it was played. Conductor Herbert von Karajan felt so strongly about this new development that even before we had marketed our full range of players and before there were many compact discs in the shops, he and I made an appearance together to talk with international journalists in Salzburg and later in Tokyo about this new development and its importance.

Some of my colleagues in electronics say that the laser is one of the greatest inventions of the century, as important as the transistor, the integrated circuit, and latter-day large-scale integrations. I agree. There is no doubt that laser technology has changed and will continue to change our lives for many decades. The first impressive uses of laser technology that the public was aware of were in industry and in medicine—the use of lasers in surgery was a quantum leap over the days when only the scalpel was available to aid the cool judgment of a master surgeon. It took men of vision to bring the laser from the laboratory and hospital to the living room. Now we are using it in digital, optical, and audio equipment, where it delivers optimum sound and picture fidelity, but this is only the beginning of what can become a revolution in the home, in which the laser will be the key to a long list of new devices, from burglar alarms to information and command systems.

The use of the laser to read a digital disk has been advanced to storage systems, where a single small 4.7-inch diameter disk can be programmed to hold about two hundred and seventy-five thousand pages of text. The entire Grolier Encyclopedia is available today on a small disk, and by punching buttons on your keyboard you can have instantaneous access to any page you want. It is now possible to put all sorts of information on such a disk and store it for retrieval later. This opens up great possibilities for researchers, for libraries, for publications. Applications for companies are limitless, for inventories and for storing enormous amounts of data of all kinds that can be retrieved almost instantly. This kind of device linked to, or as part of, a computer linked by telephone to a data base anywhere in the world will be a combination of remarkable power. We have barely scratched the surface in the applications of laser technology, computers, and communications.

My son Masao is in charge of home and personal computers for Sony, and he is impatient with us sometimes because he thinks top management isn't putting enough effort into his division. "I am under pressure every day to come up with new ideas for the use of the computer in the home," he says, "but it is a hard business. People visualize a stand-alone computer with a disk drive and a keyboard like a typewriter. It may be difficult to convince people they need a computer, but an information-gathering and -processing machine is different and that is our target. Everybody has a television and a telephone, and if you add a computer immediately you have the makings of an information system. You just need to add the software.

There is no question that the whole world is going in that direction."

I am sometimes amazed that as technologically progressive as we think we are in top management, young people coming up through the lower ranks today often scold us for being slow to pick up on the new technologies. I guess we did the same thing in our day. "A couple of decades ago," Masao says, "the senior people in this company passed down their know-how to the younger ones. The older managers knew the analog technology inside and out and they were idolized, and rightly so. But today some of our newly graduated people know more about digital technology, more than their seniors, so they pass their know-how up; it is a completely new development."

One of our strengths at Sony is that we do not structure our company so rigidly that the NIH (Not Invented Here) syndrome applies. The expression refers to the reluctance of some arrogant managers to accept any idea for which they cannot take credit. This is sometimes a problem in traditional Japanese companies with rigid structures. Although some of our best ideas have come from the graying heads at the top, we have always found vitality in the lower echelons and have encouraged and rewarded it, and so it will be, with perhaps more emphasis, in coming years. Many of the technological breakthroughs we have made, from the transistor to the Trinitron tube and on to our high-density television systems, have been made by persistent young people who were given their heads to follow a hunch.

We are headed in the direction of new communications systems in the nineties and beyond. Satellite dish antennas are already popular in the United States for home use, and this will change broadcasting, because with even a small parabolic antenna, the amount of information that can be brought into the home from many different sources is enormous. This will require more versatile VCR or laser disk systems able to store the information for later use. It will have an impact not only on broadcasting and broadcasters, but also on their advertisers.

Some of the cable companies in the United States began scrambling their signals so that people with satellite dishes who do not have an authorized unscrambler cannot receive their picture. But basic electronics technology is so open that there are few secrets, and clever technicians have figured out how to build unauthorized unscramblers.

We have seen the example in the early days of computers of how smart young people could break into some of the most carefully protected computers, and so I believe information security will become an even bigger problem as we move into the next century, especially as even the new smaller computers will be able to operate at blinding speed, making millions of computations in seconds.

In the here and now, the standard black plastic long-playing record is giving way to the CD. It is a change just like the move away from the old 78-rpm standard-play record to the LP. Small home television cameras in the eight-millimeter tape format will soon become the standard camera for the amateur, just as the larger format Betamovie and VHS cameras shoved eight-millimeter film cameras into the back of the family closet. Now a high-powered video camera small enough to fit in one corner of an attaché case, and all self-contained, with a cassette smaller than a standard audio cassette, will make fine, sharply focused pictures even in low-light levels. This is an evolution very much like the change from the clumsy old folding-bellows still cameras and awkward sheet-film holders to the compact thirty-five-millimeter cameras so widespread today. Those thirty-five-millimeter cameras will be replaced by cameras like our Mavica filmless camera, which uses a charged coupled device to digitize the picture on a small spinning disk, with no chemical processing to worry about. Mavica and similar filmless cameras are not on the market for the general public yet, but as a professional tool, as in the case of the trans-Pacific Olympics pictures for *Asahi Shimbun*, they are proving very versatile.

In video we now have high-definition TV with 1,125 scanning lines (vs. 525 lines in the United States and 626 in Europe), which gives the TV picture the sharpness and quality of a good still photograph. I think we will not only provide finer pictures in people's homes, with less strain on the eyes, but also revolutionize the motion picture business with this new kind of TV. With conventional TV the brightness is too low for movies, but with our new advances, TV cameras and videotape may one day replace the big old thirty-five-millimeter film movie cameras just as electronic news gathering with small videotape cameras replaced the sixteen-millimeter film cameras once carried by TV news teams, and U-Matic video tape recorders replaced the broadcasting studio sixteen-millimeter projectors.

Director Paul Shrader shot a portion of his film *Mishima* in videotape as an experiment and was very pleased with it. The videotape gives instant playback on a scene, unlike conventional film, which needs to be processed chemically. Some directors are using video cameras while they shoot a scene in film to get a quick look at it to determine whether they have to shoot the scene again, and this is resulting in savings already. Francis Ford Coppola estimated that he could cut production costs as much as 30 percent with videotape, and a lot of that is time saved. Videotape images can't yet be projected on to the big theater screens; they must be transferred to film. But the possibilities for video movies have excited technicians in Japan and abroad. Special effects, dubbing, erasing, splitting screens, and other popular techniques being used in film today are much easier to do electronically on tape. Using electronic, digitalized techniques, you can make Superman fly without wires. I believe that Sony technology will be widespread in filmmaking before the turn of the century.

People who saw ABC's super-slow-motion video during the 1984 Olympics were seeing the results of a Sony Super Motion video system based on high-definition TV technology. It makes slow motion possible at one-third the speed of conventional slow motion and with less blurring.

In other technological areas of video, Sony was awarded an Emmy in 1984, which I was happy to accept on Sony's behalf, for a new video recorder with mass image storage capability specially suited for computer graphics. It was our fourth Emmy. (The first was for Trinitron in 1973; the second for U-matic in 1976; and the third for one-inch helical-scan videotape recording in 1979.) In 1985 *Billboard* magazine gave us its Trendsetter Award for our revolutionary small D-5 compact disc player. We demonstrated our JumboTRON with its giant 82-by-131-foot TV screen at Science Expo '85 in Tsukuba, Japan, and have begun installing models with somewhat smaller screens in the U.S. We're still making radios, too, including the world's thinnest AM-FM unit, which is only four millimeters thick and weighs only thirty-three grams, just a bit more than an ounce.

We are selling technology on our own new MCZ method of producing high-quality silicon crystals for very large-scale integrations to companies in the United States (Monsanto Electronic Materials Company), Japan, and Italy. We and RCA Astro-Electronics have arranged for Sony to market advanced communications satellites in Japan, and we are on the market in North America with units that combine computer, TV, and communications technology.

In fact, as I look ahead toward the next century, it strikes me that we are working on some of the very techniques that have the most promise of ensuring mankind's survival. In my company, we have no specific technology in aerospace, although other Japanese companies are becoming more and more involved in this; some parts of Boeing wide-bodied jet planes are made in Japan, and design and engineering on new kinds of engines are proceeding rapidly here in cooperation with British and other European companies. Japan's new H-series of three-stage rocket boosters will be available for putting two-ton satellites in geostationary orbit in the 1990s. But those areas that are expected to receive the greatest emphasis—optoelectronics, digital technology, video technology, and laser technology—happen to be our specialties. Just where this will take Sony is a matter for the imagination. I don't think there are any other companies that are as specialized in all those areas. However, I often remind my colleagues that other companies have also been looking into these fields, so the leadership will go to the company that manages its technology best. It is not safe to assume that just because we have all this technology everything will be OK. But since we very clearly have this advantage, we have to see how we can best make it bear fruit. We have poured billions into our technical laboratories for R&D, and others have watched us and taken advantage of our up-front investment by moving into our field after we have pioneered it, but we cannot change this. I have no intention of complaining to anybody. We have boasted about our capability in these crucial areas, and now the responsibility is on management in the next fifteen years to see what we can do. We would have to be asleep if we did not produce any fruit from such a lush orchard.

III

We had a meeting of department chiefs one Saturday in Tokyo, and somebody asked me whatever happened to our slogan "Research Makes the Difference." He hadn't seen it in our ads lately. We got to talking, and I said that if we just kept saying "research makes the difference," our people might start to think that research is enough to keep the company prosperous. It is not. I used the example of the French. France is a country that believes "research makes a difference," and thus they have many unique things. The design of the Caravelle jet passenger plane with the engines in the rear was a novel idea that was copied and capitalized on by many aircraft makers, but the French didn't profit from it. They failed to improve and develop their original design and they lost control of it. Citroën produces a unique car with hydraulic suspension, a very versatile concept, and with a unique style. But they have had problems and could not market this car in very large numbers. France makes advanced weapons systems like the Exocet, which sank a British warship during the Falklands war, atomic weapons, ships, supersonic fighters, and a powerful rocket booster, Ariane, to put satellites in orbit. (We Japanese do not make weapons except in small quantities for our own defense and we are prohibited from exporting anything with "war potential" under our constitution, so we are out of this competition.) The French also have a high-speed train, the TGV, which is faster than our bullet trains, but it is to Japan that other countries have come to ask for high-speed rail technology.

The British invented the modern jet aircraft engine (Germany had a jet engine toward the end of the war, but was defeated before they could develop it beyond use in one fighter plane, the Messerschmitt 262, which was produced only in very small numbers). The British built the first jet airliner, the Comet. But the Comet had an unhappy history, and England lost its lead in engines and airframes to the Americans.

My point is that it is unwise merely to do something different and then rest on your laurels. You have to do something to make a business out of a new development, and that requires that you keep updating the product and staying ahead of the market. Our research director once mentioned the importance of cross talk between R&D and the business side, sales and

so the research projects came together at about the right time.

But some projects, such as the high-resolution plasma display worked on by one of our researchers, have been set aside. In this instance, as I said earlier, we invested some venture capital in the project, which the researcher decided to pursue outside of Sony. At some future date, we and others may benefit from it, but I could not justify the continuing investment in this research.

IV

Once a year we hold our own technology fair—we call it our Technology Exchange Convention—at which all of our divisions and the project teams set up booths just like at a trade show. Only Sony people are admitted, and invitations are tightly controlled. Last year six thousand Sony employees from Japan and overseas visited the displays. Here they can see the state of our research and technology, and they can often find things they can use in their own work. We display process equipment as well as materials and demonstrations on the status of research. Engineers and technicians are on hand to answer questions, and sometimes visitors leave their calling cards and collect brochures and make appointments to exchange information, just as at a regular trade show.

There is no way of knowing exactly how much we have saved by these conventions, but we have learned that by keeping a close eye and a tight control on R&D and using it with a minimum of duplication—except where we think it is worthwhile to try more than one approach to solve a problem—we can be more effective in allocating our funds. It would be very good if the future goals were clear and simple, for example, how to make a new kind of video recorder. But when the challenge is to produce new kinds of systems, even if you start working with the idea that a certain type of system would be best, you could be wrong, because such systems are not yet familiar to us. Computer companies, for example, are always having problems with that sort of thing. When you design a computer, you simply can't think of it as a single device with limited use outside the system of people's lives. As I said earlier, in the not-too-far future, a computer will have to be able to hook up to larger networks of information, into systems for home security, weather forecasting, financial affairs, shopping, and so on. Making the bits and pieces of such a system will not serve a company well; a successful company will have to come up with the full systems that are needed. In the future we will no longer be able to do business as we once did, when we made things thinking that they would be useful only in themselves, such as videos and tape recorders. We made them believing that people would find them useful, which they were, and that people would really discover their need for them, with each item as an end in itself. But such thinking in tomorrow's world will not be good enough—it must be broader.

I would like to see the day come soon when all of the worldwide patent information will be assembled in one data bank. Today, it is an enormous job for every company to keep track of all the information about other companies' patents. It could be put on optical disks, and constant updating would be possible. It would be a great advantage to companies everywhere if this could be done and hooked into the worldwide information system, so that the new patents could be scanned by anyone interested in a license anywhere in the world.

The precise direction in which all this will head by the end of this century is hard to guess. Obviously, by the end of the century the information systems we are starting on now, combining television, computers, and communications, will become commonplace in the home. We are in the midst of a cultural and social revolution. And it may be more and more difficult to impress people as time goes on, because even today, although the fact that we can pick up the phone and dial directly all the way around the world is a wonder to people of my generation, younger people whose memories do not go back very far don't seem to give it a second thought.

The director of our research labs at Sony, Makoto Kikuchi, says the invention of the solid-state device was the start of the science of modern electronics, a true technological revolution. The evolution that developed from that breakthrough, to the very large-scale integrations (VLSI) of today, are all part of the same revolution. It is about time for a second electronic breakthrough, and we are all thinking about it. What will there be after the VLSI, and how will we move into a whole new generation of devices that can contribute to our survival? Large-scale integrations are fascinating, but as physicists we know there is a limit to how far we can go and should want to go with this technology, even though we are still producing new technology in integrated circuits and other devices, selling equipment to make them, and licensing technologies to other companies. I have already mentioned our development of a new way of making very high-quality silicon single crystals, and we expect even better results when we do it in zero-gravity on a future space flight. We have come a long way with integrated circuits, and some say we might be coming near the limit of their development. In producing these devices the techniques we have used for etching the circuits onto the chip have progressed through lithography, photo-lithography, short-wave-length photo-lithography, and electron beam photo-lithography. Miniaturization reaches its peak in these chips. What will be next? How much more will we continue to pack onto a piece of pure silicon?

Kikuchi believes that a new generation integrated circuit should be much more than an expansion or extension of what we now have. He thinks the approach would be to take a giant step: layer the device, making the first layer photosensitive and the second layer function the way the human eye transmits data to the brain; the next layer would contain some logic; and the last layer or layers would contain pattern recognition. In other words, this new device would be a simple kind of mechanical brain. "The VLSI we have today," says Kikuchi, "are too simpleminded for the work that they will have to do in the future."

He is particularly intrigued by the idea of the biochip and by work in molecular electronics. A half-step has been taken in this direction motivated by U.S. naval research. Kikuchi is intrigued by the possibilities opened up by the discovery of the photochromic effect. If you select a certain large organic molecule that is transparent and colorless, and you bathe it in ultraviolet light invisible to the human eye, the photons of the ultraviolet will kick off one of the electrons of the molecule and the molecule will twist itself and turn blue. When you shine visible light on it, it goes back to its original state, losing its blue color. So there you have the basic two-state (on or off) memory, the basic building block of electronic technology.

Since Kikuchi thinks current technology is only good for another ten years, he is accelerating work in many fields to be ready for what is needed next. His worry is that there may not be enough scientists interested in basic research. But we are both optimistic. One of the reasons for our optimism is the steady increase in the number of Japanese papers cited as references in the *Journal of Applied Physics*, from 2 to 3 percent in 1960 to over 30 percent today. His pessimism, not completely shared by me, is that while Japan's contributions in improving process technology, such as dry etching, focusing of lasers, and so on, is making a major contribution, when it comes to opening completely new fields, our scientists are still catching up. Although we are proud of having one Nobel Prize in physics from our own Sony laboratories, Japan has only won a total of three Nobels in physics. However, as I have pointed out before, when it comes to turning ideas into reality, we have been very successful and very creative.

Several years ago, we had one of our regular company international scientific conferences at the lab at Atsugi near Yokohama. The British staff came with a theoretical idea on digital video tape recording. Six months later, at the next meeting, a Sony engineer from the Atsugi lab showed up with a working model of the British design. Our foreign colleagues were astounded. "We could wait ten years to do something like that," said a British staff member. "This would never happen in Britain." Kikuchi pointed out that even at Bell Labs when they get an idea they try it out first on a computer. Here it is the normal reaction of a researcher to say, if the idea sounds good, "Let's make one and see how it works!"

The technology that will help the world's people to survive is not all in the hands of the world's scientists and engineers. But we have great ability to develop that technology. We proved that during the oil crisis. It seemed for many years as though the appetite for oil would just grow and grow. I could envision in my mind a virtual pipeline of tankers, bow to stern in both directions, stretched from Japan to the Persian Gulf. In those days I flew over the Nagoya shipyard in my helicopter while they were building the drydock for the construction of a one-million-ton supertanker. Another million-tonner drydock was built in the harbor at Nagasaki, and there were predictions that if this kept up the oil wells would be pumped dry in our lifetime. But before a single mammoth tanker could be built, the embargo came and everything changed, and, as I said earlier, it was eventually beneficial. Because we learned to conserve, we survived the crisis, prospered, and learned how to advance on even less oil than before.

We are using nuclear fuel to generate about 26 percent of our electric power in Japan, a much smaller percentage than in France, but a higher percentage than in the United States, and this despite our "nuclear allergy," the understandable awe and fear our people have of this incredible power that destroyed two of our cities and hundreds of thousands of lives in a mere flash. We have three national nonnuclear principles: that the nation will not make, maintain, or introduce nuclear weapons. Our own nuclear-powered demonstration ship, which has been a commercial failure, is being put out of service. The visit of nuclear-powered American warships was once greeted by riots in the streets. Today there are protests, but they are less dramatic and rarely violent. Even after the accident at Chernobyl in the Soviet Union, it is understood that nuclear power for peaceful purposes can be a benefit. As new nuclear power plants are built, there are protests, but in the end, at least so far, the plants have been built because the people understand that the power is essential and contributes to our ability to survive.

I appeared on the Live Aid rock show in 1985 in Japan to appeal for aid to Africa's starving people. People are starving not only there, but in many other places on earth, and yet I know that there is the technology available to feed everybody. At the Science Expo '85, one of the major demonstrations was a tomato plant with more than twenty thousand tomatoes on it. The plant grew from a single seed and lived on very little water that was fortified with nutrients, which kept recirculating in a closed loop system called "Hyponica."

I don't think we can feed the world only tomatoes, but this demonstration, and many others I know of, proves that marvelous things are possible if we apply ourselves and we care. If we can figure out how to accomplish the task of feeding the world, we may end up with a population problem and a space problem, which might yet lead to another food problem. But I am optimistic enough to believe technology will solve all these problems.

Some people have said that the postindustrial society is

here, and some predict that we cannot expect technological innovation anymore, that we will have to live smaller lives, with less satisfaction and luxury. I don't believe it. My prediction is that we can enjoy our lives with less energy, less of the old materials, fewer resources, more recycling, and have more of the essentials for a happy and productive life than ever. Some people in the world, especially the Americans, will have to learn something of the meaning and spirit of *mottainai* and conserve more. Step by step, year by year, we must all learn how to be more skillful and efficient in using our resources economically. We must recycle more. As to the expanding populations, that will be a challenge to everyone, for they will have to be fed, clothed, and educated. But as the standard of living of a people increases, the population tends to level off, people live a different way, acquire different tastes and preferences, and develop their own technologies for survival.

In the United States and Europe, the steel makers or computer manufacturers or automobile companies periodically say they cannot compete with foreign technology, and their reaction always is to put people out of work. I have already explained how the Japanese companies attempt to avoid letting any workers go, but try to use them to bring the company back to health. When the electronic analog technology began to give way to digital technology, we did not fire our analog engineers or put ads in the paper to hire digital engineers. Our analog engineers eagerly learned a new field. They had to, to survive. Learning new technologies is a way of life for us in Japan, and others will have to do it; it is not possible or desirable to cling to the past.

JAPAN

AND THE WORLD

Alienation

and Alliance

I

Relations between modern Japan and the rest of the world have often been stormy, and it is no surprise that today the United States and the European community are locked in a cycle of recurring problems over trade with Japan. I think we should recognize and be grateful that our problems are not yet so badly politicized that we cannot sit down and talk about them rationally. But this situation is like a chronic illness, and we must find a way to cure it. Obviously two nations like the United States and Japan, which share more than eighty billion dollars in trade and together account for more than 30 percent of the world's goods and services, are bound to have some problems, because of the very size and diversity of that trade. And it is always easier to blame the other person for a problem than to look at your own faults. This has too often been true on both sides of the Pacific.

254

We think differently, and the way we look at the problems that cause these never-ending difficulties between two great nations is often very different. There are also crucial differences between our systems. Traditional ways of doing things, right or wrong, exist on both sides. And there are problems that don't have anything to do with race or culture or history or tradition, but with human attitudes that are very easy to understand.

Before Ronald Reagan took office as president of the United States, one of his advisers came to Japan to get some ideas for formulating Reagan's Asian and, specifically, defense policies. He talked with some leading Japanese figures, and in one conversation with a Tokyo economist, he linked trade problems with defense and said he thought Japan should build some warships and give or lease them to the U.S. Navy. The economist told him he thought that this would probably not be possible because of article nine of Japan's constitution, which renounces war and prohibits us from maintaining any war potential or exporting it. Mr. Reagan's friend and adviser said, "Well, then, change the constitution." Very easy to say, but very difficult for any democratic nation like Japan, or the United States, to do. (Actually, the American framers of our constitution expected that Japan would write its own once the Occupation period was over, but the present one has become so ingrained that any talk of changing it is viewed with suspicion, as though any changes would automatically bring back the bad old days of the militarists. I think it is shortsighted of Japan's politicians, who should have the courage to change what needs to be changed. After all, the document was not even written by Japanese.)

Americans and Europeans seem to think that their idea of how the world trading and monetary systems work and should continue to work should be universal, especially in the business world, and that since they believe they invented the game the rules should never be amended. The system up to now, they believe, has served them well, and there is no need to change. Moreover, some American and European businessmen still look at the Japanese as newcomers, as novices who should still be paying tuition to the school. What they don't want to face is the fact that we are not only in the same school; we have joined the faculty.

Japan's Economic Planning Agency recently made a detailed study of important economic trends and extrapolated them to the year 2000. This study shows that the United States will continue to lead the world and will produce 19.6 percent of the world's gross national product. The Soviet Union will contribute 12.5 percent, and Japan will be third with 11.9 percent. The next largest economy, West Germany, will contribute 5.9 percent, and China will have 5.3 percent of the world's production. France will contribute 4.3 percent, and Britain 2.9 percent. The world economic map looks very different from 1960, when the U.S. produced 33.4 percent, the Soviet Union 15 percent, and Japan only 1.8 percent. But today the U.S. has dropped to 22.4 percent and Japan has risen to 10.1 percent. This indicates clearly that Japan's industrial prowess and economic power cannot be ignored within the world trading system and that it is worthwhile for nations to try to understand what Japan is all about and to listen to what she has to say.

In today's fast-moving and interdependent world, we have to look for ways to get to know each other better; we need to talk with, exchange views with, and attempt to understand each other. We can argue and dispute, but we must approach each other as equals and do it with the objective of learning about, and trying to solve, our problems. I know it is difficult for some Westerners to believe that an Oriental country has reached such economic heights—Japan is the only one, so far— but it was not done with mirrors, and the system will not collapse tomorrow. Japan is in the world community for good and is contributing in a worthwhile way to the welfare of the world's people. That is why I have devoted so much time to participating in binational and multinational groups concerned with trying to find means of understanding one another.

In Japan we live under conditions of high density and we know we have to give some leeway, some freedom, to our competitors. We must make compromises. The sense of compromise is a key element of our legal system and of our relations with one another. We know that in many situations we have to sacrifice some of our desires. In the United States, there is little of that sense of compromise, as far as I can tell. Americans more often than not—or at least the ones I have met these past forty years—tend to be convinced of the correctness of their own opinions, their own way of doing things. History has shown them to be very good at many things, and, after all, we have learned a lot from America. But I think Americans must learn to compromise and listen more.

In Japan the most successful leader in business is not the man who goes around giving detailed instructions to his subordinates. It is the man who gives his subordinates only general guidelines and instills confidence in them and helps them to do good work. With this attitude he gets more original performance and new ideas.

If you go through life convinced that your way is always best, all the new ideas in the world will pass you by. Americans tend to think that the American system is the way things should work all around the world, but they should not be blind and deaf to how things are done in other countries. Many American companies that have seriously studied the way things are done elsewhere have improved their productivity and stabilized their work force by combining what they learned abroad with their own ideas.

When General Motors entered into its joint venture with Toyota Motor Company to make small automobiles in California, the first agreement of its kind, the actual operating of the plant was left up to the Japanese partner so that GM could study Japanese management methods and how they worked in the United States, a very wise move.

I suppose it is natural when something goes wrong to look for the blame somewhere else, seldom at home. During the height of American complaints about Japan's closed markets in telecommunications I happened to be at the same meeting in Hawaii as Bill Brock, who was then the U.S. special trade representative. We began talking about the issue and he said right away, "There is a huge imbalance in telecommunications equipment. Japanese equipment sales in the United States are eleven times higher than American telecommunications equipment sales to Japan!" He was shocked by this big figure, as he should have been. "Why don't the Japanese buy our equipment?" he wanted to know.

In 1985, the market for telecommunications equipment in Japan at that point was not nearly as open to foreign vendors as the American market was to foreign makers of this kind of equipment—that much was true. But it seemed to me that the Japanese market was about to open wide because the Japanese telephone monopoly corporation was in the process of becoming a private corporation. I was right, too. Despite some residual problems, Japan and the United States are now the two most open telecommunications markets in the world. As a matter of fact, to cite one simple example, Japan is the only nation in the world outside the U.S. where you can buy a U.S. telephone, plug it into the phone jack in your house, and use it. Unfortunately, most American phones are now being made in Singapore.

But I had something very serious to say to Mr. Brock. "You know, Mr. Brock," I said, "the kind of equipment we are talking about is not equipment bought by the general public; it is goods bought by experts in high-technology equipment who know their field very well. These people do not buy on a whim or impulse or based on only surface appearance or price." He had to agree with that. "So if the American telecommunications equipment makers produce such good equipment that you think the Japanese should be buying it, why are the American telecommunications operators buying Japanese equipment instead of American equipment? You should be asking the American companies this question instead of blaming us for selling too much." I reminded him that you cannot sell what people do not want to buy.

When I helped General Motors make their first capital investment in Japan, I thought they would use their Japanese partner to help sell GM cars in Japan instead of continuing to rely on only one agent to sell their cars all over the country, as they do to this day. Instead GM asked their Japanese partner to make engines to send to America, and they eventually asked them to send a small car to the U.S. They later wanted an exception from the voluntary restraint agreement that Japanese makers made to help the American industry, so they could get even more cars. So did Lee Iacocca of Chrysler, who was for a while one of the most outspoken advocates of drastically reducing Japanese exports to the United States. (As it turned out, a 1986-model Japanese small car imported by GM won the highest rating for fuel economy of any car sold in the U.S.)

I think this is not the way for American industry to develop its own competitiveness and solve the trade imbalance problem. I gave a talk recently at the Massachusetts Institute of Technology, and I pointed out that our plant in California supplies 85 percent of all our TV sets sold in America; the rest are small sets we send from Japan. And we even export picture tubes from America to our factories in Japan. Dozen of Japanese firms are operating in the U.S., making cars and trucks and auto parts, musical instruments, machine tools, electronic devices, television sets, zippers, soy sauce, and for these companies it is something of a compromise to be producing there. I know, because we sacrifice some profits on goods made in the U.S. for that market compared with goods we ship from Japan. We do have an advantage in speed of delivery, of course, and there are other advantages, but Japanese companies producing in the United States are contributing to the U.S. economy in many ways: Japanese imports are reduced, jobs are created, technology transfer takes place, and service networks are developed.

At the same time, American semiconductor companies now producing in Japan send large quantities of goods to the United States, either to their own companies, like Texas Instruments and Motorola, or to be sold to other companies. But those shipments increase Japanese exports and add to the trade imbalance. About a third of what Japanese companies sell to the U.S. is industrial products bought by American companies, not sales to consumers. As a matter of fact, the latest 1985 figures show that among exports from Japan to the U.S., nineteen billion dollars, or about one-third of Japan's total exports to the U.S., represent shipments of U.S.–affiliated companies' original equipment made here with U.S. company names on it, and parts. Also, many companies from European Economic Community countries have major tie-ups for original equipment manufacture in Japan, and those shipments are included in the export figures from Japan, as of course they should be. Companies in West Germany, Britain, France, Belgium, and the Netherlands sell Japanese-made copying machines at home with their own corporate name on them, for example. The United States and Italy have companies selling machine tools the same way. The U.S., France, Britain, and West Germany have companies marketing construction equipment made for them in Japan. And three American robot makers have their robots made here.

I think it is also worth saying, while I am on the subject, that contrary to the general perception, there are literally thousands of American and European companies doing business in

Japan. The American Chamber of Commerce alone has nearly six hundred member companies, and one hundred and fourteen of the two hundred largest companies on the Fortune 500 list hold majority ownership in their Japanese subsidiary. MITI figures show that operating profits, as a percentage of sales, of foreign subsidiaries in Japan are consistently higher than those of Japanese corporations in the same business.

It appears to me that if foreign companies have their problems competing with Japan, it is often as much a failure of that industry as it is a success of Japanese industry, and Americans or Europeans should not blame Japan for making good and attractive products. I realize it was once impossible, then very difficult, in the past to establish a wholly owned business here or even a joint venture, but whatever the historical justification or lack of one, times have changed, and many of Japan's critics are woefully out of date. I mentioned earlier that no American companies at all were interested in our compact disc player technology, not a single one, and yet this is the technology of the future, with standards agreed upon by all the major Japanese and European makers.

While we are moving into the next generation, American companies are clinging to the old twelve-inch black analog record, which will soon be as outmoded as the standard play 78-rpm record is today. When others cannot see the opportunities and refuse to get into a business, this gives us a great advantage. But I dislike it when there are complaints then because somebody else had the foresight to go into the business and capture the market. American companies should not turn their backs on this technology and give it up, because it will lead to many other applications, not just the reproduction of music.

Ironically, some of the technology that made this new recording breakthrough possible was pioneered in the United States, but American companies nowadays seem more interested in service industries than in turning new technologies into attractive products that will be enjoyed by a vast number of consumers. A theme that I feel must be struck over and over again is the danger to America of exporting its production. Rather than devoting their attention to making products competitive over the long haul, many American managers are still prone to looking for good merchandise at the lowest prices to produce quick profits. This results in a growing number of American firms seeking Japanese and other makers as the source of supply of products with American brand names. A certain amount of this kind of sourcing may make good sense for a corporation and even for world trade. But the danger is that a manufacturer might be forfeiting his rights and responsibilities.

While many Americans seem willing to ignore the arrival of a new era, the French have a punitive approach to it. I must confess I admired their shrewdness and wit when they decided they would slow the shipment of Japanese video cassette recorders into the country in 1983. They made the port of entry for VCRs the tiny inland town of Poitiers, where the French finally stopped the ancient Saracen invasion, and they stationed only nine customs agents there. They required the agents to examine each set very carefully before approving it, reducing the number of Japanese sets allowed into the country to, well, not even a trickle, hardly a drip. Of course the government was free to move the customs location anywhere it pleased. But putting it where they did, the site of the Battle of Tours, which stopped an invasion in the year 732, is very witty and typically French.

At the time, the French and other European makers had been bringing OEM (products made in Japan with the European makers' names on them) sets into Europe, but they had been slow to develop their own, with one or two companies being exceptions. Because of my experience over the years, I was not surprised to see that their first reaction against us was to raise the tariff; when that failed to stop the flow of goods, they virtually shut down imports by the Poitiers plan. The Germans got really upset about this, because they didn't want their goods stopped at Poitiers. They said openly that if products from EEC countries also had to pass through Poitiers, they would get mixed up with Japanese products and they would be paying the same penalty. Originally that was the intention; the French said all products had to pass through Poitiers. But under pressure from the Germans, the French relented and ruled that only products from non-EEC countries would have to go through Poitiers. That meant Japan alone was the target. We knew it, of course.

Actually, I was amused by the Poitiers stunt. French audacity is a great strength, and I think Japan should have a little more of the same kind of boldness in its diplomatic and economic relations. A French minister of trade, though, very unwisely said during that time, "We can live without Japanese products." Well, of course. I mean, I suppose Japan can live without French cognac and champagne and the $1.2 billion worth of goods we imported from France that year. (Japan sold $1.9 billion worth of goods to France in the same year.) It is just not wise for government officials to speak that way. Otto Lamsdorff, who was then the German economics minister, and I were chatting about it at the time and he joked, "Why don't you Japanese retaliate by making the inspection point for cognac at the top of Mount Fuji?"

Japan still has some confusing and complicated barriers to trade, but Japan is the only major industrialized country that is actively moving to open its markets, step by step, always forward, never backward, while some others have been reinforcing their protectionist practices. I find many Americans think there are no American barriers to trade, when in fact there are many—almost half of what we send to the United States is under some form of restraint. But I have to say here that it is true that the U.S. is the most open market in the world, overall, and I think it is important for the future of world trade that it remain that way. I said so to Ronald Reagan in 1985, when I was in the U.S. on a successful mission to convince several states to abolish worldwide unitary taxation of foreign subsidiaries. Of course Reagan did not need my advice; he is very clearly on the record as a champion of free trade. And I have vowed to do what I can to help, as I have during the past forty-odd years.

If you try to avoid or soften competition by political intervention, you negate the whole concept of the free trade and free enterprise system. I have been lobbying in Japan to increase healthy competition by eliminating government intervention through old regulations that still exist. It is only by competition that the dynamism of the free enterprise system can be maintained. Therefore, those of us in management must not be tempted by the easy solution of looking for government help in suppressing competition. We must see that competition is fair and try to be frank with each other in order to understand both sides of the situation clearly. This does not mean that if you "understand" the Japanese point of view you will always, or even most of the time, agree that it is right. But it is more constructive to air the issues than simply to decide that you are right and that there is no need to hear any other viewpoints. We have to remember, after all, that this is not war; we are in business, and you cannot do business with a warlike enemy, so we should all try to talk common sense.

There are attitudes among even well-meaning people that have nothing to do with attempting to understand what is happening in the world today. I have had American and European parliamentarians tell me that they understand the issues and even concur on some points with the Japanese, but that they have to face political reality and must appear to be tough before their constituents who may have lost jobs "because of Japanese exports." An American senator may very easily talk about letting Japanese automobiles sit on the dock in Yokohama, but as long ago as 1983 there were 111,550 Americans directly employed by Japanese subsidiaries in the United States, 21,700 in Europe, and 27,000 in Asia. And that does not include the car dealers or electronics dealers and salesmen and servicemen in the field working for their own companies and selling Japanese goods. Of course, those employees may not be in the senator's constituency.

A few years ago, at the Japan–U.S. Businessmen's Conference in Hakone in the foothills of Mount Fuji, Mike Blumenthal, the former secretary of the treasury, who later became chairman of the Burroughs Corporation, and I decided we didn't want to eat the buffet dinner one night. I took my wife, and we grabbed Orville Freeman, the former secretary of agriculture, and his wife, and went to a steakhouse for a fine dinner and an evening of good conversation. The next day at our meeting my friend Blumenthal made some of the most preposterous statements I had ever heard on the subject of the yen and dollar exchange-rate issue. He repeated the old and untrue argument that the Japanese were maneuvering behind the scenes to manipulate the yen rate so it would remain undervalued. I spoke out very forcefully on the subject and took issue with Blumenthal.

Investigation by the U.S. Treasury later failed to find a shred of evidence that the Japanese were manipulating the yen, and the then–treasury secretary Donald Regan said so publicly.

At the Hakone meeting my countrymen were very much surprised to hear this jarring note of disagreement in the midst of the bland and pleasant conference. At these meetings the Japanese usually like to sit politely, saying little or nothing, and thus fail to make new friends. That is a major Japanese problem, to my way of thinking. At the recess, some of the younger Japanese came up to me and said they appreciated my defense of the Japanese position, but some of the older Japanese came to me shaking their heads: "You were rude to our guests who have come from so far away to be with us," they said.

That evening the Japanese were in for another confusing scene. We had a reception on a boat on Lake Ashi, and a Japanese TV crew came aboard and asked me for an interview about the conference. They said they wanted an American to join me in the interview. So while they were setting up, my wife went to Mike Blumenthal and asked him to join me for the interview. He agreed and we discussed our difference of opinion on television. Some of the Japanese were surprised that after our argument in the meeting we could still be friends. For the Japanese, disagreement often means the end of a friendship. Often the Westerner will argue with you, I keep trying to explain, just because he is a friend. When they shut up and refuse to discuss something, then the real danger point has arrived. If Westerners and Japanese are ever going to understand each other, the Japanese will have to be as frank as the Americans are in discussing problems and putting forth their viewpoints. We have been very poor at this in the past, businessmen as well as politicians, and we do not seem to be learning fast enough.

II

In 1962, the Federal Communications Commission was giving us some headaches by requiring all TV sets to have a UHF tuner as well as the standard VHF tuner, even though there were very few UHF stations broadcasting at the time. We were making several models of very small sets, including our famous Tummy TV, a battery-powered micro TV with a four-inch screen.

Fitting a mechanical rotary UHF tuner dial into such a small unit in addition to the standard VHF dial was quite a challenge, and I thought the additional money we had to spend for the UHF feature would not pay off because of the limited use of the UHF channels. (Later, with improved technology, we were able to put all channels on one electronic dial and so the problem disappeared.)

Newton Minow was chairman of the FCC at the time the UHF ruling was made, and as a person interested in Japan he later joined the Shimoda conference. When I was introduced to him, I said something like, "Mr. Minow, I don't like you. You have caused me a lot of trouble even before we met." I was only half joking, of course. He invited me to explain myself and I told him the story. To this day, he often reminds me of those first words. Well, we became good friends, and when I went to Washington to introduce the U-Matic video tape recorder there, I invited Minow to our party. He asked if he could bring a friend, and of course I said yes. The man he brought with him was Henry Kissinger, who was then a policy adviser at the White House. Minow told me that this man Kissinger would be a very important person in the future. We chatted for about fifteen minutes, Kissinger and I, and got to know each other a bit. A couple of years later, when he was secretary of state, we met again at a reception in Tokyo and I was flattered that he remembered me. I didn't expect him to recognize me but he took one look and said, "Hi, Mr. Morita."

By then the trade problems between Japan and the United States were a central topic of conversation. In fact, many nasty things were being said about Japan in the United States because of the bilateral trade imbalance between Japan and the U.S. Some people were accusing Japan of sending a torrent of merchandise to the U.S., which was forcing Americans out of jobs. Some manufacturers complained that they couldn't meet the competition and that the Japanese market was closed to their goods. Many of the accusations were really unfair, and some were, unfortunately, true, but I was worried about the total effect of the trade dispute on our broader relationship. I had already established Sony Trading Corporation, and we were actively bringing foreign products into Japan. Our overseas managers were instructed to look for items that would likely sell on the Japanese market. And I was also advising the government and industry associations at every opportunity on the importance of increasing imports and opening Japanese markets to foreign products.

At the reception where I encountered Henry Kissinger in Tokyo, we moved to the edge of the reception room and had a long chat. At one point I told him something that I believe very sincerely: "You know, Mr. Kissinger, we Japanese feel very close to the United States. We have felt that way for a long time, and that is why the war was such a terrible tragedy that should never have happened. My concern today is that in the United States you sometimes mistakenly identify your friends as your enemies. Japan has been, basically, a solid friend of the U.S. for over one hundred years, with the tragic exception of the war. We have joined in a strong defense treaty. We are firmly among the free countries of the world, and the presence of such a politically stable and economically sound country itself contributes to the security of the Pacific and Asia, and this is vital to the United States. We have always wanted to be part of the free world, to keep Communism away from Asia.

"When I was a young student I was taught that Communism and the Soviet Union were the chief dangers to Japan. The United States was never, never considered a potential enemy in those days. My hope, Mr. Kissinger, is that the Japanese and Americans will work to see that we do not make the same mistakes that made us enemies in the past." Historically, I was referring to the American law that stopped Japanese immigration into the United States, the high tariffs the U.S. put up against Japanese goods, and the cutting off of Japan's oil lifeline in order to force Japan to pull out of China. If both sides had not made mistakes, perhaps Communism would not be so prevalent in Asia today.

A few weeks later I got a letter saying that Kissinger was very impressed with our talk, and since then I have seen him many times on his trips to Japan, which he makes frequently, and I have been able to introduce him unofficially to some Japanese who carry weight in government and business. Kissinger is very much interested in Japan's future, and last year we had a little buffet dinner at our house to which we invited the second generation of some of the top Japanese business leaders so he could get an idea of what the coming leaders of Japan are thinking about.

I have tried to get the message across in my private way as a concerned citizen of Japan and a friend of the United States that this relationship is too precious to allow it to be damaged from either side. I have gotten to know others in the U.S. administration such as Cyrus Vance, when he was secretary of state, and Harold Brown, who was secretary of defense, and I knew George Shultz as a fellow member of the Morgan International Council before he was secretary of state in the Reagan administration, to name a few, and my message is the same to them as to congressmen, senators, and the many American businessmen I know: the stakes are very high for our two nations and our goal should be harmony.

We also have to realize that one of the basic problems in our relations is that politicians on both sides of the ocean have to run for office and cannot ignore their constituencies. This is one of the strengths of democracy. Sometimes it is a weakness, too, but one we have to put up with and try to understand.

Constituents in a certain industry will complain that they would be hurt by imports and ask for protection, and once it is given it is hard to give it up. We know, because approximately 44 percent of the goods we export to the United States are under some form of restraint, either "voluntarily" or through quotas or tariffs. Most Americans do not realize this, I have found.

As I said earlier, Japan is coming to grips with the trade problems caused by her own protectionism and is liberalizing all sectors of the economy, except some parts of the agricultural sector, which is one area where almost all countries have trade barriers, including the United States. It has taken Japan a long time to see that this liberalization of the markets was not only necessary but also good for Japan. Our sense of conservatism and caution and the nagging sense of vulnerability kept us from rushing ahead and doing many of the things that were demanded, especially in the area of capital liberalization.

But the pace has been gradually accelerated, and now American and European security houses have traders on the floor of the Tokyo Stock Exchange, and foreign banks are in the lucrative trust banking business and are more and more in the mainstream of Japanese financial activity. The Japanese yen is being used increasingly as an international currency, and even if some aspects of liberalization worry our most conservative ministries and bankers, progressive things are happening. Of course, we Japanese do not feel comfortable with the kind of wide open, frontier spirit deregulation that the United States went through in the early eighties, when banks and savings and loan associations went into freewheeling promotion and many collapsed and the government had to bail them out with public money. We are also worried about America's overextension of credit and the huge deficits the U.S. has built up.

A very wise Japanese once said that if a monkey falls from a tree, he may be bruised or embarrassed, but he can pick himself up, dust himself off, and he is still a monkey. But when a grand and powerful politician loses an election, he is just an ordinary mortal like everybody else.

Any democratic political system automatically becomes domestically oriented because any politician has to be loyal to his constituents or lose his job. It is disastrous to fall from the political tree, so to speak. It is no surprise, then, that both American and Japanese politicians are basically worried about their own citizens—I won't say their own hides. Our economic and industrial system matured more rapidly after the war than we expected, and I suppose it was a normal impulse on the Japanese part to protect its growing industries as long as possible, but Japan has been moving out of its protectionist mode.

Japan has been opening up at an increasing pace in the mid-eighties just when new protectionist talk is echoing through Europe and the United States, and Japan's old policies are sometimes blamed for it. In the decade of the sixties, the American economy increased more than 2.5 times, but the Japanese gross national product more than quadrupled. The pace leveled off in the seventies and the eighties, and now that Japan has arrived, our economy is healthy and growing much more slowly but still satisfactorily, despite some severe problems. Our productivity is very strong still and it is increasing faster than that of most other countries. Although we are moving slowly into more of a service economy, our exports are still about the same as in the past, about 13 to 15 percent of our GNP.

As I have said, we have not found it easy to make the moves necessary to bring us to where we are today. Under our parliamentary system, it would appear that the prime minister of Japan has a great deal of power, because he is the president of the ruling party, the Liberal Democratic Party (LDP), which has been in control and has given us political stability since 1955. The prime minister makes statements in international councils, like any good leader, and he can have personal relationships with world leaders, like Prime Minister Yasuhiro Nakasone developed with President Ronald Reagan and many others, but making good on the promises is more difficult than it would seem.

After Nakasone made his promises to President Reagan to accelerate the opening of Japan's markets to foreign goods, he surprised many Japanese and American skeptics with remarkable success in moving the bureaucracy and the rest of the government establishment to come up with a program of market-opening measures, including tariff reductions, an end to non-tariff barriers, and the opening of government enterprises to foreign vendors. This seemed all the more remarkable because it is often the bureaucracy, not the political "leadership," that really makes Japan tick. Most of the legislation that is introduced into Japan's parliament comes from the bureaucracy, not from the political leaders of the LDP. Often the political leaders are too busy fighting each other for power to be involved in some of the more complex problems of the day, with which the capable bureaucracy deals.

We are fortunate in having such a good professional bureaucracy, representing the cream of our universities. But the problem with it, in my view, is that while these professionals are superb technocrats, they generally know nothing else as well as they know the affairs within their own ministries, and since the system promotes from within, there is never any new blood at the upper levels to bring in fresh thinking.

The tax people, for example, are very good at making the tax system work and devising rules and regulations, but they know nothing about business or about how ordinary people earn their living, and without much control from above, except from other bureaucrats at rival ministries, we end up with an unrealistic system that overtaxes some and undertaxes others. But achieving tax reform in Japan is as difficult or more difficult than in any other democratic country because money questions are so vital to everybody.

When I returned to Japan to handle the affairs of my late father's estate in 1964 I learned a lot about this. The tax appraisers came and evaluated everything, including antiques and artworks. During the appraisal I learned that if you have a nice Japanese garden with a fine tree or particularly well-shaped and artistically placed rocks, they will assess them at a high value like works of art. Imagine paying inheritance tax on a rock in the ground! No wonder we Japanese say family wealth all goes to the tax collector in three generations.

Realizing their weaknesses, like company presidents without any control over various divisions, most prime ministers of Japan have had difficulty trying to make any dramatic changes. Foreigners do not realize what an intricate thing it can be to accomplish seemingly simple things in Japan's bureaucracy. The ministers appointed by the prime minister, usually for political reasons to satisfy one of the factions within the party, come and go, but the bureaucrats they must work with are dedicated to maintaining the system, the status quo. Consequently, very often orders from above are considered and analyzed and debated to death or until another minister is appointed.

The opening of Japan's markets came at a time when we in the business community were pressing very hard for it with the government and the bureaucracy, because we had contact with the realities of world public opinion and with the opinions of the international businessmen and consumers we deal with every day. Most bureaucrats have little contact with our reality. Japan had taken many small but important steps toward open markets, but because it was taking so long, many Americans had the idea that there had been less progress than there had been.

The most activist prime minister in the postwar period, Nakasone, said in 1985 that Japan's bureaucracy was too sheltered, and its elite tradition, learned from the British and French, was too well learned. Nakasone said that after he took over his high office he ordered many vice ministers—the key bureaucrats—to travel abroad, some of them for the first time. He called many of them into his office to tell them directly what he expected of them, a rather bold move for a Japanese prime minister who is usually expected to represent, rather than really lead, the government. And he encouraged many ministries to promote internationally minded people to more influential jobs. "I have bashed many of these vice ministers," he admitted with a smile, during a speech in which he also said how intelligent a species the Japanese bureaucrats are.

In 1986 he took a giant step forward and made a personal pledge to President Reagan that he would do his best to implement an ambitious program devised by a blue-ribbon committee calling for drastic changes in the Japanese economy and the nation's life-style. This commission, headed by former Bank of Japan governor Haruo Maekawa, recommended that the nation shift emphasis away from its export orientation and develop an economy geared more to internal demand, which would, among other things, make Japan, already a creditor nation, a much greater importer of the world's goods. The recommendations would take a long time to implement fully, if ever formally adopted, but more and more the thinking in Japan's internationalist business community is along these lines.

It is difficult for the bureaucracy to give up anything; the system resists change. For example, when the national telephone system was privatized in 1985 we in the Electronics Industry Association of Japan, which I headed, had to deal with an example of this reluctance. As a government corporation, the old telephone company, known as NTT, was under the jurisdiction of the Ministry of Posts and Telecommunications (MPT), which was actually a sort of parent to NTT. But as a private company, NTT is under MPT control only as a regulating body. Under the new deregulated phone system, as new technologies come into play and new local area networks and other communications systems are set up, MPT will be directly involved with technology standards, as the American FCC is, and with approving new equipment. Therefore, MPT will have to be aware of new technologies that are being developed.

But the Ministry of International Trade and Industry (MITI) has industry technology as its province. And so it is obvious that the problem of crossed boundaries of responsibility and bureaucratic territoriality poses a huge potential problem. If it is difficult for foreigners to understand this system, it is no less difficult for many Japanese. In some long and drawn out negotiations with the Americans over trade, it has happened that a ministry would hold off making an agreement until the very last minute so that there would not be enough time for another ministry to step in and try to change what had already been decided. During the long period of seeming inaction, the foreign negotiators have often accused the Japanese of stalling. To have understood the tactic might have calmed everybody down, but it might also have tipped one ministry's hand to a rival one.

I don't suppose this sort of thing will be a complete surprise to students of bureaucracy around the world. My point is that politics in a democracy, whether in Japan or in the United States, is still basically the same.

In the past when we discussed U.S.–Japan trade relations, we often talked about the perception gap between Japan and other nations. Today, with the increased exposure of businessmen to other cultures, the old perception gap has narrowed. But the trade problems exist because they have become politicized, and now it isn't necessarily differences in perception but differences in government systems and the way they operate that cause troubles. I call it an inter-bureaucratic problem.

In Japan the bureaucracy is institutionalized. It is a powerful organ that is consistent, so consistent that policy once established is implemented continuously no matter who the changing ministry officials are. In the United States when a new administration takes office, thousands of people in government change jobs. This doesn't happen in Japan. And so while international businessmen are beginning to understand each other, governments are still behind the times, at odds with each other, failing to resolve even what may be considered a trivial problem by the businessmen directly involved in it. In the modern language of the computer generation, we lack an interface to help us get business and governments moving on the same problems with the same level of understanding.

In Japan, we sometimes think that we manage some aspects of the government-industry relationship better than the Americans. When we have a declining industry, we try to protect it while it is being phased out; then when it is phased out, and when the workers are retrained or hired elsewhere, there is no need to protect the dead industry or its workers. Sometimes it takes a long time to do this. There are still plenty of problems in Japan, such as featherbedding in the national railway system, which has about twenty-five thousand "surplus" employees. Several thousand are being retrained right now for new jobs in other industries, in a plan to rationalize the giant system. There are scores of government boards and commissions set up to regulate and judge and control agencies and activities that don't exist anymore. But we no longer protect industries that others can do better, more economically, or more efficiently, with the exception of those agricultural areas that most countries still protect.

I was chatting with the late prime minister Masayoshi Ohira before he went off to one of the industrialized nations' summit meetings, and I urged him to speak out in defense of Japan's policies. He replied, "Well, I know what you mean, but my English is not really very good and. . . ." He was too modest about his English ability, I thought. "I don't speak well enough to say freely what I would want to, so I just do it the Japanese way," which is to say virtually nothing or attempt to make your points by indirection or polite suggestion.

I said to him jokingly, "Well, if you are going to do it the real Japanese way, please go fully dressed in traditional clothing." That way, I told him, people will recognize you as being different and will pay more attention to you. They will listen more closely and maybe they will make more of an attempt to understand you as a real foreigner. This idea does not run counter to my view that the Japanese must become more internationalized—it reinforces it. So often we try to avoid being seen or speaking out. But if our leaders go to international conferences dressed in Western clothes and pretend to understand what is going on, they will miss a lot.

Prime Minister Nakasone and his foreign minister, Shintaro Abe, know English very well, but very few of our senior politicians can comfortably speak English, the international language. The same problem exists with many senior Japanese businessmen, although the second generation of leaders is more at home in international settings.

I tried to make the point with Mr. Ohira and others that unless you can join in with the international group on their own terms, then it is best to proclaim your difference so you can be noticed and listened to seriously. Japan's intention of opening its markets to the world is serious, but we have had difficulty getting enough foreign firms to come in and make the effort, because they felt the investment might be too great, or it would take too long to become profitable. I thought foreign firms needed some extra stimulation.

In 1972, when I founded Sony Trading Corporation, I put ads in prestigious publications in the United States and Europe, looking for products to sell, and we got more than three thousand inquiries immediately. Our two-page ad in *Time* magazine said, "Sony wants to sell U.S. products in Japan. . . . Japan is a foreign country to U.S. businessmen. However, it is a domestic country to Sony and we know both its market and its potential." We now have a group of over forty shops called "Sony Plaza" selling foreign consumer goods, and we are on the lookout for more imported items to sell. Apart from that, when the prime minister urged all Japanese to buy more foreign goods in 1985, we joined scores of other companies in pledging to do so. As an added gesture, we began shipping American-made Sony Trinitron color picture tubes from our San Diego plant to Japan for assembly in Sony sets to be sold in Japan.

The stand of the Japanese government in its economic relationship with the world is that openness of its markets is the rule and restrictions against imports are invoked only as a rare exception to the rule. The hope is, of course, to keep the exceptions as few as possible. But in reality even the prime minister and the other top politicians who created this fine declaration cannot live by it completely because they are, after all, politicians in a democracy.

Here's an example: even while Prime Minister Nakasone was having so much success in opening up Japan's markets to foreign goods, one of the restricted agricultural imports (an exception to the rule, we might say) was a plant called arum root, or sometimes devil's tongue, which is used to make an ingredient, *konnyaku*, that we Japanese enjoy in sukiyaki and in many traditional boiled dishes. One of the prime growing areas for domestic arum root is Gumma Prefecture in central Japan, which happens to be the home constituency of two of the most influential politicians in Japan today: Prime Minister Nakasone himself and former prime minister Takeo Fukuda, who is very influential in ruling party politics.

It is a danger when Americans and Europeans become too emotional without thinking rationally about the problems. Japan is America's best partner today, and Japan simply cannot live without the U.S., because it is the biggest market for us, our biggest supplier of raw materials, food and feed grain, technology, ideas, and fads. At the same time, Japan is America's best overseas customer for agricultural products and its best partner, industrially, technologically, and marketwise. We are cooperating in hundreds of technology agreements, including defense technology, and the trade between our two countries is the biggest two-way flow across an ocean in history—eighty-four billion dollars in 1984. Many Americans just do not realize how dependent we are on each other, and, in fact, the loss of American manufacturing jobs cannot be a comfort to Japan or any other country.

But eventually, Japan, too, will lose manufacturing jobs in large numbers—we have done so already (in aluminum smelting and shipbuilding, for example)—as service sector jobs open up and new and different kinds of manufacturing jobs come on stream. There should be a way for American and Japanese policy to dovetail so that we could foresee problems and figure out how to face them in advance. When a strong dollar caused a big trade deficit and forced American industrialists to say they were losing competitiveness and must close factories while soaking up Japanese dollars to help finance the deficit (about forty billion dollars in 1984 alone), we found ourselves in a vicious cycle. Lashing out emotionally could solve nothing. The major industrial governments realized this in 1985 when they tried to gain some control over exchange rates, especially the yen-dollar rate, which to my mind should be the main and most crucial concern of the trading world today. But the initial moves caused serious problems because the movement was too fast.

Early in the 1960s, world trade was at a crossroads, and America led the free world into the Kennedy round of trade negotiations. That brave action avoided a serious split of the world into trading blocs. Nations sat down together and decided to drastically reduce tariff barriers to trade. In doing this, they accelerated the growth of all the countries that participated. But many of us realized then that nontariff barriers, trade restrictions, and so-called voluntary restraint agreements, surcharges, import quotas (and even domestic tax laws) continued to restrain world trade and would have to be eliminated. We were then protecting some quite healthy enterprises and politically touchy territory.

It seemed to me at the time that with two-thirds of the world's population living at a very low economic level, the developed world had a responsibility and opportunity to help bring them into a higher economic sphere, which would be a benefit to everyone. After all, the people of developing countries have the right to enjoy the benefits of an advanced civilization, better food, clothing, education, and entertainment, but we in the developed world haven't done enough to help them. This is shortsighted of us because they are our future strength, allies, coproducers, and customers. I am reminded of the story of the two shoe salesmen who visited an underdeveloped country. One cabled his office, NO PROSPECT OF SALES BECAUSE NOBODY WEARS SHOES HERE. The other salesman cabled, SEND STOCK IMMEDI-ATELY INHABITANTS BAREFOOTED DESPERATELY NEED SHOES. We are too much like the first salesman, and we have not moved on this need to help the Third World. Japan's overseas development assistance, while growing, is still inadequate and even the government admits it. But in a broader sense, neither the free world nor the Communist bloc has done enough.

I was invited in 1969 to testify before the subcommittee on U.S. foreign economic policy of the Joint Congressional Economic Committee. My picture had been on the cover of *Business Week* magazine holding our newest Sony Micro Color TV, and I guess I was something of a target as a result of the trade problems. I spoke about the need to remove nontariff barriers around the world and the parallel need to help move the underdeveloped nations into the mainstream of world economic life by focusing resources not on capital investments such as highways, dams, steel mills, and national airlines, but on the human resources of the countries and on developing a desire within these nations to become second Japans.

After I had read my prepared statement, I hoped to be excused, but there were questions from some of the congressmen. The Japanese press said I was "grilled" by angry congressmen, but I didn't think of it in those terms. One of them asked me about the establishment of Sony, and I answered him. Then he said, in very lawyerlike language, "I will ask you whether it was possible for us Americans to start a firm in Japan when you started Sony in Japan."

I said, "No, it was not possible."

"But Sony has now established a firm in America. Why is it that America is not allowed to enter Japan?"

I gave a rather long-winded answer, but I think I made my point. "Immediately after the war America looked like a giant in the eyes of penniless Japan," I said. "The Japanese had a fear complex that giant America's free inroads into Japan would immediately outmarket them. Whatever the reason, as long as they have this fear complex, they will feel resistant toward liberalization.

"Free trade is an ideal, and Japan keeps its face turned toward this direction. But as the American government has to consider the situation in making political utterances, the Japanese government, which is adopting a highly planned economy, sometimes finds itself in a difficult position. Personally, I feel that the government's moves for liberalization are slow, but I think it is certain that things will be free eventually." I didn't think then that it would take quite so long as it has.

I have often said that a booming Japanese economy is the greatest weapon against Communism that the free world has in the Pacific or anywhere else in the world. It is unfortunate that Japan's slow way of doing things seems unfair to the kind of "victim consciousness" that the U.S. has developed where Japan is concerned. America is a country of humanism and emotion. Americans like to favor the underdog. According to some Japanese scholars, the power of the American press, indignant at Spain's treatment of tiny Cuba, aroused the national consensus that led to the Spanish-American War. American sympathy for China's Chiang Kai-shek as the underdog in the war with Japan (dramatized by his charming, American-educated, English-speaking wife), turned into a national consensus that eventually helped to drive the United States and Japan to war.

I think the old Avis car rental slogan, "We're Number 2, So We Try Harder," is a perfect example of this American humanism. But America is not number 2, Japan is, and very glad to be it. However, as Japan moved from underdog against Russia to bully in China, to aggressor against the United States, to disastrous defeat, and then to number 2 in the world, American attitudes about Japan had to undergo many changes. Even number 2 may seem too big for comfort to some. On Capitol Hill, which I have visited often, there are politicians who go through dramatic emotional swings, making sensational speeches and statements for the press that they feel are good for their political campaigns. It seems to me that American politics has too much of this kind of grandstanding. We cannot see the facts for the rhetoric. And that is what worries me about the direction in which our relations are headed.

In 1919 the American Congress was carried away with emotion and passed the Volstead Act that outlawed all alcoholic drinks. Common sense today tells us that it was a stupid thing to do, and certainly there must have been millions of Americans who felt it was wrong at the time—probably including many congressmen and senators—but they went along with it. The law was broken by millions of Americans who would never have dreamed of doing anything else illegal. The Volstead Act was repealed in 1933.

What this taught me is that public opinion can move American policy. If a really negative feeling sweeps America about Japan, there can be trouble everybody may regret. Once such a trend moves too far it is very difficult to stop. And the fact that Americans too often seem to believe that they are right is a complicating factor. The United States will not likely pass a Japanese prohibition law, or repeat the mistakes of the thirties, but both Japan and the U.S. should be aware of the dangers of emotionalism and pettiness in our relationship that could lead to economic and political problems.

I have been dealing with Americans for many years and they are always in a hurry. It is common to hear in America: "There's no time!" "Do it now!" "He who hesitates is lost!" America was swept into Vietnam on this kind of emotional rush. American politicians said the United States must do this in Vietnam for the sake of the peace of the world. They lost perspective. Once the Americans love something they love it too deeply, and when they hate something they often go too far in their hate. Many foreign friends of the U.S. feel this way about America.

Take the case of China, for example. For a long time, the United States did not want to recognize that China existed, even though nearly one billion people lived there. America tried to isolate China because it didn't like the country's politics. And so in recognizing the Taiwan government, it tried to punish the Beijing government by pretending mainland China did not exist. Anybody who bought a Chinese-made trinket in Hong Kong on a vacation trip could be in trouble if he or she tried to bring it home to the U.S. in those years. Diplomatically, it was as though a third of the world's people did not exist. During that time, Japan did not recognize Communist China either, and we had no official diplomatic relations. But our people went to China often. Many went back and forth and did business and made contacts and did news reporting. And then suddenly America changed its mind. Richard Nixon went to China. Without telling anybody in advance, including China's closest neighbors, such as Japan, which had been following a policy supportive of the U.S., Nixon suddenly recognized the existence of a billion people.

In Japan we are still the inheritors of an agrarian cultural tradition and philosophy, which are influenced by nature and the change of the seasons. Perhaps because of this we are not a hasty people. We have thousands of years of history and tradition and that is why we are not pleased when we are treated as newcomers by such a young—even though great—country as the United States. We have a proverb that says everything changes in seventy days, which counsels us not to be hasty, not to overrespond, not to react too quickly. There ought to be a middle ground between the two approaches, the too hurried and the too slow.

WORLD TRADE

Averting Crisis

I

Shortsighted statesmen and businessmen around the world see their problems in bilateral terms: American businessmen are worried about their problems with Japan, and Japanese businessmen worry about how they can cope with the complaints of American and European governments and businessmen.

The other day I heard a joke about an American and a Japanese who were walking through the jungle together when they saw a hungry lion running toward them. The Japanese immediately sat down and began putting on his running shoes.

"If you think you can outrun a hungry lion," scoffed the American, "you are a fool."

"I don't have to outrun that hungry lion," said the Japanese. "I only have to outrun you!"

But the lion we face, our coming crisis, is global. We can't run away from this lion. I believe the world economic trading system is in great peril and the squabbles over specific trade issues and between countries only mask the real problems that are below the surface. Solving these small pieces of the problem do not serve us at all.

I believe the main problem is with our money. In order to have economic activity in a free and open economic system, you have to have buying and selling at appropriate prices. The prices will be affected by supply and demand, of course. That's the simple basis of the free economic system.

If I sell a product worth a thousand yen to someone in the United States or Britain, I expect to be paid the dollar or the sterling equivalent of a thousand yen. The rate at which that exchange is made must be fair and should reflect the relative competitiveness of the different nations' industries, because I believe that industry should be the primary factor in setting the value of the nation's money.

As an industrialist I know that competitiveness has to be balanced and that the exchange rate acts as the balancing mechanism. At the Bretton Woods conference in 1944 exchange rates were fixed by international agreement. The rates were based on the economic realities of that time and the foreseeable future. Japan's rate was set at three hundred and sixty yen to the U.S. dollar during the immediate postwar period, and it remained at that rate until 1971 even though our nation's industrial competitive power increased greatly. Our Japanese currency, then, was undervalued when compared with other currencies. A weak yen against a very strong dollar, for example, made Japanese goods cheaper in America, and it encouraged Japanese companies to export. This led to mounting trade imbalances in Japan's favor. Because of the strong dollar, U.S. exports became quite expensive.

When U.S. president Richard Nixon devalued the dollar in 1971, all currencies, including the yen, were allowed to float free of the old fixed-rate limits, and the yen immediately became about 15 percent more expensive against the dollar. I thought that it was proper for an upward valuation of the yen to take place. In fact, many businessmen thought of the floating system as a potentially superior one to the fixed-rate system because it could continually balance nations' industrial competitiveness.

I saw an analogy for what I thought the new system would

be in the handicap system used in golf, in which the capability of each player is balanced against that of other players. Every year the golfer's handicap is adjusted to reflect any changes in the player's capability. A player can win or lose even with his handicap, which can range from zero to thirty-six, but he knows that the game is fair because everybody is playing within a fair system.

I thought the floating system would, by international agreement, be monitored, and that rates would not be allowed to fluctuate too far or to be influenced artificially. What we didn't count on was that a factor other than the competitive power of our goods—namely, money traders—would begin to affect the value of world currencies. No mechanism had been set up to monitor the system and, figuratively speaking, to set the handicaps. Money speculators used one criterion only for buying one currency and selling another—profit. This resulted in a constant changing of rates that had nothing to do with industrial competitiveness. For those of us engaged in world-wide trade, it was as though some bully had come swaggering onto the golf course and was changing our handicaps after every hole.

In this situation the price of our goods became a matter virtually beyond our control. To illustrate the problem, suppose, for example, we listed the price of a television set not at a specific dollar, yen, pound, franc, or lira amount, but at whatever the price ten shares of Sony stock would be on the day you bought the set. Who would buy under such circumstances while the stock is being traded and the price is fluctuating each day? Who could manufacture under such circumstances?

For industrialists, money is a scale. We use it to measure the economic activity of our companies, our assets, our inventories, and even the results of human effort. When prices are set by factors other than the competitiveness of the products made, there is inevitably a withering of our confidence to invest. I am a firm believer that the foundation of the economy lies with a nation's industry. In order to invest wisely we must be able to predict the return we can reasonably expect on our investment. If we can't forecast the return, it takes a very good sixth sense, or perhaps a dash of foolhardiness, to invest. If we reach the point where there is no investment, industry will collapse. If industry collapses, money will lose all its meaning and then even the financial markets will collapse.

It worries me that today some industrialists have begun to take part in the money trading game. Since they cannot forecast the return on potential investments, many industrialists have stopped investing in their own companies and are investing a lot of energy, time, and money in acquisitions and mergers. Companies have become a commodity to be traded, bought, and sold. This is not the natural and rightful role of industry, which is to better existing products and create new ones. Looking at the situation as a Japanese, I cannot believe employees of such companies have much desire to work. How can a sense of loyalty and harmonious productivity be cultivated in such an environment, when management is concerned more about whether they are taking over another company or being taken over? The outlook is not encouraging. This is why I continue to talk loudly about the need for a new exchange-rate system based on industrial values rather than money markets.

The oil shocks of 1973 and 1979 were a great blow to the world monetary system as vast amounts of money were pooled in the oil-exporting countries. Under Reaganomics, the U.S. tightened the money supply and raised interest rates to stop inflation. Large amounts of Japanese currency went to America in the form of investments, seeking the benefit of those high interest rates. In fact, money from all over the world came pouring into the United States. This made the dollar stronger, cheapened all other currencies, made bigger American government spending possible, and bigger debt accumulation, too. The world money game was on in earnest.

I have written earlier, maybe not with too much sympathy, about how many American businessmen must run their businesses with greater and greater profit foremost in mind, always with the fear that their stock price may drop if their quarterly dividends do not show constant improvement. In this atmosphere, when the pursuit of profit gets stronger and stronger, managers are forced to seek the easiest ways to make a profit. Two dangerous things have happened: some managers have found they can make more money more easily by trading money rather than goods; others have found that manufacturing where the cost is cheapest gives them the best chance to show profits quickly, even if it means moving production offshore.

This phenomenon is leading to what I call the hollowing out of American industry. America's industrial establishment is being reduced to a mere shell, and the same is happening all over Europe. Some Japanese firms may soon face it also. Many are beginning to export production. American companies like Motorola, Texas Instruments, Fairchild, and many others have moved production facilities to Japan or added new facilities here. Yet congressmen in districts where jobs in these companies have been lost in the U.S. complain about Japan being responsible for the decline in American employment. In 1984, IBM Japan was the biggest exporter of computers from Japan. One reason American firms move to Japan or buy high-tech parts from Japan is to take advantage of the skills available here now that quality labor, not merely less expensive labor, is needed. But Sony, on the other hand, has been able to find the skills we need in America and in other countries. Employing our production technologies, and using our longer-term business philosophy, we can make money where domestic companies often flee, because they demand quick and consistent profits.

In the fall of 1985 I took a trip to Europe with Yoshihiro Inayama, the chairman of the Keidanren (Japan Federation of Economic Organizations), and we met many Europeans who were boasting, "There are no new ideas made in Japan. We make the ideas, right here in Europe." I said to one such, "Look, there is no sense in boasting that you have ideas. I mean, everyone has some kind of ideas that people agree are good. The important thing is how you are going to interpret that idea in your industry. Japan has been working hard in that area. You haven't, so don't boast too much."

European nations appreciate scientists—we all know that. Many of the greatest "American" scientists have their roots and even received their education in Europe; it has been one of the great strengths of the United States. But whereas in the U.S. and in Japan equal appreciation was given to engineers—the people who translate scientific breakthroughs into usable goods—many European countries traditionally tended to shun this hands-on discipline, engineering, through a sense of snobbishness. European engineers for a long time were considered "merely" craftsmen. It was America and Japan that recognized their crucial importance. Universities in both countries developed good engineering departments. Lately, however, emphasis on university engineering studies is higher in Japan than in the U.S., where (and this is connected to the U.S. emphasis on litigation) law currently seems more intriguing to American youth.

As concerned as I am about the trend toward the expansion of trade in currencies at the expense of the expansion of the trade in goods, this lack of interest in keeping up with the need for changing technologies and production of new kinds of goods concerns me too. The problem is far deeper than simply the fact that the dollar and the yen are unreasonably valued. In 1986, U.S. senator Thomas Eagleton made an impassioned comment at a breakfast meeting of the American Chamber of Commerce in Tokyo in answer to a question about the decline of America's industrial capability. Eagleton said the United States had to protect its industry and expand it, and he vowed that the U.S. would never allow itself to become a nation of mere service trades. The context of the senator's statement was that Japan must do more to correct the trade imbalance between the two countries—otherwise the U.S. might turn protectionist. I sympathize with his frustration, but the fact is that what must be done to help the U.S. depends more on the U.S. than on Japan. Exporting production and playing the money game are not the ways to ensure a strong and healthy industrial plant in the United States.

Recent treasury secretary Donald Regan was formerly chairman of Merrill Lynch Pierce Fenner and Smith, Inc., which is a big player of the money game. The philosophy of the monetarists, handicapped by not knowing anything firsthand about industry, is that a strong dollar is best for America, and that the problems of an imbalance of currencies will correct themselves naturally over time. When James Baker took over from Regan in the Treasury Department in 1985, he grasped the problem immediately. In one of his first speeches he staked out his position, saying that unless we change the exchange system in the world and correct the abnormal situation of the strong dollar, the problem of this wide imbalance of currencies will plague us. That led to the first of the Group of Five (G-5) meetings of finance ministers from Japan, the U.S., the U.K., France, and Germany on the subject that resulted in a readjustment in exchange rates in 1985.

The attempt by Baker and the Group of Five produced a sudden, too drastic swing in exchange rates, rocketing the yen to historically high levels in record time, making a reasonable adjustment by business virtually impossible. In a little over half a year, after central banks of the G-5 nations intervened by selling other currencies to lower the value of the dollar, the yen zoomed more than 35 percent against the dollar, a stunning rise that was difficult to cope with, especially for small- and medium-sized firms. Although Japanese makers of export goods raised their prices because of the rise of the value of the yen, we were dismayed to see many American companies raise their own prices as well, creating an inflationary trend.

As well-meaning as the G-5 action was, it is obvious to me that the world cannot depend upon arbitrary policy coordination between countries to keep exchange rates realistic. Nations must get together to create a new international mechanism to stabilize rates. And the pursuit of monetary profits through mere speculation rather than productive endeavor must be discouraged.

Leaders of the seven industrialized nations meeting at the Tokyo Economic Summit in May 1986 did not take any significant action on exchange rates. But they recognized the problems inherent in wide fluctuations of rates, and by agreeing to monitor the situation they moved a step toward what I hope will be a resolution, but I was disappointed that they didn't go farther and set up a formal mechanism for monitoring the rates or call for a meeting to consider a new system.

How much can be accomplished by intervention and for how long? The money that is being shipped around the world by the money merchants is enormous compared with the amount that Japan or any other single country can use to intervene. So the money game players of the world are biding their time, thinking that sooner or later things will get better for them. If the amount of funds available to central banks for intervention in the market to influence currency rates is insufficient, the system may begin to falter and chaos may ensue. That is why I insist on the need to change the exchange system once again.

Nobody knows what a "fair" set of exchange rates would be, and I have no magic prescriptions either. But once a year the International Monetary Fund could meet and agree to adjust currencies to the current realities, allowing for a small and reasonable amount of fluctuation between preset limits below and above the optimum figure. We in industry put tremendous effort into reducing the original cost of a product by as little as 1 or 2 percent, but under the current system the value of our money can fluctuate as much as 10 or 15 percent in a single day, wiping out all our attempts at economy. This saps the will to work, to innovate, and a fundamental incentive in a free economic system is being lost. It is difficult to do business and make plans for the future without knowing what the value of your money will be.

Our decision to invest in a manufacturing plant in San Diego was made despite such uncertainty. When Kazuo Iwama was president of Sony America he was very strong, as was I, for a domestic TV plant, even though the economics didn't look very good. The yen was still fixed at three hundred and sixty to the dollar (it was being traded on the black market for as little as four hundred and twenty to the dollar), and American companies like RCA, Zenith, and Admiral were going offshore to produce their television sets, to places like Mexico and Singapore. Iwama and I, who had the most experience in the American market, felt that for us, it was better to go in the opposite direction, that is, to go to the U.S. because that was where the market was.

But to produce the sets in those days before the integrated circuit, we knew we had to do a lot of manual operations on the sets, at higher American labor rates, and we, of course, had to build a plant, which we estimated would cost us at least twenty-five million dollars. Junichi Kodera, who was to be our first San Diego plant manager, was brought back to Japan, and we set him to work evaluating and projecting the current and future costs of operating in the U.S. That project team knew that integrated circuits were on the way and would soon be replacing transistors and that in about three to four years, as the number of components of each set decreased, assembly time would decrease, too, which would compensate for the increased wages we would be paying in the United States compared with Japan.

But that was the only light at the end of the tunnel. Kodera says today that when he came to our management committee with all his figures and projections, he was very pessimistic. Based on the exchange rate of three hundred and sixty yen to the dollar, even though we could see a dramatic business turn-around in three years, the numbers at the time, in August of 1971, didn't justify building the plant. But Ibuka and I were heading the management committee then, and we knew the figures; we also felt, however, that this move would prove a wise one in the long run. We knew the cheap yen could not last forever. We surprised Kodera by not even asking about the numbers. We told him we were going ahead. We sent him to our main TV assembly plant at Ichinomiya to get briefed on the latest production systems in preparation for his job in San Diego.

Later that same day, August 16 (it was still August 15 in the United States), President Nixon announced a change in U.S. monetary policy, in effect devaluing the dollar and raising the yen value against the dollar by 15 percent. Nixon temporarily suspended the pledge to convert dollars held by foreign central banks into gold or other monetary assets. He cut back on foreign aid and slapped a 10-percent surcharge on all imports. It was an amazing turn of events that suddenly made the projections on the San Diego operation look very much better. And although we were committed to going ahead with the plant, even if it meant financial difficulty for a few years, we were thrilled with this good omen for our future, enabling us to manufacture products that would carry the label, "Made in U.S.A."

It is ironic that in Europe, socialist prime minister François Mitterrand seems to be the only leader who understands the need to change the exchange rate system. He has said often that the current exchange system is wrong and that he wants to apply the European Monetary System (EMS) to the dollar and the yen.

The European countries that trade with each other in the EMS maintain fixed exchange rates that are periodically adjusted by the EMS. Trade with nonmember nations is conducted at foreign exchange market rates and can fluctuate greatly, but inside the group there is coordination and freedom from any great swings caused by currency speculators or unrelated events.

Imagine, we are getting this sound free market advice from the head of a socialist government, and the heads of states who say they believe in a free economy do not understand this. I think it is ironic and dangerous.

I have the same problem in Japan. I have tried very hard to stress this point. The money experts, however, are shortsighted. They say, "We cannot do this." Or, "Oh, that would be too dangerous." They seem to lack creativity, imagination.

When I suggested to experts in the Ministry of Finance in the past that we must intervene in money markets, buying yen to make the yen stronger, they would say, "No, we cannot intervene, the amount of money we can spend to prop up the yen by buying it is so small." But after the G-5 decision was made, the Bank of Japan intervened and it worked very well in helping to raise the value of the yen.

I spoke about this need in America, too, before it happened. The money experts there said, "How can we go back now to a fixed rate? If we cannot change back to the fixed rate, the floating system that we have now is the best we can do. There is no other choice." I got angry. I said if we engineers were to think that the systems we have today are the best we can devise and that we have no other alternative, we would stop all innovation. We scientists and engineers work constantly to come up with new ideas. The day we make an invention is the day we begin to work to improve it, which is how technology has developed to this point. I responded to one expert by saying, "If you people say that because you cannot change back to the fixed rate system, the floating system is the only choice and that there are no other alternatives, then you are showing yourself to be lame before the whole world."

A main challenge to the world trading system is the rebuilding of the American industrial structure. I believe there are signs that it is beginning, but there are contradictory signs, too, of industries that are giving up and blaming their failure on others. Although many Americans proclaim that service industries are the future of American business, it is obvious that no nation can give up all of its crucial industrial infrastructure, and, as the senator says, become a nation of fried chicken restaurant franchisers. But I do not see Congress making this kind of recovery a priority.

Protectionism, the stifling of free trade, is a curious way to expand free trade, but too often that is the short and oversimplified answer that congressmen in America and government officials and parliamentarians in Europe come up with. I have been saying to my government for years that we should be telling the United States that what is wrong with American industry is not Japan; it is an American problem. Even Lee Iacocca has admitted that. I have long felt that instead of stifling our trade through so-called voluntary restraint agreements, as we have in automobiles and some other fields, it is much better to have forthright protectionist legislation. At least that way the people who impose the restrictions have to face up to what they are doing. They can no longer see themselves as free-traders.

A couple of years ago, when we were being bashed very hard on trade, I told the prime minister, "If you are so close to President Reagan that you are on a first-name basis, please say more to 'Ron' about where the problems lie, that America is very much to blame for her problems, not just Japan," and he said something about not wanting to act the villain. I said, "I act the villain very hard whenever I go to America. I try to say things that will get people's attention and get them thinking clearly about our problems."

Konosuke Matsushita, the founder of Matsushita Electric, and I wrote a book in 1976 called *Yuron*, or roughly, "Voicing Our Concern," a book about the need for excellence. When we were about to have it published he called me and asked me whether I thought that his criticisms in the book might somehow be bad for the nation's business. I said, "No, sir, if we keep our mouths shut in the interest of good business, Japan may crumble to pieces and nobody will be able to say why." Actually, criticism can hurt business, but seeing things from many viewpoints is important for businesses, for individuals, and for nations, too. Japan was ruined in World War II because she saw only her own point of view.

For a decade or longer, whenever the Americans and Europeans have told us our market is not fully open to imported goods, our government responded by saying, "We will work on it." And then tariffs would be relaxed, some nontariff barriers would be dismantled, edging the Japanese market open a bit more. When the next complaint came, we devised plan two, taking more of the same steps. And finally after plan eight it still is not enough. All of these plans will not solve the trade imbalance. Japan's market is opening too slowly—I have said that often. However, the main ingredient in the trade imbalance has been the problem of exchange rates. And this situation did not begin to show any improvement until the G-5 meeting, and then the pendulum of rates swung too far and raised the yen to record, and unrealistic, highs.

My point is that we Japanese should have been more adamant about exchange rates and more candid in identifying the reasons for the trade imbalance, instead of just ducking our heads and painstakingly eking out market-opening measures, which everybody knows will not solve the trade imbalance. Japan's attitude when it comes to international negotiations is very poor. We never seem to be holding our heads up high and saying sincerely just what we think.

In 1979, together with our former foreign minister and ambassador to the U.S., the late Nobuhiko Ushiba, we held the first U.S.–Japan Economic Relations Group meeting. There were eight private citizens on the panel, and the American side was headed by Robert Ingersoll, former ambassador to Japan. At that time, American congressmen were talking about trade reciprocity. Some people were demanding that anything that is allowed in the United States in business should be allowed in Japan, and vice versa, and they called that reciprocity. The concept we of the so-called "Wisemen's Group" came up with was not reciprocity, but equal national treatment. Our view prevailed. What we said was that when in Japan, all foreigners can engage in all the activities open to the Japanese; in the U.S. the Japanese can do what the Americans are allowed to do.

But most of the Americans I know seem to believe that since the U.S. has the least restrictions, America should set the standard for everyone to follow. We said in our group meetings, however, that to allow people from other countries to have privileges in Japan that even the Japanese themselves cannot enjoy is impossible. Reciprocity would mean changing laws to accept foreign systems that may not suit our culture. In our report we said, among other things, that "Japanese negotiators should speak up more, countering American criticism as squarely as possible, to minimize misunderstandings or misperceptions of their position. When the United States Government criticizes Japanese policy or makes specific requests, the Japanese government should respond with rational explanations of its positions and counterarguments instead of saying nothing, appearing to acquiesce, or simply saying 'no.' "

I believe the future of our world trading system depends upon increasing, not stemming, trade. Right now Japan is digging her own grave in this regard. If the trade imbalance does not change, then the reaction from abroad will be to demand greater and greater restrictions on Japanese exports. We have to get to the root causes of these problems and not just react to what appears to be the problem on the surface. American industrial competitiveness must return. We are soon approaching the point, because of the loss of American manufacturing, where the U.S. may need Japan and her exports as much or more than Japan needs the U.S. market.

Some American analysts have said that Japan will slow down, that Japan is losing the work ethic, and so on. Many Japanese, too, especially a lot of the oldtimers, think that we have lost our sense of loyalty or that people now work only so that they can play. People's states of mind change through the course of time, but despite some natural generational changes in attitude, Japan's work ethic is very firmly in place.

Japan's position has grown stronger and more important in the world, so we can no longer live quietly in a corner with only our own needs in mind. If we are going to say something, we have to say it in a way that the other side will understand. We are not used to this, even though today we are the world's second largest economy. But if we are going to get along with our neighbors, it is necessary for us to do things differently. We have problems with the Americans, and they are hard to deal with because Americans get so emotional. But in my experience with America and Americans, I have found that if you are straightforward and convincing they will listen and they might even change their minds.

II

We have struggled hard to expand our business and to do business in other countries by the rules of those countries. Learning how to do it was not easy, and frankly, until recently I have not seen many American companies or European companies making similar efforts.

Moving into the European market was not easy for us. We sent young men with creative minds and didn't give them too many rules or instructions and no unusual benefits or special compensation packages. They performed wonderfully, proving again my contention that people do not work only for money. American companies that are moving offshore to cheaper labor zones will soon find that it is self-defeating. To move abroad to expand world trade is a noble thing. But if it means the hollowing out of the industry of your own nation, I think there is something very wrong with it.

Many foreigners complain how difficult it is to do business in Japan, but as I have said already, when I went to America for the first time I felt that it would be impossible to do well in that enormous market. In Japan we have a large percentage of the population in one relatively short band along the Pacific coast. They are almost 100-percent literate; they all speak the same language, have the same cultural background, see the same nationwide TV, read the same national newspapers. Consider how different the United States is, or England, or France. Yet these people often say they find Japan perplexing. It amazes me. We faced the challenges abroad, and I still wonder why so many companies are afraid of Japan and its one hundred and twenty million consumers. Expanding world trade will require companies to know and understand other peoples; that should be the first priority today, not protectionism. A company can sell its products abroad if those products are good and suit the market and if the company is willing to put some long-term effort into it. I have had experience in this, obviously. We faced a lot of obstacles and struggled to find the answers; it should be a lot easier today. I'd like to recount some examples.

Selling our products in Germany was a big challenge for me in the sixties. Of course, German companies were electronics pioneers, and they naturally considered that their consumer electronics were unbeatable. People all over the world held the names in awe: Grundig, Nordmende, Telefunken, to name the top ones. We had on our staff a young man named Yasumasa Mizushima, who had spent about two and a half years in New York with a Japanese trading company before joining Sony. He spoke English and a little Spanish. I had previously assigned him to Sony Overseas, in Zug, where he was busy learning French, when the idea of opening a representative office in Germany struck me. Our products were not selling well there, and our distributors didn't seem too enthusiastic about them. We found a new distributor, and I thought if we had an office there to work with the distributor we could do better in that tough market. I called Mizushima back to Tokyo and told him he had four weeks to learn German and start work on the Germany office plan. We often joke about it now; he bought a book on how to speak German in four weeks, but after three weeks we needed him to go, so I told him to learn the fourth week's lesson on the plane on the way to Germany.

Mizushima set up his office in Kiel, because that was where our new distributor was. He took a desk in the distributor's office, because that was the most convenient and cheapest way to start out, but within six months we decided to move the office to Hamburg because Mizushima was covering the Netherlands and Austria as well as Germany, and transportation from Kiel was difficult. It took three hours then to drive from Kiel to the Hamburg airport.

The German consumers didn't accept any Japanese products easily, and our distributors were not producing satisfactory results. Mizushima, who by now had learned a surprising amount of German by studying at night school, paying his tuition out of his own pocket, recommended we open our own company. I knew what kind of effort he had put into the work so far, and I had confidence in him. He used to take the German office correspondence home with him at night, translate it with the help of a dictionary, and bring it in to have his secretary check it each morning, in addition to his schoolwork and his company work. When he suggested we establish the Sony Deutschland sales company, I put him in charge of designing the project and selling it to the home office, which he did.

In the first group of seventeen people hired for the new company, only one knew what kind of a company Sony was when he applied for the job, and that man was a service technician who had worked on some of our products. Our approach to the market was to promote an image of quality. We began by selling high-quality amplifiers and receivers and tape recorders and a brand new product—a digital clock radio—in only the best electronics shops. When Mizushima first went to Germany no Sony product sold more than one thousand units a month, but within a few months sales of the clock radios alone were more than three thousand. As the Sony name began to become known, department stores and mass sales companies began to ask for Sony products, but we turned them down. Mizushima was under pressure from Tokyo to accept more and more orders, but he stuck to his guns and continued to promote the Sony image of expensive high quality. I visited every three months or so, but refrained from giving Mizushima unasked-for advice. He was only about thirty years old and was running a sixty-million-dollar business. He allowed himself to buy a company Mercedes at the end of the first year.

Our German employees increased in number to over one thousand and caught the spirit of our enterprise. They worked hard, for long hours. We gave them promotions and responsibility. Many of our employees were given authority and responsibility they could never have gotten in a German company at their young age and with their level of education. Ironically, we took advantage of a handicap in the beginning, which was that we were unknown and we could not recruit university graduates, who would find this little foreign company lacking in prestige. And so we had marvelous, energetic young people holding important jobs in this new company who appreciated the opportunity to succeed even though they did not come equipped with a degree from a famous university. We applied my philosophy of disregarding school background, and it worked in Germany as well as in Japan. Mizushima would spend long hours, as in Japan, dining and drinking with his colleagues and building up a sense of sharing. (The Sony Deutschland operation is very successful to this day and is now managed by Jack Schmuckli, a Sony executive who has amply demonstrated that a non-Japanese can run a major Japanese subsidiary.)

We had to adapt our operations and our products to the European market in order to be successful there. In many countries, such as in Scandinavia and in Belgium and France, we at first appointed manufacturers, technically competitors, to be our agents, because they had good sales capability and good names. Most of them were small family companies, such as Gylling Company in Sweden, a fine company that was very good in office communications and tape recorders, black and white television, and printed circuit boards. In Denmark we worked with Eltra, also a small maker of tape recorders, and in Finland with Helvar, another fine, small company. We had complementary products to fill out the sales lines of these and other companies we joined. Eventually, some of these companies we worked with changed into trading companies, because they could not compete with the European manufacturing giants, but they stayed in our "family." Eltra is now Sony Denmark.

In Holland, Anton Brandsteder very boldly and effectively promoted Sony products in the Dutch market, right under the nose of the giant Philips company, from our earliest days. In Canada we had the trust and faith and good business judgment of Albert D. Cohen, Sony's first overseas distributor, who began selling Sony products in the fifties, beginning with our very first transistor radio.

To supply the right products we had to know the markets. I sent another young man named Nobuyuki Idei to Europe as our marketing manager, who found that resistance to Japanese products was high, partially because our products looked and sounded different from the European models. Also, European TV has different standards, and in the early sixties, before the PAL system was made a standard, there were four different standards, so we had to design a set that would accept any of four standards at the push of a button. The sound had to be modified, because, for example, the German language has many guttural sounds, and so we had to come up with a kind of European sound for our radio and TV speakers.

In the beginning, too, there was a great deal of resistance to our spare, modern styling of straight lines and square corners; European products were more rounded and used a lot of wood. We had some meetings on this subject and considered making different designs for Europe, but I finally decided that if we were to try to emulate European styling we would look like imitators, so it would be better to retain our own style. Our products became popular because they were distinctive, and soon the clean lines of Japanese design influenced European styling.

I wrote earlier that we had much trouble creating our own sales company in France. Idei used to joke while the two-year struggle was going on that he didn't know it was so hard to get a French divorce. Even after we had separated from our French partner and we had opened our showroom on the Champs Elysées, our former partner complained to the French government that we were showing products not sold in France, which was then against the law.

It is curious, but the French government tries to control all investment in the country, no matter how small. The government is always trying to protect the nation from foreign industry, yet the French people are very eager to get foreign goods. It is much easier to sell to the French people than the Germans. We have persevered, despite the customs roadblock

at Poitiers, and we opened a tape manufacturing plant in Bay-
onne in 1981, another at Dax Pontonx in 1984, and had a compact disc plant in Alsace under construction in 1986. We had
a lot of help in France from Jacques Dontot, who was the honorary chairman of the Electronics Industry Association of France
and became the first president and director general of Sony
France. Giscard d'Estaing helped to open doors for us when we
began our negotiations to open a manufacturing operation in
France, and our relations since those early difficult days have
been fine.

Getting our own operation going in the U.K. was not very
simple either. We had as our distributors the Debenham Group,
Ltd, a fine old firm, but one that could not service a company
like ours with our big hopes for the future. When I sent Masa
Namiki to London, he discovered that the Debenham company's wholesale division could only assign three agents to Sony
and they had to cover about six hundred dealers. Namiki went
through the phone book and got a list of about two hundred
and fifty leading dealers and visited them all. He found that
Japanese radios and tape recorders were considered cheap and
unreliable. Unfortunately for us at the time, we were making
a small number of transistor radios in Shannon, Ireland, but
were not getting good quality. The local content laws required
30-percent local parts, and we could not get quality parts.

We shut down the Shannon factory and started our U.K.
sales company in London in 1968, after Namiki and I had worked
on it for two years. Unlike our experience in dropping our French
agent, the termination with Debenham was gentlemanly; they
offered us all sorts of help, and when we took five people from
their staff into our new company, they did not ask for a termination fee or goodwill money. We started in the U.K. with
Namiki and seven other people in a tiny office in Wigmore Hall
and later set up regional sales offices in Kent, Birmingham,
Bristol, Manchester, and eventually in Glasgow, Scotland. By
1970 we had a distribution center in Slough near Heathrow
Airport and a service center there. Then we moved from Wigmore Hall to Hounslow, a small town also near Heathrow.

Learning to work with the English was quite a problem
at first. Namiki assigned one of his salesmen to be district
manager in Kent, but the salesman refused the appointment
graciously because he couldn't bear to leave his rose garden in

Surrey. Namiki didn't understand it at first; to turn down such an offer would be unheard-of in a Japanese company. Later he was invited to visit the salesman's beautiful garden, and after a tour of the rose beds, Namiki said, "Now I understand."

It was in an era before trade frictions had begun when Namiki suggested we open a manufacturing plant in Britain. We could see our U.K. business growing, and in 1971 we projected that we might get our share of the market up to 7 or 8 percent. Together with the other Japanese importers we could conceivably reach 10 percent or more by 1975 or 1976, and that could mean trouble from domestic makers and politicians. We gave Namiki the green light to investigate possible plant sites and make a proposal for a British manufacturing operation. He examined a lot of the country—Scotland, the northern border country, the Newcastle area, East Anglia, and Wales—and talked with many local officials about the sites, about taxes and the kinds of inducements they were offering for plant locations, such as tax holidays, leaseback arrangements, even wage supplements.

I did not tell Namiki that the Prince of Wales had urged me to look at Wales when and if we decided to manufacture in Britain, and I was as surprised as anybody when Namiki came up with the recommendation for Wales. Clearly, it was the best site. It was close to the big markets, such as London, Birmingham, Manchester, Bristol. We also knew that a motorway, or highway, was being planned and that transportation from the port of Southampton by road and rail was good. We also got a good package from the government. After Namiki had made his recommendation, which we accepted, I told him about the prince, and though we actually started production at the Bridgend plant in June 1974, we held the official opening in December, when the prince could be present.

We were of course worried about strikes in the U.K., and what a transit strike, for example, would do to our production, so we made sure our employees got to work despite transit strikes or slowdowns by using our own buses to pick them up and bring them to work every morning. We did away with any notions of hierarchy at the plant, as in Japan, by having no special dining room for executives or supervisors and no reserved parking places. Of course we wanted everybody to wear our Sony jacket, and there was some resistance at first from our service engineers, who in Great Britain traditionally wear a long white smock. We didn't make wearing the jacket mandatory, but before long just about everybody was proud to be wearing the jacket, including the men in the white smocks. The notions of hierarchy broke down.

In the United States we didn't even have to advertise for workers when we established our plant at Rancho Bernardo Industrial Park north of San Diego. Of course our name was known by the time we broke ground and finally opened in August 1972. Hewlett-Packard, NCR, and Burroughs were all manufacturing there, and they assured us that hiring was very easy. We set up a temporary office to take applications after ground-breaking in 1971—we got a lot of publicity as the first such Japanese venture in the United States, so the "advertising" was free—and we had quite a backlog of applicants to interview when we were ready to hire.

We did run an ad for managers in Chicago, and the plant manager, Junichi Kodera, interviewed twenty applicants, all experienced people with other companies such as RCA and Zenith, but the more we thought about it, the more we realized that hiring a manager with experience in TV was not such a good idea. We wanted our new operation to use the same basic methods we used in Japan, although we knew we would have to modify them somewhat, but we insisted that we had to have the same quality from the first set off the end of the assembly line that we got in Japan. People with TV manufacturing and assembly backgrounds in U.S. companies, I thought, might have trouble adapting to our system. To make sure we wouldn't have any conflicts with old habits, we decided not to hire anybody who had TV or home appliance background. We got our managers from other manufacturing fields and trained them the Sony way in Japan. We also hired our first assembly-line employees from among those who had had no experience in manufacturing operations.

We had difficulties at first, of course. Our assembly-line workers were mainly women who had not worked on this kind of job before. We interviewed each one carefully several times before we made the selection. Each supervisor and the prospective employee who would work on that team could look each other over before the hiring took place. We hired only thirty people for the core group, and we began by assembling sets from parts shipped from Japan. We knew we would have difficulty doing things our way from the beginning, because there was a need for written instructions for each operation. In Japan our basic assembly manuals were never updated because people stayed on the various line jobs for a long time and they learned and taught the newcomers how to do each operation or group of operations. Changes in technique were constantly being made without being written down in any manual.

We also discovered that sometimes new employees couldn't keep up with the pace and might miss an operation. In Japan if someone misses doing something the next person down the line will catch it and correct it. But we discovered in San Diego, working with our new employees, that we could not depend upon the people down the line automatically to look for and correct earlier mistakes or omissions. So we devised a system in which an operator who couldn't do a certain operation would mark the missed operation, not as a penalty, but in order to alert another station to finish the job. Solving problems like this took three or four months.

We found our American workers, like the British and French workers, to be excellent after training. But our system at San Diego had a built-in flaw. We had set up our pay scales to compensate more for the most difficult jobs: one pay rate for an entry-level assembly-line job, a higher pay scale for a different and more difficult job on the line, and a still-higher one for line jobs adjusting the sets after assembly. Naturally, worker morale was high, and they wanted to move up to the top job category and get the highest pay rate. In Japan workers are content to move between jobs on the line, and they are paid by seniority, not by job classification, so we did not have the problem that developed in the U.S., where we found that we could not get our repair rate below a certain point because our basic assemblers were all newcomers just learning the job and naturally were missing operations. To minimize job hopping, we adjusted the system in San Diego so that a worker could stay on the same job and earn more money. Some of those early employees are still with us. They are our core staff at San Diego. We have not laid off a single employee there, even during the difficult period after the 1973 oil embargo.

I wrote earlier about how we had to be more demanding in our specifications to get the American workers (and British, too) to give us the standard we wanted. We found a higher diversity of dexterity among the American women on our assembly line than among Japanese women, so we had to compensate for it, finding the right person for each job. I visited the San Diego plant very frequently in the early days and often the management would ask me to give a talk to the employees, usually taking about ten minutes at lunchtime. I would tell them about the Sony philosophy, or about whatever popped into my head. Mainly, I wanted to be visible to them, to show them that the company was not faceless, and to make them feel like members of our family, which they are. Kodera and the others who were running the plant said it became easy to manage because top management was so well known to everybody.

III

In this way we expanded our trade and development overseas. While doing it, I was always conscious of reactions to the volume of our trade, as in Britain and the United States, where it seemed not only logical but also prudent to create employment in the places where we sell our products. This has been a main problem abroad for Japanese makers, whose success in manufacturing and marketing attractive consumer products has caused so many problems. Sometimes our critics talk of "torrential" exports from Japan and complain that they cannot compete. It is a complex subject, of course, but for years I have been unhappy with the situation in which we become the only suppliers, or we get so far out ahead that none of our competitors abroad can catch up.

When we began making tape recorders in Japan, we held all the crucial patents and we had 100 percent of the market. But it might have been self-defeating to continue that monopoly. We began licensing, and soon we had only 30 percent of the market, but it was a much bigger market. It gives us no sense of comfort that there is no domestic American maker of video tape recorders or compact disc players; in fact it bothers me a lot, because with competition we could expand the market and hasten the development of new models. Without competition there is less incentive to innovate.

It would be good to talk about this with our competitors, but antitrust laws in the United States make it impossible for heads of competing businesses to get together and discuss future trends and mutual problems. By contrast we have been doing this very thing in a friendly manner in Britain for a number of years. Lord Thorneycroft, the chairman of Pye Electronics, headed the British delegation and Sony's Noboru Yoshii headed the first Japanese delegation.

We started these conferences because of my concern about one nation's industry getting such a long lead on the rest of the world's industry back in the late sixties. This was dramatized to me in the early seventies when we began doing research on video tape recording (VTR). We joined with Philips to work in the same direction on this project. To me, VTR was the next logical product while color TV was reaching its peak. Obviously, we were not the only people working on the new technology; many companies had started R&D and were already filing patent applications on the recorder. Even though it seemed clear to the Japanese makers that VTR was going to be big, there was a reluctance in America and in Europe. Only Philips and a couple of other firms were interested. Philips seemed to be in a hurry and moved into the consumer market with a machine that was not right for home use, I felt, and they were not successful with it. They finally licensed from Japanese companies. In the meantime we had perfected our product and other Japanese companies followed. Then the same American companies that had never even bothered to do the spadework and make the investment to get into the market themselves began buying OEM products from Japan, and some of them were complaining to their congressmen that Japan's exports were becoming "torrential."

I tried to convince my colleagues and competitors that to avoid future trade problems it would be better to have European makers and American makers aware of the future prospects and available technology, as well as estimates of the probable public demand for specific kinds of products for the coming decade. With this knowledge, they could do their R&D on their own and be able to compete. If they could not compete, they wouldn't have much to complain about, since they would have had the benefit of the judgment of their competitors about which way the market was heading.

What will the consumer need in the next ten or twenty years? This is what I felt top management should be concerned with—the future technological trends, which technologies will be useful, or necessary, and what kind of standards we should be thinking of. This kind of talk could only benefit consumers, it seems to me.

I proposed such a meeting in a chat with Viscount Etienne D'Avignon, who was then vice president of the Commission of the European Communities in charge of industrial affairs. He was visiting Tokyo, and we talked about trade problems and cooperation in industry, and I gave him some suggestions. I told him that Japan was working on products that would not be on the market for at least ten years. With video, for example, I told him, "Ten years ago everyone in Japan was working on video. When we introduced it at Sony, everyone followed. But look at your European industry. Because almost nobody was working on video, no company had products ready to market when the Japanese companies began selling them. Your importers began buying these machines from us in large amounts, and then you get angry and refer to our exports as a type of torrential downpour."

I told him I didn't want to dwell on the past, but I said, "Your companies just do not know what will happen in the future. We are thinking about directions ten years from now and your industry should be doing the same. Why don't you arrange with Japan to get those at the top of related industries to sit down together and have discussions?" He thought it was a good idea. I also discussed it with Dr. Wisse Decker, then the chairman of Philips, Europe's biggest electronics maker. He was in favor of it also.

Back in Tokyo I discussed the idea with Shintaro Abe, a top politician, who was then minister of MITI, pointing out that naturally we would not be talking about prices or market share. But such a meeting, I felt, should be sponsored by governments, not the industry associations of the nations, in order to avoid any antitrust complications. I proposed that a record of our deliberations would be made, and it would be available to companies that did not attend. Formally, Abe asked the Keidanren to get involved through the relevant committee, and they agreed. Then Abe contacted D'Avignon, and in 1982 the first meeting was held in Brussels. The second meeting took place in Tokyo in 1984 and the third in London in 1985. These meetings have helped us understand each other better, for one thing. But I am not sure that they are breaking down the traditional patterns of European business behavior.

Years ago I was told by a European friend that if you had a fine book manuscript and you knew you could sell one hundred copies of the book, the European publisher's reaction would be to print ninety-nine copies. To print one hundred and one copies, said my friend, would be going against the European sense of propriety. The Japanese view is this: we would keep printing those books and sell as many as we could. The more we printed, the cheaper the price could be, and with promotion and education, we could create more demand and get more books into the hands of more and more people.

Our view of our business is that when we develop a new process, or a new device, we want to make something with it. If we look upon an invention merely as something clever, or as an academic exercise, it is of little benefit to anyone. We believe it is important to use the technology we have to create products that people can use. This is my theory of the three creativities: the creativity of technology, of product planning, and of marketing that I mentioned earlier. The electronics industry has a unique advantage: because of technological advancement, we can create completely new things—the auto makers can't do it, the furniture makers can't do it, the airplane makers can't do it. We can make things that didn't exist before and show people how these things can enrich their lives.

But I must say the first meeting of competing companies in Europe had its trying moments. At our first session, the Japanese side made various presentations on future technologies. A European delegate said, "Wait a minute, you are not talking about consumer electronics at all—you're talking about high technology. That has nothing to do with consumers."

I responded, "Oh, no, that is where the mistake is. You see, in ten years what you now call high technology will be in use in the hands of consumers."

He still didn't get it. "You mean that in ten years' time high technology and the consumer industry will become one?" he asked.

"No," I said, "it's not quite that way. In ten years' time, what we call high technology will be different from today's high technology. So what we call high tech today will soon become ordinary, usable technology in the hands of the consumers, perhaps your customers." Only a few years ago, nobody could imagine that they would have lasers working for them in their home.

I think we finally got through to them in that first meeting after this exchange, and the subsequent meetings have been smooth. I have repeatedly stressed that industry must promote broader trade through new technology and that the owners of the technology should spread it with licensing. In the compact disc case, Sony and Philips jointly licensed many other people, and that is why the business is expanding, although it has been slower than it should have been as a result of initial reluctance from some fainthearted managers. I am encouraging people in other industries to work as diligently as we are on R&D, inviting them to join us to create a market. We are not getting enough takers from America and Europe, but we really learned about this from America and Europe, where they have forgotten their own lessons.

Another example of the impediments to expanded trade is the unitary tax that is on the law books in several states in the U.S. This tax requires a company subsidiary of an overseas firm to report its worldwide earnings and to be assessed on the basis of the total company's business rather than on just the business transacted in the state. Submitting all this bookkeeping in itself is a costly thing, and paying high taxes on a subsidiary that is losing money even if the company as a whole is making a profit does not seem fair. I have always felt that business should pay its share of taxes and abide by all the laws and rules of the host country. But the unitary tax, which was championed by Edmund Brown, Jr., when he was governor of California, seemed to me to be an attack on foreign business. A handful of other American states had passed similar laws or were planning them, and some of us in the Keidanren decided to speak up about this. A survey of member companies in the federation showed that of eight hundred and seventy companies, about one hundred and seventy of them were either thinking of expanding into the United States or had plans to do so. But the unitary tax made every potential investor think twice before committing himself to establishing a plant in the U.S.

At the time, there were about twenty representatives of American states with offices in Tokyo, and we talked with all of them, explaining our thoughts about investment in facilities in the U.S., making it plain that it was our consensus that the unitary tax would be an impediment to investment and that that would mean no new jobs or construction contracts or any new tax revenue for the states at all. We also wrote to all the governors of unitary tax states, and every one invited us to come and visit his state. In 1984, we put together three delegations to visit the U.S., not as an anti–unitary tax task force, but as a Keidanren "committee to investigate the investment situation based on the environment." We visited twenty-three states, almost half of the U.S., dividing up the states among us. My group was given some of the most critical states, including Oregon, Indiana, and California.

Much to our surprise, and despite a lot of the critical talk we had been hearing from Washington, our reception was tremendous. In Oregon the governor publicized the visit through the media, including TV. The state used five helicopters and took us in pairs to see potential plant sites and to give us a look at the landscape. They treated us generously.

I was called upon to make a speech at every stop. The point I tried to make everywhere was that we are working to increase world trade and to decrease the trade imbalance between Japan and America in a practical way. By producing products in America, I said, direct exports from Japan will decrease and jobs will be created in America. This would mean that more taxes will be paid, and so I felt this was something that should be welcomed as a benefit for all of us.

"Our committee has as its goal the promotion of investment," I said in Oregon. "It would be too much for each company to go to America and investigate these possibilities, so we decided to summarize what we found out and report to our member companies. Therefore, I ask you to give us lots of information. Among the information I need to know is what you intended with the application of the unitary tax." The tax, I said very plainly, is considered an unfair tax.

Oregon governor Victor Atiyeh turned to me and said, "I agree with your feeling about the unitary tax. I will support what you say, so please pursue your efforts to seek its abolition." He said the Oregon law would definitely be amended. But I said to him, "Your word alone that it will be stopped will not be enough, because I realize you have a legislature to contend with. I cannot report back as the leader of this group that the governor of Oregon asked us to please trust him when he says this tax will be discontinued." Perhaps I underestimated the Oregonian politician, but as it turned out, the unitary tax in Oregon was repealed very soon after our visit.

We had many successes, and today the major holdout for the tax is still California. They started it and so they still have a lot of pride to swallow. And former governor Brown is still convinced that the tax is right and proper. He says he believes big corporations do not want the tax because they do not want to tell the truth about their business. It is simpler than that: they just don't think the tax is fair and do not want to pay money based on an unfair calculation of their profits for the privilege of creating employment and stimulating the business environment in foreign states. California's current governor, George Deukmejian, has said that in the long-range view the unitary tax is not a good thing for California. But the tax has not been repealed as of this writing.

In some states, like Massachusetts, the law was on the books but never enforced, and the Keidanren group that went there did not push for its elimination. I guess I would have done so; I always push to the limit, to make sure there is no ambiguity. You never know how politics or public sentiment can change. In America, I learned long ago, you have to have things written down and signed.

Near the end of our mission, while we were visiting New Jersey and Missouri, I left my group and flew to Washington with a Keidanren mission colleague. We went to the White House, where we spoke with Vice President George Bush and were invited to see the president. We had our pictures taken with him, and then he asked us to sit down. I began to tell him about Keidanren and our investment mission and how Japanese businessmen had decided to take the initiative in balancing trade and he said, "You people are concerned about the unitary tax, aren't you?"

I said, "Yes, that's right, Mr. President," and I explained how the problem was resolved in one state. I had brought along a copy of a pledge that had been signed in Indiana. "This is how it turned out," I said. I knew that in Indiana the governor and lieutenant governor and many other officials were Republicans, so I said, "These are very good people," and we got a laugh out of it. Then I said, "The same thing will someday happen in California," which is Mr. Reagan's home state, but he remained silent.

We had seen Secretary of State George Shultz, an old friend, in the hallway and he invited the whole group to visit him in his office. Again the unitary tax came up. "We all understand that the unitary tax causes problems for you," Shultz said, "so go to a state where there is none."

I said, "That's a good idea, but it wouldn't help my company, George, because when we went into California it was at a time when they didn't enforce this tax. In Florida the year after we went in they started it. If a state passes a law after we're established, there is nothing we can do. We don't know what will happen next."

"Akio," he said with a smile, "my advice is, when you build a factory next time, put wheels under it. Install 'unitary wheels.' "

Back in Japan, everybody at Keidanren was amazed with our success on the unitary tax problem, and I think we made a contribution to increased investment in the United States by making the climate there more hospitable. At the same time, it is becoming easier for foreign firms to invest, manufacture, and do business in Japan. This is as it should be. More Japanese companies are moving into the U.S. and Europe, but there still seems to be an uneasy feeling abroad about the future, and the threat of protectionism still hangs over our heads; it seems to be the first refuge of anyone with a trade grievance.

In these days of change and international communication, we must learn to talk sensibly and frankly to each other. We must try harder to understand the facts about our trading relationships, neither ignoring our conflicts nor allowing them to become too quickly politicized.

Because a war over trade is unthinkable today, every nation must face changes that will require difficult decisions. Japan is now going through a painful period of adjustment as we work toward redirecting our economy away from its traditional heavy reliance on exports. Other nations have experienced their own economic problems and will no doubt experience more. We are going to have to learn to share the pain if the world's economic system is to adjust to new realities and become more equitable.

The world economic system has slipped out of our control; increasingly, our economies are at the mercy of financial opportunists. Entire companies have become objects of exchange for the money traders, and great, old businesses are eating up their own assets in pursuit of quick profits. Some nations are crushed under debt burdens they cannot hope to liquidate. And as some industrialists invest in the money trading game instead of the future, the ability of some countries to produce their industrial necessities is diminishing rapidly. None of this activity is helping to create the better, more stable world we say we want.

It is time to get together as a world community to remedy the situation. It has been more than forty years since the war, more than four decades since the International Monetary Fund met at Bretton Woods and helped to set the free world on the economic road we have traveled so successfully for so long. We now have to create an up-to-date system for our own survival. Heads of government and heads of state, supported by the private sector, must take this upon themselves. Revising the system will require great political and moral courage.

I believe there is a bright future ahead for mankind, and that future holds exciting technological advances that will enrich the lives of everybody on the planet. Only by expanding world trade and stimulating more production can we take advantage of the possibilities that lie before us. We in the free world can do great things. We proved it in Japan by changing the image of the words "Made in Japan" from something shoddy to something fine. But for a single nation or a few nations to have accomplished this is not enough. My vision of the future is of an exciting world of superior goods and services, where every nation's stamp of origin is a symbol of quality, and where all are competing for the consumers' hard-earned money at fair prices that reflect appropriate rates of exchange. I believe such a world is within our grasp. The challenge is great; success depends only on the strength of our will.